Perry
   Collective bargaining
and the decline of the
United Mine Workers

COLLECTIVE BARGAINING AND THE DECLINE OF THE UNITED MINE WORKERS

by

CHARLES R. PERRY

INDUSTRIAL RESEARCH UNIT
The Wharton School, Vance Hall/CS
University of Pennsylvania
Philadelphia, Pennsylvania 19104
U.S.A.

8-91

Foreword

The bituminous coal mining industry has long been a stormy part of the American industrial relations scene. As a result, books and articles dealing with collective bargaining in this industry were once rather abundant. In recent years, however, and particularly during the quiet decades of the industry's labor relations, 1950-1970, labor developments in the coal fields went relatively unnoticed.

Recent coal industry negotiations have featured long strikes and weak union leadership, a far cry from the days of iron rule by John L. Lewis. Other aspects that have changed include the great increase in importance of western coal mining where the United Mine Workers are only an insignificant factor. The result is a dwindling in importance of this once mighty union which now has under contract only a little more than 40 percent of bituminous coal production.

Professor Charles R. Perry examines the current industrial relations picture in bituminous coal mining in depth. He shows the chaos which has resulted from the disunity in the union and among the employers, and he chronicles the bungling intervention of the Carter Administration and its secretary of labor which probably greatly added to the size of the settlement of one long strike, and may have prolonged it as well. Whether the new, seemingly stronger leadership of the United Mine Workers and the current mine owners can change the discouraging performance of the 1970s and early 1980s remains to be demonstrated.

This book is the first of a series which the Wharton Industrial Research Unit is undertaking in an effort to fill, at least partially, the gap which has resulted from the dearth of modern studies concerning employee relations in particular industries. Whereas once such works were a feature of industrial relations literature, new studies of this type have been rare since 1960. The Industrial Research Unit has in process books dealing with the construction, trucking, textile, and printing industries and hopes to sponsor others which will shed light on the current employee relations scene.

The author of this study, Dr. Charles R. Perry, Associate Professor of Management and Industrial Relations at the Wharton School, and Senior Faculty Research Associate in the Industrial Research Unit, has many publications to his credit, including the widely discussed *Operating During Strikes*, No. 23 in the Unit's Labor Relations and Public Policy Series, plus two books and several articles on employee relations in education. Professor William H. Miernyk, West Virginia University, as the outside reader, strongly recommended publication and made valuable suggestions. The book was edited by Patricia L. Dornbusch, assisted by Richard D. Freeman and Kate C. Bradford, who also compiled the index. Mrs. Margaret E. Doyle, who retired December 31, 1983, after thirty-one years of devoted service, handled the administrative matters. Research was sponsored by a grant from the Pew Memorial Trust and from funds supplied by membership in the Industrial Research Unit's industry Research Advisory Group. Editing was underwritten by the John M. Olin Foundation, Inc., and publication by the J. Howard Pew Freedom Trust.

As in all works published by the Wharton Industrial Research Unit, the author is solely responsible for the research and for all opinions expressed, which should not be attributed to the grantors or to the University of Pennsylvania.

HERBERT R. NORTHRUP, *Director*
Industrial Research Unit
The Wharton School
University of Pennsylvania

Philadelphia
January 1984

TABLE OF CONTENTS

LIST OF TABLES

LIST OF FIGURES

CHAPTER I

Introduction

The bituminous coal mining industry in the 1980s is an industry with a bright future and a dismal past. By all predictions and projections regarding the future of coal as an energy resource, the United States coal industry is poised on the brink of an era of growth and prosperity of almost overwhelming proportions. That pleasant prospect stands in marked contrast to the industry's fortunes over the past three decades, an era of decline and adversity of almost equally overwhelming proportions. By contrast, the United Mine Workers of America (UMWA) and its industry bargaining partner, the Bituminous Coal Operators' Association (BCOA), in the 1980s are two institutions with a bright past and a dismal future. In 1980, UMWA-BCOA national agreement tonnage accounted for less than 50 percent of total coal production, down from 70 percent in 1970 and 90 percent in 1950. To make matters worse, the UMWA-BCOA bargaining relationship, which had been a model of serenity and stability in the 1950s, had become a model of conflict and chaos in the 1970s, as evidenced by strikes in each of the last six UMWA-BCCA national agreement negotiations, in contrast to peaceful settlements in each of the six preceding sets of negotiations.

The divergent past fortunes and future prospects of the industry and of its "unionized" sector are the focus of this study. Specifically, the study identifies the forces and describes the processes that account for the decline of the UMWA-BCOA segment of the industry and the deterioration in the UMWA-BCOA bargaining relationship during a decade of industry growth after having survived almost two decades of industry shrinkage. The ultimate purpose of this effort is to establish a basis for enlightened speculation regarding the future of unionism and collective bargaining, in general, and of the UMWA and UMWA-

1

BCOA multiemployer bargaining, in particular, in the bituminous coal industry over the remaining two decades of this century.

THE STUDY

There are few industries in the United States with a longer or more colorful history of labor relations than bituminous coal mining, and among those, only railroads can rival mining in the extent of government involvement in labor relations. There are equally few industries in which labor relations have been as volatile as they have been in coal mining, particularly over the past forty years. The decades of the 1950s and 1960s were periods of tranquility totally unlike the turbulent decades that preceded and followed. What the 1980s and 1990s will bring remains to be seen, but it will undoubtedly have a profound influence on the future of the UMWA and the BCOA.

The history of labor relations in coal mining prior to 1950 has been the subject of extensive scholarly research and is not a major focus of attention in this study except as it relates to subsequent labor relations developments. Until very recently there had been little scholarly interest in the history of labor relations in coal mining after 1950, and it is one purpose of this study to fill that gap.[1] Beyond describing what has happened over the past thirty years, the study endeavors to identify the basic economic and institutional forces and changes that have shaped the course of labor relations from 1951 to 1981 and that seem likely to shape the course of labor relations in the brave new world of 1984 and beyond with a view to answering two interrelated questions: (1) What is the future likely to hold for the UMWA and BCOA as forces in the industry—decline, stability, or growth? and (2) What is the future likely to hold for the UMWA-BCOA bargaining relationship—confrontation, coexistence, or cooperation?

The study is divided into three basic segments. The first (Chapters II-V) deals with the changing economic, technological, demographic, and geographic character of the industry and context of UMWA-BCOA relations over the past thirty years. The second (Chapters VI-X) describes the basic institutional frame-

---

[1] One notable exception is William H. Miernyk, "Coal," in Gerald G. Somers, ed., *Collective Bargaining: Contemporary American Experience* (Madison, Wis.: Industrial Relations Research Association, 1980). *See also* Paul F. Clark, *The Miners' Fight for Democracy* (Ithaca: New York State School of Industrial and Labor Relations, Cornell University, 1981).

work in which the UMWA and the BCOA have conducted their bargaining relationship and analyzes the changes and constants in the character and role of the various players in what has come to be the triennial passion play of UMWA-BCOA negotiations. The third (Chapters XI-XIV) focuses on the process and results of UMWA-BCOA negotiations from 1951 through 1981, with special emphasis on the 1977-1978 and 1980-1981 UMWA-BCOA National Bituminous Coal Wage Agreement negotiations. The final chapter draws together the findings of the preceding chapters in an effort to map the future course or courses of labor relations in the bituminous coal mining industry—a difficult task at best, as many students and observers of the industry discovered in 1981.

The study draws on a wealth of quantitative data on the operation of the bituminous coal mining industry in its discussion of the economics and technology of coal production over the past eighty years. Specifically, the study draws heavily on industry statistical data reported in the *Keystone Coal Industry Manual* [2] and compiled for the President's Commission on Coal and published in its *Coal Data Book*.[3] In looking ahead to the future of the industry, the study draws on the report of the World Coal Study, *Coal—Bridge to the Future*,[4] and the abundance of articles in the press on the current economic condition and future economic prospects of the industry, such as the six-article series in the *New York Times,* "Coal's Future: Promise and Reality," published in the fall of 1980.[5]

There is, by comparison, relatively little hard data on the demography and geography of the industry and only limited qualitative data on the character of the industry's employees and

---

[2] *1980 Keystone Coal Industry Manual* (New York: McGraw Hill, 1980).

[3] President's Commission on Coal, *Coal Data Book* (Washington, D.C.: U.S. Government Printing Office, 1980).

[4] Carroll L. Wilson, *Coal—Bridge to the Future: Report of the World Coal Study* (Cambridge, Mass.: Ballinger Publishing Co., 1980.

[5] Ben A. Franklin, "Coal outlook troubled despite high hopes," *New York Times,* November 16, 1980, p. 1; Robert D. Hershey, Jr., "Gasification plant arising amid many snags," *New York Times,* November 17, 1980, p. 1; Philip Shabicoff, "Effort to soften environmental rules likely," *New York Times,* November 18, 1980, p. D-1; Agis Salpukas, "Surge in coal exports tied to investment," *New York Times,* November 19, 1980, p. D-1: Robert D. Hershey, Jr., "Fuel conversion stirs conflicts," *New York Times,* November 20, 1980, p. D-1; Ben A. Franklin, "New effort to make mines safer," *New York Times,* November 22, 1980, p. D-1.

employers and on the special character and circumstances of the
industry's western segment. Indeed, the remarkable growth and
different character of coal mining in the Rocky Mountain West
has been one of the best kept secrets of the past thirty years in
terms of both the scholarly literature and national press. In order to fill these voids, heavy reliance was placed on interviews
with union and industry personnel both in the East (UMWA and
BCOA) and particularly in the West (non-UMWA and non-
BCOA), supplemented by a review of the publications of the
relevant unions—most notably the *United Mine Workers Journal.*

There is an ample body of scholarly literature on the institutional character and role of the UMWA and government in the
organization and bargaining system of the industry prior to
1950. The policies and politics of the UMWA over that period
have been widely analyzed in works such as Baratz, *The Union
and the Coal Industry,*[6] as have been the politics and problems
of government intervention in coal-mining labor disputes in works
such as Blackman's *Presidential Seizure in Labor Disputes.*[7]

The twenty years of labor peace that began in 1950 were accompanied by apathy among scholars and the press toward the
UMWA and the government. That apathy lasted until 1971, when
internal political strife and external economic problems with wage
controls once again brought the UMWA and the government back
into the limelight where, thanks to continuing political problems
within the union and government interest and involvement, they
have remained. The result has been a rebirth of press interest
in the affairs of the union and government as they relate to the
industry's bargaining system. Such reports constitute an important source of information for the study, as did Weber and
Mitchell's account of the 1971 coal case in *The Pay Board's
Progress,*[8] the Bureau of Labor Statistics (BLS) 1977 and 1980
reports on *Collective Bargaining in the Bituminous Coal Industry,*[9] and the Bureau of National Affairs (BNA) *Daily Labor*

---

[6] Morton S. Baratz, *The Union and the Coal Industry* (New Haven, Conn.:
Yale University Press, 1955).

[7] John L. Blackman, Jr., *Presidential Seizure in Labor Disputes* (Cambridge, Mass.: Harvard University Press, 1967).

[8] Arnold R. Weber and Daniel J. B. Mitchell, *The Pay Board's Progress*
(Washington, D.C.: The Brookings Institution, 1978).

[9] U.S. Department of Labor, Bureau of Labor Statistics, "Collective Bargaining in the Bituminous Coal Industry," Report 514 (November 1977) and
Report 625 (December 1980).

Report coverage of government actions and statements in conjunction with extensive involvement and ultimate intervention in the 1977 coal negotiations. Further insight into that involvement and intervention was sought through interviews of the top UMWA and BCOA negotiators in the 1977 coal negotiations.

There is virtually no descriptive or analytical information on the organization and operation either of the BCOA or the western segment of the industry as participants in the industry's industrial relations system. It was not until after the conclusion of the 1977 UMWA-BCOA negotiations that press interest was focused on the internal workings of the BCOA, attention which has since grown, particularly with the threatened withdrawal of some members in 1980. Similarly, western collective bargaining received little national press attention until 1980, and then only on a limited scale. Those two voids have been filled by information gained through interviews with industry personnel both in the East and in the West. In both cases, those interviews netted sets of perceptions from specific viewpoints that had to be woven together to provide a picture of the whole institutional cloth— a task that proved to be difficult, given the complex and fragmented character of both institutions.

There is certainly no dearth of information on the results of BCOA-UMWA negotiations since 1950. The bituminous coal mining industry has been the subject of a BLS "Wage Chronology" that dates back to 1933-1934 and that has been expanded since 1977 in the aforementioned reports on *Collective Bargaining in Bituminous Coal Industry*. In addition, the Weber and Mitchell account of the 1971 coal case and subsequent Council on Wage and Price Stability contract-cost analyses provide valuable settlement cost information on agreements concluded between 1968 and 1978. Copies of all agreements concluded since 1950 were obtained and analyzed to trace the "noneconomic" results of negotiations, as were copies of judicial decisions handed down in cases arising out of those results—most notably, *United Mine Workers of America v. James A. Pennington*[10] and *Amax Coal Company v. NLRB.*[11]

Except for BLS data on strikes, there is relatively little press or other public information on the process through which UMWA-BCOA agreements were reached prior to 1977, when for the

---

[10] United Mineworkers of America v. James A. Pennington, 381 U.S. 657 (1965).

[11] Amax Coal Company v. NLRB, 103 L.R.R.M. 2483.

first time in over twenty-five years coal negotiations became big news, as they continued to be through 1981. In addition, in both of those sets of negotiations, the parties were not shy about issuing formal statements and press releases to present their case to the world as well as to each other. In addition to a review of such information regarding the public posture on the parties, the study draws on intensive interviews with those involved regarding the private processes and priorities of the parties in their struggles to reach agreement in 1977-1978 and 1980-1981.

Those interviews, the results of which form much of the basis for discussion of the institutional context and course of union-management relations in recent years and for predictions regarding the future of those relations, were conducted initially in 1978 and 1979 and focused primarily on developments in 1977 and 1978. Follow-up interviews were conducted in 1980 and 1981 and focused on developments in the 1980-1981 coal bargaining round. In an effort to encourage interviewees to speak frankly, particularly about possibly painful or sensitive "internal" matters, all were promised confidentiality and anonymity. Given such assurance, most appeared willing to talk openly, but some remained obviously reluctant to "air dirty linen" to an outsider, necessitating a certain amount of reading between the lines. Overall, what emerged was a fairly detailed and complete picture of the UMWA-BCOA labor relations system but a less detailed picture of the labor relations system of the unionized western and nonunionized eastern segments of the industry—systems deserving of intensive research in their own right given their combined dominance in total coal production in 1980 and possibly in the foreseeable, if not indefinite, future.

CHAPTER II

The Economics of the Industry

The stated energy policy of the United States, first adopted in 1974 in response to the 1973 energy crisis and subsequently reiterated with every ensuing crisis, called for coal production of 1.2-1.5 billion tons per year by 1985—a level 2-2.5 times the 600 million tons of coal produced by the bituminous coal mining industry in 1974. That scenario would seem to have made it inevitable that by 1980 the industry would be enjoying unprecedented growth and prosperity. In fact, however, that is not the case. The last half of the 1970s did produce an increase in the demand for coal, but not of the magnitude envisioned by the government or anticipated by the industry. As a result, at the end of 1980 "at least 100 million tons of annual production capacity [lay] idle for lack of a market, and most of that idle capacity [was] in the Eastern half of the United States where most UMWA-National Agreement mines are located." [1]

THE DEMAND FOR COAL

Coal has been mined commercially in the United States for over 200 years, but it was not until after the Civil War that coal mining began to assume the role of a major industry. The energy needs of a rapidly expanding railroad industry and growing industrial economy during the late 1800s and early 1900s fostered rapid growth in coal mining. Thus, by 1920, bituminous coal mining was well established as an important and basic industry in the United States. In that year, the industry employed more than 600,000 workers to produce over 500 million tons of coal. [2]

---

[1] "Bargaining Statement By Bituminous Coal Operators Association," *Daily Labor Report*, No. 15 (January 23, 1981), p. F-1.

[2] *1980 Keystone Coal Industry Manual* (New York: McGraw Hill, 1980), p. 690.

The 1920-1950 period was one of both adversity and prosperity for the industry. The demand for coal failed to grow appreciably during the 1920s and then fell precipitously with the onset of the depression. The industry nadir was reached in 1932, when the industry employed approximately 400,000 workers to produce only about 300 million tons of coal.[3] Thereafter, the demand for coal grew gradually during the remainder of the 1930s and then dramatically with the advent of World War II. The industry zenith was reached in 1947, when annual production exceeded 630 million tons before falling back to a level of about 500 million tons in 1950.[4] Technological change enabled the industry to produce 500 million tons of coal in 1950 with a work force of about the same size (400,000) required to produce 300 million tons of coal in 1932.[5]

The 1950-1980 period was much like the 1920-1950 period (see Table II-1). The demand for coal failed to grow during the early 1950s and then declined precipitously with the onset of the 1958 recession. The industry nadir in this second coal bust came in 1961, when annual production reached a postwar low of 400 million tons. Thereafter, the trend of coal production was upward to a level of 550 million tons in 1971, and 800 million tons in 1981. The trend in industry employment in the postwar period was consistently downward from a high of 440,000 in 1948 to a low of 125,000 in 1969 before the growth of the industry and the passage of the Coal Mine Health and Safety Act combined to produce growth in employment to a level of about 250,000 in 1979.

The growth in the demand for coal over the past twenty years, while a pleasant relief from the downward trend of demand in the 1950s, has done little more than enable the industry to hold its own in the U.S. energy market. In 1980, as in 1960, coal accounted for approximately 20 percent of the nation's energy supply, in marked contrast to the situation in 1950, when coal accounted for 40 percent of that supply.[6] Government projections, however, foresee an increase in the market share of coal

---

[3] *Ibid.*

[4] *Ibid.*

[5] *Ibid.*

[6] U.S. Department of Commerce, *1981 U.S. Industrial Outlook* (Washington, D.C.: U.S. Government Printing Office, 1981), p. 111.

TABLE II-1

Bituminous Coal Mining Output and Employment,
1950-1980

Year	Production (tons)	Employment	Mines
1950	516,311,053	415,582	9429
1951	533,664,732	372,897	8009
1952	466,840,782	335,217	7275
1953	457,290,449	293,106	6671
1954	391,706,300	227,397	6130
1955	464,633,408	225,093	7856
1956	500,874,077	228,163	8520
1957	492,703,916	228,635	8539
1958	410,445,547	197,402	8264
1959	412,027,502	179,636	7719
1960	415,512,347	169,400	7865
1961	402,976,802	150,474	7648
1962	422,149,325	143,822	7740
1963	458,928,175	141,646	7940
1964	486,997,952	128,698	7630
1965	512,088,263	133,732	7228
1966	533,881,210	131,752	6749
1967	552,626,000	131,523	5873
1968	545,245,000	127,894	5327
1969	560,505,000	124,532	5118
1970	602,932,000	140,140	5601
1971	552,192,000	145,664	5149
1972	595,386,000	149,265	4879
1973	591,000,000	157,800	4650
1974	603,406,000	166,701	5247
1975	648,438,000	189,800	6168
1976	678,685,000	202,280	6161
1977	691,344,000	221,428	6077
1978	665,127,000	242,295	6230
1979	776,299,000	224,203	6300
1980	823,644,000	232,900	6400

Source: *1980 Keystone Coal Industry Manual* (New York: McGraw Hill,
1980), pp. 685, 690; *1982 Keystone Coal Industry Manual*, p. 729.

to about 25 percent by 1985, when domestic demand for coal is
projected to exceed one billion tons.[7]

The Market for Coal

The market for coal is international in scope, but foreign sales
historically have accounted for only about 10 percent of U.S.
coal production. The remaining 90 percent of coal production is
consumed domestically in four basic "end-use" sectors: (1) elec-

---

[7] President's Commission on Coal, *Coal Data Book* (Washington, D.C.:
U.S. Government Printing Office, 1980), p. 15.

tric utilities; (2) coke plants; (3) industry and transportation; (4) residential and commercial. The distribution of domestic coal consumption among these four "end-use" sectors in 1950, 1960, 1970, and 1980 is presented in Table II-2.

TABLE II-2
U.S. Coal Consumption by End-Use Sector,
1950-1979
(in percent)

Sector	1950	1960	1970	1979
Electric Utilities	18.6	44.5	61.2	77.3
Coke	21.8	20.4	18.5	11.3
Industrial	37.3	24.2	17.2	9.7
Residential	23.3	10.3	3.1	1.3

Source: U.S. Department of Commerce, *1981 U.S. Industrial Outlook* (Washington, D.C.: U.S. Government Printing Office, 1981), p. 118.

The single largest source of demand for coal, by far, is electric utilities, which today consume almost 80 percent of all coal used domestically and are the only domestic end-use sector that used more coal in 1979 (529 million tons) than in 1950 (92 million tons). The remaining 20 percent of domestic consumption was split almost equally between coke plants, which burned 77 million tons of coal in 1979, down from over 100 million tons in 1950, and all other industrial, commercial, and residential uses, which in 1979 consumed 75 million tons of coal, down from almost 200 million tons in 1950. Projections of demand by end-use sectors, through 1981, foresee no change in this basic pattern of growing absolute and relative coal use by utilities and shrinking absolute and relative coal use by other domestic consumers of coal.[8]

The data on coal demand by end-use sectors clearly indicates that the past, present, and very probably the future of the coal and electric utility industries are closely linked. Specifically, the fortunes of the coal industry over the past two decades have been, and over the next two decades will be, heavily dependent on the fuel source choices of utilities in the generation of electric power. Overall, those choices have been sufficiently favorable over the past twenty years to enable the coal mining industry to grow and maintain its share of the energy market despite declining demand from other end-use sectors. Those favorable choices, how-

---

[8] U.S. Department of Commerce, *1981 U.S. Industrial Outlook*, p. 118.

ever, were not distributed evenly across the utility industry, as is indicated in the following characterization of trends in the use of coal by utilities since 1960.

> Within the utility sector, regional shifts occurred in the use of coal due to prices and government regulations. Eastern utilities, historically the largest market for coal, greatly reduced their use of coal in the 1960s after the deregulation of residual oil imports to the East coast. At the same time, labor disputes, mining regulations, and technological bottlenecks doubled the costs of Eastern deep-mined coal. Western utilities meanwhile turned to coal, as cheap low-sulfur coal from strip mines became a less expensive alternative to further hydroelectric development. Air quality regulations were less strict in the West than the East, and for the most part, the low sulfur content of the coal made scrubbers unnecessary.[9]

The 1970s did not produce a reversal of the trend of the 1960s in the fuel-use choices of electric utilities. The rising cost of oil and gas in the 1970s has not yet achieved a substantial increase in the "coal burn" of utilities at the expense of other fuels primarily because eastern utilities have not greatly increased their use of coal. In the short run, any such increase would require the conversion of existing noncoal-burning facilities —a time-consuming and expensive process. The cost and risks of undertaking that process have been substantially increased by the environmental problems associated with the burning of coal and pollution-control requirements imposed on coal-burning facilities by the government in an effort to abate those problems.

The demand for bituminous coal for coking remained fairly stable between 1950 and 1970, at a level of about 100 million tons per year before dropping to a level of only 75 million tons by 1980.[10] The domestic demand for metallurgical coal for coking, most of which is mined underground in the East, has been weakened by the generally depressed state of the steel industry. It has also been weakened by the cost of compliance with Environmental Protection Agency (EPA) and Occupational Safety and Health Administration (OSHA) coke oven emission standards, which have raised the price of domestically produced coke and increased the attractiveness of imports as a source of coke. The fact that in 1980 "over 20,000 miners [were] laid off" and "many mines have closed, and more are expected to close" is

---

[9] *Ibid.*

[10] *Ibid.*

largely attributable to the depressed state of demand for metallurgical coal.[11]

The demand for coal for industrial, commercial, and residential use declined dramatically during the 1950s, from almost 300 million tons in 1950 to under 150 million tons in 1960, owing to the growing availability of oil and natural gas, which are easier and cleaner to burn than coal.[12] The shrinking availability and increasing price of these fuels during the 1970s have not yet been sufficient to offset the inherent advantages of oil, gas, and electricity over coal as energy sources in the industrial, commercial, and residential sectors. Thus, the coal-fired locomotive and coal-fired commercial or residential furnace, which consumed almost 180 million tons of coal in 1950, have become historical relics, which by 1979 consumed less than 10 million tons of coal, and seem likely to remain such.

Foreign demand for coal from the United States historically has been relatively constant in absolute amount and concentrated on metallurgical rather than steam coal. The report of the World Coal Study predicted a dramatic change in that situation over the next ten years in projecting U.S. exports of 30-60 million tons of steam coal by 1990 in contrast to an estimated 10 million tons in 1977.[13] The boom in foreign demand for steam coal anticipated by the World Coal Study has not yet materialized, but there are some encouraging signs. The National Coal Association, which in early 1979 asserted that the United States was becoming "a dumping ground" for low-cost foreign steam coal, reported in mid-1980 that "American steam coal exports which were 'effectively zero' in 1978 rose to 2.5 million tons last year and may soar to between 7 million and 12 million tons this year." [14]

The Future of Coal

The bituminous coal mining industry entered the 1980s hopeful but skeptical regarding its prospects for substantial growth.

---

[11] "Bargaining Statement," *Daily Labor Report*, p. F-1.

[12] U.S. Department of Commerce, *1981 U.S. Industrial Outlook*, p. 118.

[13] Carroll L. Wilson, *Coal—Bridge to the Future: Report of the World Coal Study* (Cambridge, Mass.: Ballinger Publishing Co., 1980), p. 244.

[14] Ben A. Franklin, "Constraints inhibit coal boom," *New York Times*, June 24, 1980, p. D-5.

In June 1980, the *New York Times* characterized the situation in the industry as follows:

> Public commitments by government officials to the doubled consumption of coal in place of oil . . . have become a fixed, if unfulfilled, part of the energy rhetoric in this country since 1974. Then, former President Richard M. Nixon in his "Project Independence" plan made the first "Dig we must" proposal to turn the vast bituminous reserves of the United States into what mining executives like to call the "Saudi Arabia of Coal." But despite the fact that his two successors in the White House also delighted the slump-prone coal industry by calling for doubled production by 1985 in energy scenarios of their own, not even the coal industry believes it anymore.[15]

The basic barrier confronting the industry in achieving the destiny set for it by national energy policies and scenarios is the environmental problems associated with the burning of coal —problems which thus far have made coal a "demand limited" energy resource. The *New York Times* presented the problem as follows:

> The root difficulty with coal, it is widely agreed, is not mining it. Notwithstanding the industry's bitter complaints about safety and environmental "constraints" . . . the main problem for coal is in burning it. The objective, endorsed by three presidents, of 1.2 to 1.5 billion tons of coal a year by 1985 is widely regarded as unattainable because burning coal is so polluting . . . . As a result, in the economists' argot, coal is "severely demand restricted." And as a further impediment, coal is hard to move over the nation's largely decrepit rail system.[16]

The basic hope for the industry rests in a substantial increase in the coal burn of electric utilities at the expense of alternate fuels. The prospects for such an increase in the near future are not particularly good, as conversion to coal requires large capital expenditures for land as well as equipment for the handling, storing, and burning of coal, and for compliance with antipollution regulations—regulations which "may increase the cost of each new coal burning plant by half again."[17] The prospects for an increase in the coal burn of utilities at the expense of oil or gas over the long term seem more favorable. The Powerplant and

---

15 *Ibid.*, p. D-1.

16 Ben A. Franklin, "Coal's time of frustration," *New York Times*, May 5, 1979, p. 31.

17 *Ibid.*

Industrial Fuel Use Act of 1978 (PIFUA) requires that new large industrial and utility boilers use coal unless oil or gas is "substantially less expensive," unless there are site restrictions on coal use, or unless air quality regulations prohibit the use of coal. More importantly, coal has cost advantages over natural gas and residual oil estimated at 50 and 150 percent respectively, in 1981.[18] The Department of Commerce concluded that "this price advantage. . . . and the coal conversion mandate of PIFUA are expected to result in substantial increases in the use of coal by . . . electric utilities."[19] The fact that the law is silent on the use of nuclear energy, and that nuclear energy enjoys a price advantage over coal in power generation, may well mean, in the words of the *New York Times*, that "coal's hope of gaining a substantially greater share of the electric power fuel market will likely turn on coal's cost compared with nuclear energy."[20]

The second hope of the industry for substantial growth in demand is the world market. The prospects for increasing worldwide demand for coal over the next ten years are excellent. The prospects that the United States will fare well in that environment in competition with other developed nations with large coal reserves, such as Australia and South Africa, however, are less clear. The competitive success of the U.S. coal industry in the world market will depend on the relative price of its coal and its reliability as a supplier of coal—two variables in which the labor relations of the industry have played, and will continue to play, an important role. A second potential impediment to competitive success in the world market, as in the domestic market, may be the lack of adequate, efficient facilities for the movement of coal, as there is little capacity at most U.S. ports for the efficient loading of coal after it arrives over "the nation's largely decrepit rail system."

There appears to be little hope for any real growth in the demand for coal in the domestic industrial, commercial, and residential markets. Barring a miraculous rebirth of the steel industry, it is hard to foresee any increase in the domestic demand for high-grade metallurgical coal for coking or other industrial uses. The domestic demand for steam coal for industrial, com-

---

[18] Robert D. Hershey, Jr., "Coal—the other glut," *New York Times*, May 16, 1982, p. F-28.

[19] U.S. Department of Commerce, *1981 U.S. Industrial Outlook*, p. 119.

[20] Franklin, "Coal's time of frustration," p. 31.

mercial, and residential use can be expected to grow, but only slowly and by relatively little in the foreseeable future. The more esoteric sources of new demand for coal, such as coal gasification and liquefaction, seem destined to consume miniscule quantities of coal throughout the 1980s.

Overall, it seems that the future of the bituminous coal industry rests primarily on the nation's demand for electrical power and the demand by the nation's electric utilities for coal to generate that power. A second possible source of growth is the world's demand for coal as an energy source. In both cases, the growth that can be anticipated is likely to be concentrated, in the demand for steam rather than metallurgical coal—a prospect that can be of little comfort to the UMWA or the BCOA, since their memberships include substantial numbers of miners of metallurgical coal.

THE SUPPLY OF COAL

The excess capacity that currently exists in the bituminous coal mining industry is not a new or unusual phenomenon. The industry historically has been characterized by varying degrees of excess production capacity and the "ruinous competition" generally associated with excess capacity. The industry historically also has been characterized by a fairly consistent upward trend in productivity. As a result, coal typically has been an abundant and, until very recently, a relatively inexpensive energy resource.

In 1920, there were 9,000 coal mines in operation in the United States employing 640,000 men to produce coal at an average value of $3.75 per ton.[21] The 1920s produced a dramatic downward trend in both the number of coal mines and the value of coal that continued until 1932, when the industry reached its first production nadir. In that year, there were only 5,400 mines in operation producing coal with an average value of $1.31 per ton. Between 1920 and 1932, employment in the industry dropped from 640,000 to 400,000, and average number of days worked per year from 220 to 146, but output increased from 4.00 to 5.22 tons per man per day.[22]

The upward trend in the demand for coal after 1933 produced a parallel trend in the number of mines and in the value of their

[21] *1980 Keystone Coal Industry Manual*, pp. 690.

[22] *Ibid.*, pp. 690-91.

output. The peak was reached in 1948, when there were once again some 9,000 mines in operation producing coal with an average value of almost $5.00 per ton. Those mines employed 440,000 men working an average of 217 days per year and producing an average of 6.26 tons per man per day to mine 600 million tons of coal.[23]

The 1950s, like the 1920s, produced a clear downward trend in the number of mines in operation until by 1961, at the industry's second production nadir, there were fewer than 7,700 mines in operation. Unlike the 1920s, however, there were no parallel downward trends in average number of days worked, which varied marginally around an average of 195 days per year, or in average value of coal, which fluctuated between $4.50 and $5.00 per ton.[24] The fact that the effects of declining demand during the 1950s were concentrated on the number of mines in operation rather than hours of work and/or the price of coal is attributable directly to the policies and power of the UMWA.

The 1950s was a decade of rapid technological change in the industry—change which the UMWA both accepted and encouraged. Between 1950 and 1961, productivity more than doubled, from 6.77 to 13.87 tons per man per day.[25] That increase, coupled with declining demand, resulted in a dramatic drop in industry employment, from 415,000 in 1950 to 150,000 in 1961.

The 1960's produced little change in the basic trends of the 1950s, despite growing demand for coal. The basic trend in the number of mines over the decade continued to be downward to a level of 5,100 by 1969. The trend of productivity continued upward to a level of 19.90 tons per man per day, which when added to a slight upward trend in days worked to a level of 225 per year in 1969, permitted the industry to further reduce employment to under 125,000 in 1969.[26]

The passage of the Federal Coal Mine Health and Safety Act of 1969 has had a profound effect on the supply and suppliers of coal. One subtle effect of the law was to extend and enhance the downward trend in the number of operating mines that continued through 1973, at which time there were less than

---

23 *Ibid.*

24 *Ibid.*

25 *Ibid.*, p. 691.

26 *Ibid.*, pp. 690-91.

4,800 mines in operation. Small mines (those with annual production of less than 10,000 tons) seem to have been the primary casualties of the law. The law, however, has not prevented subsequent growth in the number of operating mines to a level of 6,000 in 1979.

The law has had a more profound and long-lasting effect on labor costs in the industry. The long-term favorable trend in productivity in the industry was reversed after 1969, as was the downward trend in employment of the past twenty years. Production per man-day, which reached almost 20 tons in 1969, fell to 13.5 tons in 1979 and employment, which reached a low of 125,000 in 1969, grew to 250,000 in 1979. The decline in productivity coupled with the substantial wage increases negotiated by the union in 1971 and 1974 put an end to twenty years of stable coal prices. The price of coal, which had been $4.99 per ton in 1969, reached $8.42 per ton in 1973, jumped to $19.23 per ton in 1975 after the energy crisis, and climbed steadily to $23.50 per ton over the next 5 years.[27]

The Mining of Coal

Bituminous coal is mined both underground and by surface strip mining. In 1900, all coal production in the United States came from underground mines, and as recently as 1940 underground mining accounted for 90 percent of all coal production. By 1950 that percentage had fallen to 75 percent, and by 1960, to under 70 percent. By 1980, surface mining accounted for about 60 percent of U.S. coal production and employed 33 percent of the industry's work force.[28]

The dramatic growth of surface mining relative to underground mining over the past thirty years is a product of three forces. The first has been the growth of demand for steam coal in both absolute and relative terms, as most coal that can be extracted by surface strip mining is suitable only or primarily for such use. The second has been the productivity advantage of surface over underground mining in extracting steam coal, as is evident in the fact that surface mining produces 60 percent of all coal using 30 percent of all coal miners. The third has been the fact that it has been affected relatively little by the requirements of the Federal Coal Mine Health and Safety Act of

---

[27] *Ibid.*, pp. 685, 690-91.

[28] Richard Green, "Employment Trends in Energy Extraction," *Monthly Labor Review*, Vol. 104, No. 5 (May 1981), p. 7.

1969—requirements which have not only expedited the closing of some smaller underground mines but also encouraged conversion of some underground mines to surface mines, resulting in a 65 percent decline in the number of underground mines in operation between 1969 and 1974.

The dramatic relative growth of surface mining over the past ten years has played an important role in the declining relative strength of the UMWA in the bituminous coal mining industry. The organizational strength of the UMWA historically has been, and continues to be, underground mining, where it represents about 90 percent of all miners. Thus far, the UMWA has been unable to establish comparable organizational strength in surface mining, where it represents only about 40 percent of all miners, for several reasons. First, the superior productivity of labor in surface mines enables operators of such mines to provide wages and benefits equal or superior to union wages and benefits. Second, working conditions in general and safety problems in particular, which long have been a basic operational concern and organizing attraction of the union, are far less ominous in surface mines. Finally, the skills required in surface mining are more like those required in road construction than those in mining, making the union vulnerable to competition from unions such as the International Union of Operating Engineers (IUOE).

The past ten years have produced a fundamental change in the geography as well as the technology of coal mining. There are three basic coal fields in the United States—Appalachia, the Midwest, and the West. The Appalachian coal field, encompassing Alabama, Georgia, eastern Kentucky, Maryland, Ohio, Pennsylvania, Tennessee, Virginia, and West Virginia, long has been the largest producer of bituminous coal and in 1969 accounted for approximately 70 percent of U.S. coal production. The midwestern coal field, encompassing Arkansas, Illinois, Iowa, Kansas, western Kentucky, Missouri, Oklahoma, and Texas, historically has played a more limited but not unimportant role in U.S. coal production, as was the case in 1969, when it accounted for about 25 percent of total production. The western coal field, encompassing Alaska, Arizona, Colorado, Montana, New Mexico, North Dakota, Utah, Washington, and Wyoming, historically has not been a major factor in the industry and was not in 1969, when it accounted for only 5 percent of U.S. coal production.[29]

---

[29] President's Commission on Coal, *Coal Data Book*, p. 93.

The major geographical change that has taken place in the industry over the past decade has been a consistent and dramatic, absolute and relative growth in western coal production (see Table II-3). Western coal production doubled in absolute amount between 1969 and 1973 and did so again between 1973 and 1977. As a result, its share of total U.S. production climbed from 5 percent in 1969 to 10 percent in 1973 and 20 percent in 1977. By 1979, western coal production totalled 181 million tons and accounted for 23.4 percent of U.S. coal production and by 1982 was expected to total 290 million tons and account for almost 33 percent of U.S. production.[30]

The dramatic growth of western coal production over the past ten years, like the growth of surface mining and not unrelated to it, is the product of several forces. The first has been the basic economic growth of the Rocky Mountain West and the growing demand for electric power that accompanied that growth. The second has been the existence of sizable reserves of bituminous, subbituminous, and lignite coal that can be mined at the surface as a potential source of energy to generate electric

TABLE II-3
Bituminous Coal Production
by Region, 1969-1980
(thousand tons)

Year	Total	Appalachia	Midwest	West
1969	560,505	394,928	139,857	25,720
1970	602,932	417,846	149,941	35,145
1971	552,192	373,582	136,303	42,307
1972	552,192	387,249	157,528	50,609
1973	591,738	374,797	156,411	60,530
1974	603,406	377,719	150,208	75,479
1975	648,438	396,487	162,118	89,833
1976	678,685	406,162	161,955	110,568
1977	688,575	389,850	163,130	135,595
1978	665,127	369,903	146,188	149,036
1979	776,299	424,691	170,183	181,425
1980	823,644	398,864	215,703	209,077

Source: President's Commission on Coal, *Coal Data Book* (Washington, D.C.: U.S. Government Printing Office, 1980), p. 93; U.S. Department of Energy, Energy Information Administration, "Energy Data Report," January 22, 1982.

---

30 Hershey, "Coal—the other glut," p. F-28.

power. The fact that those coal reserves generally were of lower quality than eastern coal was more than offset by the fact that they were easily surface mined and contained less sulfur than eastern coal, thereby making coal a more cost competitive fuel source in the West than in the East. Finally, the West was better able than the East to "solve" some of the problems of shipping and burning coal for electric power by not shipping it to or burning it in urban areas, choosing instead to burn it on-site in "mine-mouth generating plants" and to ship the power generated therein.

The growth of western coal mining also has played an important role in the decline of the UMWA, whose power base historically has been and currently continues to be concentrated in the major coal-producing states in the East and Midwest—Pennsylvania, Ohio, Indiana, Illinois, West Virginia, Kentucky, and Virginia. Thus far, the UMWA has not been able to extend that power base into the rapidly growing coal-producing states in the West and Southwest—North Dakota, Montana, Wyoming, Colorado, Arizona, New Mexico, and Texas. The UMWA is fairly strong in underground mining in the West, but such mining accounts for only about 10 percent of total production as compared with over 50 percent in the East. Its position in surface mining is far more tenuous in that it represents only a very limited percentage of the work force and competes with at least three other unions in organizing and representing surface mine workers—the IUOE, the International Brotherhood of Electrical Workers (IBEW), and the Progressive Mine Workers (PMW).

The Future of Coal Mining

It seems virtually inevitable that the last two decades of the twentieth century will be ones of growth for the coal mining industry in the United States. That growth, however, is not likely to be as rapid or as easy as was foreseen in the "energy scenarios" of the 1970s. In part, the limitations on industry growth will be limits reflecting the environmental problems associated with the burning of coal and the logistical problems associated with the transport of coal by rail, ship, or pipeline. Those environmental and logistical problems are unlikely to disappear or be overcome by government energy policies such as the Powerplant and Industrial Fuel Use Act of 1978 (oil back-out) or the Energy Security Act of 1980 (synfuels).

There are also potential supply limitations on industry growth. The problem at the moment may be more a matter of burning than of digging coal, but in the long run that may not be the case. The historical supply elasticity of the industry, as manifested in the fluctuations in the number of operating mines and number of days operated, no longer exists. The basic character of coal mining has changed from a labor-intensive to a capital-intensive operation, as have the regulatory requirements imposed on the mining of coal. As a result, the opening of a mine is now a far more expensive and risky undertaking than was the case in 1950 or even 1970.

The stubborn refusal of the demand for coal to grow as projected in national and international energy scenarios over the last half of the 1970s has tended to diminish the enthusiasm of coal producers for development and expansion of coal mines. Nonetheless, the most recent projections of planned expansions in capacity foresee the development or expansion of over 300 mines, to add some 525 million tons of production capacity between 1980 and 1988, with 90 percent of that new coal production destined for use as steam coal.

The projections of development and expansion of coal mines during the 1980s indicate that the basic trends of the 1970s will continue. Most (70 percent) planned expansion in capacity will come in surface mining which by 1988 should account for two-thirds of U.S. coal production. Similarly, most (70 percent) planned expansion in capacity will come in seven western states —Colorado, Montana, New Mexico, North Dakota, Texas, Utah, and Wyoming—with approximately 90 percent of the expansion of capacity in those states coming in surface mining and almost 50 percent of that increase coming in the state of Wyoming. (See Table II-4.)

The projected continued absolute and relative growth of surface mining in general, and western surface mining in particular, will further move the production of coal away from the historical and institutional heartland of the bituminous coal mining industry—underground mining in the East. That growth and movement, however, is not assured and may well be limited by the effects of the Federal Surface Mine Control and Reclamation Act of 1977, which sets minimum standards for the reclamation of the surface-mined land. Most mining states had enacted legislation requiring reclamation of strip-mined land prior to 1977, but the requirements of those laws were highly variable. As a re-

TABLE II-4
*New Coal Mine Developments and Expansions
by Region, State, and Mining Method,
1978-1988*
(millions of tons)

Region	State	Deep	Surface	Total
Nation		224.52	541.60	766.12
Appalachia		96.50	30.40	126.90
Midwest (except Texas)		62.20	33.65	95.85
West (including Texas)		65.82	477.55	543.77
	Arizona		8.00	8.00
	Colorado	21.39	12.05	33.44
	Montana	.25	64.70	64.95
	New Mexico	1.50	34.80	36.30
	North Dakota		53.80	53.80
	Texas		70.20	70.20
	Utah	35.43		35.43
	Wyoming	7.25	234.00	241.25

Source: *1980 Keystone Coal Industry Manual*, p. 696.

sult, "the growth and excesses in strip mining" during the 1970s "fueled a push for Federal regulation" to ensure some equality in reclamation requirements.[31] The legislation required to achieve that goal was enacted in 1977, legislation which the industry contended would "cost 100 to 150 million lost tons a year." [32]

The environmental problems associated with surface mining are indeed substantial, as are the costs of rectifying those problems. The basic problem created by surface mining has been described as follows:

Failure to reclaim mined land can mean permanent loss of its productivity for agricultural, recreational and other purposes. In addition, unreclaimed mine sites may create significant external problems, including: erosion and related water quality degradation resulting from steep slopes, uncompacted soils, and toxic substances; danger from collapse of highwalls and the subsidence of over-burden materials; disruption of natural drainage networks at mine sites

[31] Franklin, "Coal's time of frustration," p. 31.
[32] *Ibid.*

and interference with ground water acquifiers and downstream water rights; and disruption of wildlife habitat.[33]

The technical problems of reclaiming surface-mined land are no less formidable than the environmental problems that surface mining may create. The nature of those technical problems has been summarized in the following terms:

> Problems encountered in reclamation of surface mined land are highly area-specific. In Appalachia, the problem is one of returning the land to its original contour in such a way that the harmful environmental and health effects of acid drainage, soil erosion and water run-off are avoided. In the semiarid West, the problem is basically one of revegetation.[34]

The costs of solving these problems are substantial and highly variable, depending on geologic and climatic conditions and applicable regulations governing percent of slope allowed and amount of topsoiling required. There is little disagreement regarding the desirability of reclamation of surface-mined lands, but also little evidence to show that efforts to do so are cost-effective. Cost/benefit analysis of land reclamation efforts in six western states revealed benefit/cost ratios sufficiently low to suggest that "most of the applicable legislation has apparently been drawn with little concern for the cost to society or the benefits derived." [35]

This cost/benefit question is a particularly sensitive one in the West, where environmental interests are strong and the supply of both topsoil and water are weak. The potential cost of having to cope with these problems as well as the host of potential other political, social, economic, and environmental problems—ranging from water supply to mineral rights to extraction taxes to the building of new communities—which confront the industry in exploiting the West's vast reserves of coal may possibly slow the growth of coal mining in that region. Despite these potential costs and real problems, however, it seems unlikely that the rate of expansion of coal production will slow sufficiently in the West or grow sufficiently in the East during the 1980s to prevent the West from becoming a virtually equal partner with the East in the nation's coal supply. Barring a basic change in the or-

---

[33] Steve H. Murdock and F. Larry Leistritz, *Energy Development in the Western United States* (New York: Praeger, 1979), p. 148.

[34] *Ibid.*

[35] *Ibid.*, p. 151.

ganization and/or bargaining structure of the industry, the result will be a further lessening of the control of the UMWA
over the industry by virtue of its bargaining relationship with
the BCOA. The consequences of that development are difficult
to predict but may well have been foretold in 1977 when an
impasse in UMWA-BCOA contract negotiations failed to preclude
an agreement by western UMWA locals and non-BCOA surface
mine operators to a new contract and a 111-day strike by the
UMWA against the BCOA failed to produce a true national
energy emergency.

CHAPTER III

The Technology of the Industry

Historically, underground mining has been the dominant method of coal extraction in the United States, accounting for over 50 percent of bituminous coal production as recently as 1973.[1] Although underground mining has since lost its dominance in terms of total production, it continues to dominate in terms of total employment, accounting for over 65 percent of the industry work force in 1980.[2] The institutional significance of underground mining in industry employee relations outweighs its numerical significance in industry employment by virtue of the dominance of the UMWA in the organization of underground mine employees and the prominence of its representational activities on behalf of those employees through its bargaining relationship with the BCOA.

UNDERGROUND MINING

Underground mining is used to extract coal deposits located deep under the surface of the land. Extraction takes place below that surface and involves only limited surface disturbance. An underground mine essentially is a room or series of rooms cut into a buried coal seam which are serviced by a shaft or series of shafts through which employees, equipment, air, and coal are moved into and out of the mine. Once access to a coal seam has been established by construction of shafts or tunnels, one of three basic techniques may be used to extract coal: cutting machine, continuous mining, or longwall mining. None of these techniques involve the pick and shovel technology historically associated with coal mining—a technology that had fairly well disappeared from

---

[1] *1980 Keystone Coal Industry Manual* (New York: McGraw Hill, 1980), p. 691.

[2] Richard Green, "Employment Trends in Energy Extraction," *Monthly Labor Review*, Vol. 104, No. 5 (May 1981), p. 6.

the industry by 1930.[3] Also, none of these techniques are dependent on the manual loading of coal, as virtually all coal today is mechanically loaded.[4]

A cutting machine cuts holes into the working face of a coal seam, into which explosives are placed. When detonated, the entire working face crumbles, leaving chunks of coal which are then loaded into a car to be moved to the surface by a locomotive. Support timbers or roof bolts are then put in place under the now extended roof and the process is repeated. The cutting machine was first introduced in the 1870s, and by 1920 accounted for 60 percent of all underground coal production. By 1950, that figure had grown to over 90 percent, but now stands at only about 30 percent.[5]

The continuous mining machine is a one-man machine that claws coal directly from the seam and loads it into a conveyor to a waiting transport car for movement to the surface. As the machine moves forward into the face, support timbers or roof bolts are put in place behind it to support the newly exposed roof. Continuous-cutting machines were first placed in service in the industry in 1948, and by 1970 accounted for approximately 50 percent of underground coal production. Currently, coal mined by continuous mining machines accounts for about 65 percent of all underground coal production in the United States.[6]

Longwall mining is a technique used extensively in Europe for some time but not introduced into the United States until the late 1960s. The longwall mining process involves the use of a machine that shears slices of coal off the face of a seam. It moves forward using self-advancing roof jacks and is followed by roof-bolting equipment. Longwall mining today accounts for less than 5 percent of all underground coal production, but that percentage is expected to grow consistently and significantly during the 1980s.[7] That prospect, coupled with the rising cost of mining equipment and the capital required to purchase such equipment, has spawned a growing interest in continuous operation, which became a subject of conflict in UMWA-BCOA nego-

---

[3] *1980 Keystone Coal Industry Manual*, p. 691.

[4] *Ibid.*

[5] *Ibid.*

[6] *Ibid.*

[7] *Ibid.*

tiations in both 1977 and 1981. The *Wall Street Journal* explained the industry's interest in continuous operation in the following terms:

> The increasingly high cost of coal-mining equipment—with the particularly burdensome expense of financing equipment purchases —partly explains the industry's desire for non-stop operation. The growing use of multi-million-dollar "longwall" mining machines, which are highly productive but which require extensive start-up procedures after closings, makes the need for uninterrupted mining more compelling, in the industry's view.[8]

Productivity

Underground mining requires a larger labor force and capital investment per ton of production capacity than does surface mining. As a result, production costs per ton of coal mined underground may be as much as three times those for surface-mined coal. The offsetting advantage of underground coal is heat value per ton, which enables it to command a higher price per ton. This difference is most apparent in the prices of metallurgical coal—high quality, deep-mined coal—which in 1981 sold for about $45.00 per ton and steam coal—primarily lower quality, surface-mined coal—which in 1981 sold for about $32.00 per ton.[9]

The quality differences that segregate the markets for metallurgical and steam coal are also a factor in the market for steam coal, but to a lesser extent. The ability of deep-mined coal to compete in that market depends on its ability to remain cost-competitive with surface-mined coal as a source of electric power. There is clear evidence that deep-mined coal has been losing that battle, particularly over the past ten years. One obvious explanation is the downward trend in productivity in coal mining over that period.

The labor-saving character of technological change in the bituminous coal mining industry in general prior to 1970 has already been documented. The fact that underground mining was both a major source and basic beneficiary of that technological change is well known. The development and relatively rapid application of mechanical coal-cutting and loading in the first

---

[8] Thomas Petzinger, Jr., "Coal industry, facing UMW talks, seeks work rule changes to boost productivity," *Wall Street Journal*, December 22, 1980, p. 13.

[9] Robert D. Hershey, Jr., "Coal—the other glut," *New York Times*, May 16, 1982), p. F-28.

half of this century resulted in an increase in net tons produced per man per day from three in 1900 to almost seven in 1950.[10] The introduction of the continuous mining machine extended that trend and enabled net tons produced per man per day in underground mines to more than double by the end of the 1960s. The advent of longwall mining ultimately may have a similar effect on production per man per day, as average output per unit per year for longwall mining machines has proven to be about two and one-half times that of continuous cutting machines.[11]

The favorable productivity trend that had been a basic fact of life in underground mining, as in the industry as a whole since 1900, came to an abrupt halt in 1969 and then reversed itself (see Table III-1). Average output per man per day in

TABLE III-1
Productivity in Underground Coal Mines, 1969-1980

Year	Tons Per Man Per Day	Percent Change
1969	15.61	
1970	13.76	−11.9
1971	12.03	−72.6
1972	11.91	− 1.0
1973	11.66	− 2.1
1974	11.31	− 3.0
1975	9.54	−15.7
1976	9.10	− 4.6
1977	8.70	− 4.4
1978	8.25	− 5.2
1979	9.25	+12.1
1980	9.65	+ 4.3

Source: Data for 1969-1974: Bureau of Mines Annual "Bituminous Coal and Lignite Production and Mine Operators." Data for 1975-1980: *1980 Keystone Coal Industry Manual* (New York: McGraw Hill, 1980), p. 685; 1982 Keystone Coal Industry Manual, p. 729.

underground mines, which reached almost sixteen tons in 1969, fell to under twelve tons by 1974, and to under eight tons by 1979. According to the BCOA, labor cost per man-hour under the UMWA National Agreement increased by more than 200

[10] National Coal Association, *Bituminous Coal Data Book, 1975-1977* (Washington, D.C.: National Coal Association, 1976), p. 87.

[11] *Ibid.*

percent over that same period, resulting in a more than 400 percent increase in employment cost per ton of coal mined in UMWA National Agreements mines.[12]

The precipitous drop in productivity and rise in unit labor cost in underground mining during the 1970s obviously had to be of concern to management and to the BCOA. That concern first became manifest in the 1977 UMWA-BCOA National Agreement negotiations when the BCOA entered those negotiations with the stated position that an "area of major concern to us as we approach these negotiations has been the continuing decline in productivity." [13] That same view was expressed again in 1981 when the BCOA entered negotiations with the stated position that:

> The biggest reason for the failure of the UMWA-National Agreement segment of the industry to participate in the growth of the total coal market is the heavy cost burden that low productivity imposes on coal produced under the UMWA-National Agreement. Unless corrective steps are taken now to reduce this cost, coal mined under the UMWA-National Agreement cannot compete effectively in the coal market.[14]

Safety

Underground coal mining has never been and is not today a safe or healthful industry in which to be employed. In 1969, the year in which the Federal Coal Mine Health and Safety Act was passed, underground coal mining had the highest injury frequency and severity rates in all of U.S. industry. That record lends credence to the statement made by the Department of the Interior at the Senate Hearings on the Act that "while the coal mining industry has made great strides in its ability to extract the natural resource coal from the depths of the earth, it has lagged behind other industries in protecting its most valuable resource—the miner." [15]

---

[12] "Bargaining Statement By Bituminous Coal Operators Association," *Daily Labor Report*, No. 15 (January 23, 1981), p. F-4.

[13] Bituminous Coal Operators' Association BCOA, *Will the United Mine Workers of America Play a Major Role in Coal's Future?* (Washington, D.C.: BCOA, 1977), p. 8.

[14] "Bargaining Statement," *Daily Labor Report*, p. F-2.

[15] U.S. Congress, House of Representatives, Committee on Education and Labor, *Legislative History, Federal Coal Mine Health and Safety Act* (Washington, D.C.: U.S. Government Printing Office, 1970), p. 1.

The most serious and pervasive occupational health problem in underground mining is black lung (pneumoconiosis) contracted as a result of inhalation of coal dust. The incidence and effects of this debilitating occupational illness have been judged sufficiently serious to warrant a special federal program of mandated/ guaranteed disability benefits for victims of black lung supported by a trust fund established by law in 1977, which is financed by a tax of $0.50 per ton on deep-mined coal and $0.25 per ton on surface-mined coal. The cost of providing federally mandated black lung benefits and such other black lung benefits as are required by state laws or by the UMWA National Agreement has been estimated by the BCOA to be "an average of about $3,200 a year per active miner," excluding the $0.50 per ton federal black lung tax.[16]

The federal black lung benefit program has been the subject of considerable controversy and criticism since its inception in 1977, primarily with respect to determination of eligibility for benefits. The law specifies that those who filed disability claims for respiratory ailments prior to January 1, 1973, are to be presumed to be eligible for benefits if they worked in an underground mine for a period of ten years or more. For those filing claims after January 1, 1973, eligibility is to be determined on the basis of medical evidence of occupationally related respiratory problems. In practice, however, eligibility determination has been based on the assumption that miners inevitably would contract black lung after twenty-five years of employment in an underground coal mine—a practice that the General Accounting Office characterized as more appropriate to a pension program than to a disability program. The result has been the payment of more than $300 million in black lung disability or death benefits for claims that in almost 90 percent of the cases were not supported by medical evidence.[17]

The safety problems in underground coal mining are both numerous and, in many cases, potentially lethal. Five specific hazards, however, account for most fatal accidents in underground mines: (1) fall of roof, face, or back, (2) haulage, (3) machinery, (4) electrical hazards, and (5) explosion. The haulage, machinery, and electrical hazards in underground mining

---

[16] "Bargaining Statement," *Daily Labor Report,* p. F-6.

[17] Robert D. Hershey, Jr., "GAO urges medical evidence as basis for black lung claims," *New York Times,* August 6, 1980, p. A-10.

are serious and pervasive but not unlike similar hazards in other industries. The problem of roof falls and explosions, however, are especially dangerous hazards in underground coal mining. Roof falls result from inadequate support of the mining-area roof. Most roof support is done by use of roof bolts that place the weight of supporting the mine area roof on the overlying layers whose ability to sustain that weight is never certain. The fact that continuous mining machines, by virtue of their basic nature, operate under a distance of unsupported roof further enhances the risk of roof fall. Explosions, like roof falls, are a constant and unpredictable threat owing to the presence of coal dust and the possibility of a sudden release of methane from the working face in close proximity to the mechanical and electrical power of mining equipment.

The safety hazards of underground coal mining have long been a subject of federal government attention, but it was not until the passage of the Federal Coal Mine Health and Safety Act of 1969 that the federal government became deeply involved in regulating operating conditions in underground coal mines. The Federal Bureau of Mines was established in 1910 and given the responsibility "to make diligent investigation of the methods of mining, especially in relation to the safety of miners and the appliances best adopted to prevent accidents." [18] In 1941, the Bureau of Mines was given the power to inspect mines by the Coal Mine Inspection and Investigation Act but did not receive enforcement powers until 1952, when the first Coal Mine Safety Act was passed. The Federal Coal Mine Health and Safety Act of 1969 resulted in the creation of the Mine Safety and Health Administration (MSHA), in the Department of the Interior, which subsequently was transferred to the Department of Labor with greatly enhanced inspection responsibilities and enforcement powers relative to those formerly vested in the Bureau of Mines.

The Federal Coal Mine Health and Safety Act of 1969 provides for a system of standards, inspections, citations, and penalties not unlike that later embodied in the Occupational Safety and Health Act of 1971, which created the Occupational Safety and Health Administration (OSHA). MSHA, like OSHA, has been the target of considerable controversy and criticism regarding both its mode of operation and its ultimate effectiveness. Specifically, MSHA has been criticized for diverting attention from

---

[18] J. P. David, "Earnings, Health, Safety and Welfare of Bituminous Coal Miners" Ph.D. diss., University of West Virginia, 1972, p. 98.

prevention to compliance, focusing attention on minor rather than major problems, and forcing expensive changes in workplaces and practices that have not substantially enhanced the safety of miners.

In marked contrast to the case of OSHA and the rest of U.S. industry, there is a surprising lack of controversy regarding the adverse effects of federal health and safety regulation on productivity and prices in the bituminous coal mining industry. There is, however, and undoubtedly will continue to be, a lack of agreement as to whether those adverse effects are justified by the changes in the probable fate of workers brought about by regulation. Thus far, those changes appear to have been a decrease in fatality rates but not in the rate of disabling injuries. The fatality rate per one million man-hours in underground coal mining, which was about 2 in the 1920s, 1.5 in the 1930s, and 1.0 for the following three decades, dropped during the 1970s to about 0.5.[19] The rate of disabling injuries, however, failed to show a similar downward trend during the 1970s, remaining fairly constant at about 50 per one million man-hours (see Table III-2).

TABLE III-2

Disabling Injuries in Underground Coal Mines, 1969-1980

Year	Number	Injuries Per Million Tons	Per Million Hours
1969	8,139	23.55	48.41
1970	9,348	27.67	51.62
1971	9,529	34.44	55.72
1972	10,341	36.03	54.47
1973	9,197	32.23	47.71
1974	6,713	25.48	34.24
1975	8,733	31.40	36.45
1976	11,455	40.84	46.24
1977	11,575	45.54	50.86
1978	10,465	47.84	50.47
1979	14,467	49.38	n.a.
1980	17,525	54.68	70.70

Source: President's Commission on Coal, *Coal Data Book* (Washington, D.C.: U.S. Government Printing Office, 1980), p. 141; U.S. Department of Labor, Mine Safety and Health Administration, *Injury Experience in Coal Mining 1980*, Information Report IR 1133, 1981, p. 13.

n.a. = not available.

---

[19] President's Commission on Coal, *Coal Data Book* (Washington, D.C.: U.S. Government Printing Office, 1980), p. 139.

The Coal Mine Health and Safety Act of 1969 requires regular inspection of all mines by government inspectors and regular training and medical surveillance of miners by mine operators. The basic provisions of the statute with respect to inspections, training, and surveillance are as follows: [20]

(1) *Inspections*: All underground mines are to be inspected at least four times per year (twice for surface mines). Additional inspections may be conducted at the request of miners who assert that hazardous conditions exist at their place of employment. If a mine liberates excessive quantities of methane, it shall be inspected every five days. In the case of such a mine, an inspector is empowered to immediately withdraw all miners with no loss of pay for a period of up to one week if, in his judgment, an imminent danger exists.

(2) *Training*: Each operator is required to establish a health and safety program subject to government approval which meets specified training and retraining requirements. If an inspector finds a miner who has not had the required training, that miner is to be withdrawn immediately with no loss of pay as a hazard to himself and others.

(3) *Surveillance*: Each operator is required to establish a program of medical surveillance including a chest X-ray within 18 months after passage of Act, 3 years thereafter, and then at least every 5 years. If any of those X-rays show evidence of black lung, the affected miner may transfer to a less hazardous job at the mine without loss of pay.

The statute and regulations subsequently adopted thereunder are to establish specific standards governing maximum coal dust and noise levels and minimum ventilation, rock dusting, and electrical requirements. The basic elements of those standards, which fill 559 pages of the Code of Federal Regulations, are as follows: [21]

(1) *Coal Dust and Noise*: Respirable dust levels are to be limited to 2.0 milligrams per cubic meter; noise levels and exposures are to meet the standard set by the Occupational Safety and Health Administration.

(2) *Roof Control*: Each operator shall file a roof control plan specifying roof control and support techniques; entry width is limited to 20 feet and minimum size and spacing of supports are specified.

(3) *Ventilation*: A minimum of 3,000 cubic feet per minute of air must reach each working face and methane concentrations must be below 1.0 percent in working areas (no energized

[20] *Ibid.*, p. 218.

[21] *Ibid.*, p. 219.

equipment may be activated if the volume of methane exceeds 1.0 percent and if the volume of methane reaches 1.5 percent the mine is to be evacuated immediately).

(4) *Rock Dusting*:   Rock dusting is required within 40 feet of all working faces.

The UMWA also is involved in protecting the health and safety of underground miners. The UMWA National Agreement gives "health and safety" both prominent and extensive attention, as does its monthly journal, which provides extensive coverage of problems and disasters, particularly those occurring in nonunion underground mines. The UMWA has long expressed interest and concern regarding the dangers confronting underground miners, but historically it has not been aggressive in pursuing those interests and concerns in the halls of Congress. In the mid-1950s, a BCOA executive was quoted as praising the UMWA for joining the industry in a cooperative effort to combat, among other things, "unreasonable safety regulations." [22]   In the late 1960s, the UMWA was not in the vanguard of those pressing for federal mine safety or state black lung legislation, to the obvious dismay of many of its members.

The provisions of the UMWA National Agreement dealing with health and safety precede all other substantive provisions of the agreement regarding terms and conditions of employment. Those provisions do not deal extensively with the specific hazards facing miners or the steps to be taken to control those hazards, although they do identify twelve "special safety problem areas" and set some general requirements for solutions to those problems. Instead, those provisions place the basic responsibility for safe and healthful working conditions on the good faith of employers and, more importantly, on the vigilance of individual miners and their union representatives at the local and district level.

The National Agreement (Article III, "Health and Safety") states that "every employee . . . is entitled to a safe and healthful place to work" and that "no employee will be required to work under conditions he has reasonable grounds to believe to be abnormally and immediately dangerous to himself beyond the normal hazards inherent in the operation." An individual who believes he finds himself in such conditions and who cannot convince his supervisor of that fact has the right to be reassigned

[22] Richard A. Lester, *As Unions Mature* (Princeton, N.J.:   Princeton University Press, 1958), p. 70.

to other duties at no loss of pay until such time as the presence or absence of abnormally dangerous conditions can be definitively determined. If an individual is found not to have acted in good faith in exercising this right to reassignment, he "shall be subject to appropriate disciplinary action." [23]

Article III also stipulates that "at each mine there shall be a Mine Health and Safety Committee made up of miners employed at the mine . . . selected by the local union," which is empowered to "inspect any portion of a mine" after giving "sufficient advance notice." If, in the course of such an inspection that committee finds "those special instances" in which it "believes that an imminent danger exists" which should require the removal of employees from the area in question, "the Employer is required to follow the Committee's recommendation and remove the Employees from the involved area immediately." If a committee acts "arbitrarily and capriciously" in closing down an area of a mine, "a member or members of such Committee may be removed from the Committee." [24]

The health and safety provisions of the agreement explicitly provide for the right of international union officials to have "access to the mine" in recognition of the union's "concern with health and safety in coal mines." That right extends to international union officers and staff, and to district officers of the union in the district in which a mine is located. The three top officers of the international union are specifically accorded "the right to visit any and all mines covered by this Agreement at any time." [25]

The National Agreement (Article XVI, "Training") also contains separate, extensive provisions regarding the training of employees, which reflect accord that "effective training programs [are] essential to safe and efficient production of coal." Those provisions deal with both training of new and retraining of old employees. In both cases, training it to "emphasize health and safety with particular emphasis on local conditions and associated hazards." [26] The training provisions of the agreement also preclude the assignment of an inexperienced employee with less

---

[23] National Bituminous Coal Wage Agreement of 1981, Article III, sections (a) and (i), pp. 8-9, 15-17.

[24] *Ibid.*, section (d), pp. 10-12.

[25] *Ibid.*, section (e), pp. 12-13.

[26] *Ibid.*, Article XVI, sections (a) and (b), pp. 55-58.

than forty-five days' prior underground mining experience to the operation of "any mining machine at the face or . . . any transportation equipment, mobile equipment or medium or high voltage electricity" [27]—a ban that the BCOA in 1981 singled out as one of the provisions of the agreement that "does little for the well being of miners while standing in the way of increased productivity." [28]

The basic safety and training provisions of the National Agreement are not much different today than they were twenty years ago. The 1974 UMWA-BCOA negotiations produced some changes in manning, ostensibly in the interest of health and safety, which became something of an issue in their 1977 negotiations when the industry cited as part of its productivity problem "certain contractual changes in the 1974 contract which increased employment, but did not result in more coal being mined." [29] That scenario was repeated in 1981 when the BCOA chose to raise the question of restrictions on assignment of inexperienced personnel as a productivity issue. With the exception of such productivity issues, health and safety were not the focus of much attention in the 1981 UMWA-BCOA negotiations, despite the fact that unions publicly took the position that "increases in disabling injuries and the relatively constant rate of fatal injuries occurring in the industry force the union to seek to strengthen . . . the provisions of Article III, 'Health and Safety,' and Article XVI, 'Training.' " [30] No substantial changes, however, were made in those articles, lending credence to the BCOA view that "the UMWA-National Agreement and the Federal Mine and Safety and Health Act, and the regulations issued under that Act, contain more than enough provisions on safety and health." [31]

SURFACE MINING

Surface or strip mining is used to extract coal deposits located near the surface of the land and is fundamentally an earth-moving operation. Strip mining is a three stage process.

---

[27] *Ibid.*, section (f), pp. 62-63.

[28] "Bargaining Statement," *Daily Labor Report*, pp. F-3, F-4.

[29] BCOA, *Will the United Mine Workers of America Play a Major Role in Coal's Future?*, p. 9.

[30] "Statement of United Mine Workers President Church on Union's Bargaining Demands in Soft Coal Talks," *Daily Labor Report*, No. 14 (January 22, 1981), p. E-2.

[31] "Bargaining Statement," *Daily Labor Report*, p. F-8.

First, overburden covering the coal seam is removed. Second, once the seam has been exposed, the coal is extracted using large power shovels, bulldozers, trucks, and other earth-moving equipment. The final step, as required by law, is land reclamation designed to restore the surface of the land to something approximating its original condition.

The fundamental technological difference between surface and deep mining is clearly reflected in their respective occupational structures. Both types of mines employ substantial numbers of skilled maintenance personnel and a limited number of skilled explosives personnel, but beyond those two categories of jobs there is little occupational similarity between deep and surface mining. In conducting its wage survey for bituminous coal mining, the Bureau of Labor Statistics examines a total of thirty-eight jobs in deep mines, but only sixteen jobs in surface mines.[32] Among the key jobs in deep mines are mechanical-cutting and loading-machine operator, continuous-mining machine operator, and roof bolter; in contrast to surface mines where the key jobs are power-shovel operator, bulldozer operator, and truck driver. The basic difference between the two is perhaps best exemplified by the fact that within surveyed employment the most important occupation in terms of number of workers is roof bolter in deep mining and bulldozer operator in surface mining.

The obvious dissimilarity of jobs between deep and surface mines constitutes a potential problem to the UMWA in organizing surface miners, given the union's historical record and continuing image as a champion of the cause of underground miners. That problem, at least in the West, has been complicated by the fact that the obvious similarity of jobs in surface mining to those in heavy construction has produced a potentially formidable organizing rival in the form of the IUOE, which typically represents heavy equipment operators in construction and serves as the major source of supply of such operators for that industry.

Productivity

The quality of surface-mined coal generally is not as high as that of deep-mined coal and it does not command as high a price. The cost of surface-mined coal, however, is generally also less than deep-mined coal, in large part because of higher labor produc-

---

[32] *Industry Wage Survey: Bituminous Coal—January 1976-March 1981* (Washington, D.C.: U.S. Government Printing Office, 1978), pp. 10, 32.

tivity. In 1980, production per man per day in surface mines was almost twenty-seven tons as compared with nine tons in underground mines.[33] The productivity difference between the two types of operations has grown slightly over the past five years, but that trend may be halted and possibly reversed by federal land reclamation requirements.

Surface mining has been the beneficiary of technological advances in heavy earth-moving equipment, just as deep mining benefitted from technological advances in coal-cutting and loading equipment. In 1947, average output per man per day in surface mines was about fifteen tons.[34] By 1973, that figure had more than doubled to over thirty-six tons, but since then output per man per day in surface mines, as in deep mines, has reversed its upward trend and by 1980 stood at just under twenty-seven tons (see Table III-3). Despite the recent downward trend in output per man per day, the relatively constant productivity advantage of surface over deep mining has made productivity a far less important issue in labor relations in surface mining than in deep mining. The conflict over work rules in recent UMWA-

TABLE III-3

Productivity in Surface Coal Mines, 1969-1980

Year	Tons Per Man Per Day	Percent Change
1969	35.71	
1970	35.96	.7
1971	35.88	− .2
1972	36.33	1.2
1973	36.67	.9
1974	33.16	− 9.6
1975	26.69	−19.5
1976	26.40	− 1.1
1977	26.59	.1
1978	25.78	− 3.1
1979	26.98	4.7
1980	27.00	0

Source: Data for 1969-1974: Bureau of Mines Annual, "Bituminous Coal and Lignite Production." Data for 1975-1980: *1980 Keystone Coal Industry Manual*, p. 685; *1982 Keystone Coal Industry Manual*, p. 729.

[33] *1982 Keystone Coal Industry Manual*, p. 729.

[34] President's Commission on Coal, *Coal Data Book*, p. 125.

BCOA contract negotiations has not been duplicated in recent contract negotiations between the UMWA and the companies that are party to its Western Surface Mine Agreements. This lack of overt conflict, however, does not mean that productivity problems do not exist. One western surface mine operator, whose employees are covered by a UMWA surface mine agreement, characterized the situation in the following terms: "The basic problems and issues are the same in the West as in the East; the only difference is in their degree."

Safety

The safety record of surface mines, like their productivity record, is clearly superior to that of deep mines (see Table III-4). The most spectacular occupational safety and health problems of the industry—explosion, entrapment, and black lung—are fundamentally problems of underground mining. There are, however, other serious problems that beset both surface and underground mine operations, such as material handling, power haulage, machinery, and slips and falls. These problems take on a special significance in strip-mining by virtue of the scale of equipment used to extract, handle, and move coal within the mine site.

TABLE III-4

Disabling Injuries in Surface Coal Mines, 1969-1980

Year	Number	Disabling Injuries Per Million Tons	Per Million Hours
1969	942	4.42	21.41
1970	1,306	4.98	24.88
1971	1,525	5.50	25.79
1972	1,227	5.10	23.67
1973	1,136	4.27	19.72
1974	1,175	3.95	16.14
1975	1,650	5.03	17.14
1976	1,976	5.47	19.27
1977	2,211	5.51	18.93
1978	1,997	5.29	16.55
1979	2,198	4.55	n.a.
1980	3,163	6.69	23.70

Source: President's Commission on Coal, *Coal Data Book* (Washington, D.C.: U.S. Government Printing Office, 1980), p. 141; U.S. Department of Labor, Mine Safety and Health Administration, *Injury Experience in Coal Mining 1980*, Information Report IR 1133, 1981, p. 13.

n.a. = not available

The frequency rate for disabling injuries per million man-hours worked is about two and one-half times greater in underground than in surface mines. That difference is even more dramatic when injury rates are computed on the basis of tonnage mined, in which case the injury rate for underground mines is about eight times that for surface mines. Fatality rates are also lower in surface mines, but by substantially lower margins primarily as a result of the seriousness of the potential hazards associated with the use of large-scale, earth-moving equipment.

The Federal Coal Mine Health and Safety Act of 1969 clearly was aimed primarily at the health and safety hazards in underground mines, as is evident in the fact that it mandates inspection of underground mines four times each year as compared with only two times per year for surface mines.[35] That emphasis is even more evident in the record of enforcement of the act which between 1973 and 1978 produced almost four times as many notices of violations to underground mines as to surface mines. The emphasis of federal health and safety regulations on deep mines, however, does not mean that surface mines and surface mine productivity have been unaffected by that regulation. The concern of the UMWA for the health and safety of underground miners has been extended to its relationships with surface mine operators. The health and safety provisions of its western surface mine agreements are virtually identical to those of its National Agreement. In both agreements, the health and safety article precedes all other substantive articles, provides that "every employee . . . is entitled to a safe and healthful place to work," and promises that "no employee will be required to work under conditions he has reasonable grounds to believe to be abnormally and immediately dangerous to himself." Similarly, both agreements provide for a mine health and safety committee empowered to inspect and, in case of imminent danger, to force removal of employees from the mine.

UMWA surface mine agreements, like the National Agreement, also contain fairly extensive provisions regarding training of new employees and retraining of all employees. Specifically, those provisions require orientation programs for new, inexperienced employees of not less than four days and annual retraining programs for existing employees of not less than eight hours. The training provisions of surface mine agreements do not limit the

---

[35] *Ibid.*, p. 219.

assignment of new, inexperienced personnel, as in the National Agreement, but another provision of those agreements stipulates that "a new and inexperienced employee with less than 90 days experience in surface mining shall not be required to work alone in any areas where he cannot be seen or his cries for help heard."

Safety issues have not played a prominent role in recent UMWA western surface mine negotiations, just as they have not in negotiations with the BCOA. Safety issues, however, have played a prominent role in the union's efforts to organize surface mine workers, particularly in the West. The UMWA has made safety virtually the key issue in its organizing campaigns in the West, as in the East, and has been vocal in its criticism of the weakness of the safety provisions in coal mine contracts of its rival unions. A review of a few contracts of one of those rival unions—the IUOE—suggests the existence of only a very limited basis for such criticism in the case of that union. In those contracts, safety is explicitly covered, but not as prominently or extensively as in UMWA contracts. The safety provisions of IUOE contracts generally are less adversarial and more cooperative in character than are the provisions of UMWA contracts. Specifically, those contracts provide that the company will "maintain such safe and sanitary working conditions as are reasonably possible in view of the nature of its operations" and will "give prompt consideration to suggestions from the union concerning possible improvements therein." In lieu of the UMWA's mine health and safety committees, the IUOE contracts call for a "Joint Safety Committee" composed of an equal number of union and company representatives which is to "serve as an advisory body to the company."

The strategic advantage gained by the UMWA in its efforts to organize surface mine workers by virtue of its emphasis on safety in general, and its superiority in protecting the safety of workers in particular, remains to be seen. The fact that the UMWA does not represent even a majority of such workers suggests that safety appeals have to date not been overwhelmingly persuasive, despite or perhaps because of the intense attention focused on coal mine health and safety by federal legislation and regulation over the past decade. Whether that situation will change in the face of what appears to be diminishing public and governmental enthusiasm for federal regulation is an open question.

CHAPTER IV

The Demography of the Industry

The bituminous coal mining industry in 1980 was quite a different creature than it was in 1950 or even 1970. The consolidation that took place in the industry between 1950 and 1970 took a substantial toll in terms of both mines and miners and changed the character of the industry's employers and employees. The rebirth of the industry during the 1970s has halted and reversed the attrition process and produced a new set of changes in the character of employers and employees in the industry. As a result of those changes, the industry today has a new management, new work force, and new industrial relations climate that have created a whole new set of problems for the UMWA and the BCOA.

THE NEW MANAGEMENT

The declining demand for coal during the 1950s left the industry with substantial excess capacity and great potential for the "ruinous competition" historically associated with such excess capacity. The bargaining power and policies of the UMWA in the 1950s effectively prevented competitive pressures from taking their toll on coal prices and coal miners' wages and forced those pressures to be focused on coal costs and coal miners' productivity. The key to survival in this competitive environment was ability to mechanize—a form of natural selection that tended to favor larger mines and mine operators by virtue of their likely superior access to the capital required to mechanize. That indeed was the case as the percentage of annual production accounted for by the fifty largest coal companies rose from a low of 41.8 in the record production year of 1947 to a high of 69.2 in 1973, the year in which the number of operating mines reached its postwar low.[1]

---

[1] *1980 Keystone Coal Industry Manual* (New York: McGraw Hill, 1980), p. 686.

In 1950, there were basically only two types of major producers—coal companies and captive producers. Coal companies,
engaged solely or primarily in the mining of coal for sale in the
open market, dominated the industry in terms of production.
Captive producers, primarily steel companies engaged in the mining of coal for internal consumption, were prominent among the
major producers and played an even more prominent role in the
labor relations of the industry.

The ownership/operating character of the largest coal producers is far more complex in 1980 than it was in 1950. The
same distinction can be made between coal companies and captive producers, but a new ownership distinction must be made
within each category. There are now two types of coal companies: independents and those which are part of energy (oil)
companies, and two types of captive producers: steel and utilities,
as is evident in the list of the top fifteen coal-producing groups
in 1979 (see Table IV-1).

The growing involvement of oil companies in the coal mining
industry, by acquisition or merger or by purchase of reserves to
open new mines, over the past decade is likely to continue over

TABLE IV-1
Top 15 Coal Producing Companies in 1979

Group or Company	Operation	Ownership	Standing 1979	Standing 1970
Peabody	Coal	Independent	1	1
Consolidation	Coal	Energy	2	2
AMAX Group	Coal	Coal-Energy	3	5
Texas Utilities	Coal	Utility	4	n.a.
Island Creek	Coal	Energy	5	3
U.S. Steel	Captive	Steel	6	8
Pittston	Coal	Independent	7	4
NERCO Group	Captive	Utility	8	44
American Electric	Captive	Utility	9	17
Peter Kiewit	Coal	Independent	10	n.a.
Arch Mineral	Coal	Independent	11	n.a.
Bethlehem Mines	Captive	Steel	12	6
Western Energy	Captive	Utility	13	48
North American	Coal	Independent	14	12
Old Ben	Coal	Energy	15	10

Source: *1980 Keystone Coal Industry Manual* (New York: McGraw Hill,
       1980), p. 686.
n.a. = not available.

the next decade. Those companies possess the capital needed by existing companies to expand capacity or required to begin mining operations on their own—an option that they clearly enjoy by virtue of holding 40 percent of all privately owned coal reserves in the United States.[2] What this trend has meant to or will mean for labor relations in the industry is unclear, but it "no doubt has had an effect on managerial behavior." [3] The view of many in the industry is that this effect on managerial behavior has been growing resistance to the UMWA.

The Old Coal Companies

Independent coal companies historically have been the dominant force in the industry and within the BCOA. As such, they were the primary partner of the UMWA in the uniquely cooperative bargaining relationship that characterized the industry during the 1950s and 1960s and were the primary beneficiaries of the UMWA's efforts to utilize that relationship to stabilize the industry. That tradition of cooperation has left a lasting mark on the labor relations image, if not policies, of old coal companies, which tend to be perceived by the union as the "good guys" and by other producers as the "doves" in the labor relations of the industry.

The labor relations image and posture of independent coal companies can be explained by reference to their bargaining power. The basic product of these companies is coal to be sold in the coal market. Concessions to the union by such companies are of concern only to the extent that they result in a competitive disadvantage in the coal market. On the other side of the coin, such companies typically are not in a good position to resist concessions to the union, even when those concessions may result in competitive disadvantage, for two reasons: (1) most of all of their mines are organized by the UMWA and covered by the UMWA National Agreement; and (2) they lack the financial resources required to take a long strike in their UMWA-organized mines.

The organizational strength of the UMWA in the old coal segment of the industry is a matter of history. The older mines of

---

[2] President's Commission on Coal, *Coal Data Book* (Washington, D.C.: U.S. Government Printing Office, 1980), p. 123.

[3] William H. Miernyk, "Coal," in Gerald G. Somers, ed., *Collective Bargaining: Contemporary American Experience* (Madison, Wis.: Industrial Relations Research Association, 1980), p. 10.

the major independents, regardless of technology or geography, were organized by 1950 and covered by the first National Wage Agreement, concluded in that year. To the extent that new mines were opened by the major independents between 1950 and 1970, no attempt was made to resist the organization of those mines by the UMWA or to resist the inclusion of new eastern mines under the UMWA National Agreement. In the West, however, while there was little resistance to UMWA organization in the new surface mines of the major independents, there was resistance to inclusion of such mines under the National Agreement, which resulted in a separate UMWA Western Surface Mine Agreement. Thus, a producer like Peabody, whose eastern and midwestern surface and underground mines are covered by the UMWA-BCOA contract, has a separate contract with the UMWA covering its western surface mines.

Since 1970, however, the growth of non-UMWA coal production in the West has begun to stiffen the resistance of eastern independents to UMWA organization and control of their western mines. AMAX, the nation's third largest coal producer and a member of the BCOA, acquired a surface mine in Wyoming in the early 1970s which was organized by the UMWA. When that mine was subsequently struck by the UMWA, the company decided to operate the mine using replacement labor. As a result, the nation's largest mine is now nonunion, although the status of that mine and its employees continues to be a matter of conflict between AMAX and the UMWA.[4] Westmoreland Coal, another major independent and BCOA member, has opened both a new underground and a new surface mine in the West since 1970 on a non-UMWA basis.

The Captive Producers

Historically, steel companies have been dominant captive coal producers and the only ones to play a visible role in industry labor relations. Utilities, however, now outrank steel companies in total coal production but remain in the shadow of steel as a factor in labor relations, primarily because most captive utility production is in the West.[5]

---

[4] See "Decision of Supreme Court in NLRB v. AMAX Coal Company," *Daily Labor Report*, No. 124 (June 29, 1981), pp. D-1 to D-9.

[5] *1980 Keystone Coal Industry Manual*, p. 692.

In recent years, the steel industry has been perceived by the union and others as a "hawk" in UMWA-BCOA contract negotiations. That, however, has not always been the case and seemingly was not as recently as 1974. The changing character of steel's image and posture is a product of the changing fortunes of the steel industry. Steel companies produce coal to use, not to sell and are, therefore, concerned with both cost and continuity of supply. When the demand for steel is strong, continuity of supply takes precedence. When the demand for steel is weak, as it has been in the past five years, cost takes precedence. Thus, it is not surprising that steel played a prominent role in the BCOA's recent confrontations with the UMWA.

Captive steel mines, like the mines of major independent producers, are extensively organized by the UMWA. Despite that fact, those mines can withstand a long strike primarily because of the ability of their parent company to stockpile or, as in 1977-1978, to import coal in sufficient quantities to meet demand. In addition, the financial drain of a coal strike on steel companies is far lesser relative magnitude than in the case of coal companies. That situation, however, may change, given the apparent trend toward exploitation of coal reserves as a source of revenue rather than raw material by major steel companies.

The fact that most captive utility coal production is concentrated in the new surface mines in the West has placed that production outside the historical orbit of UMWA control. The fact that cost and continuity of production are crucial concerns for utilities has created a clear incentive to keep their captive production out of UMWA control, which most thus far have done. In the course of that process a new element has been added to the labor relations of the industry—the International Brotherhood of Electrical Workers (IBEW), which is the dominant union in the utility industry and which represents miners at Texas Utilities, the nation's largest captive coal producer.

The New Coal Companies

The most visible new entrants into the coal mining industry over the past decade have been oil companies. Their invasion of the industry has come in two stages. The first took the form of acquisition of, or merger with, existing old coal companies, which placed those oil companies that undertook such action in the role of party to longstanding bargaining relationships with the

UMWA. The second is taking the form of acquisition of previously unmined coal reserves for the purpose of opening new mines unfettered by an existing bargaining relationship.

The labor relations image of the oil companies in the union and among independent producers is that of "bad guy" and "super hawk." Consolidations Coal, which is controlled by Conoco, now a division of DuPont, and the nation's second largest coal producer, has been singled out for special attention as an energy villain.[6] Economically, the roots of the image rest on the fact that the oil companies view coal in the context of a broad energy market in which it must be, or be made competitive in terms of, not only price but also return on investment. Institutionally, the roots of this image rest in the perception by the union and independent producers that oil companies lack an appreciation for the special traditions and conditions of the industry and seem anxious either to "buy out" or "battle out" the problems that stand in the way of making coal a competitive energy resource. Thus, it is not surprising that the energy companies, like the steel companies, have been blamed for recent UMWA-BCOA confrontations over productivity issues to the point where some in the union and in the industry have come to suspect that those confrontations are part of a broader strategy to break the UMWA. That vague suspicion is accompanied by a clear conviction that oil companies are determined to keep their new mines, particularly in the West, non-UMWA, if not nonunion.

The invasion of the coal mining industry by energy companies has produced one particularly interesting new entrant into the labor relations of the entire industry—the Gulf Oil Company. In the late 1960s, Gulf acquired the Pittsburgh and Midway Coal Company, which today operates UMWA-organized mines in both the East and the West. As a matter of policy Gulf Oil does not believe in multiemployer bargaining or benefit systems and, as a matter of practice, believes in pursuing an independent course in the conduct of its labor relations—two operational principles that it imposed on Pittsburgh and Midway which has, in turn, become an industry maverick in both the East and the West.

The western segment of the industry has a large number of relatively young, regional producers not steeped in the labor relations traditions of eastern underground mining and apparently,

---

[6] Thomas Petzinger, Jr., and Carol Hymowitz, "Anxiety is growing in the coal industry over CONOCO unit's tough labor stance," *Wall Street Journal*, March 27, 1980, p. 15.

like the oil companies, they are determined not to become part of those traditions. Among those regional producers are some owners and/or operators whose background is in heavy construction. Those firms are noteworthy because, by virtue of their background, they have served as an obvious and often easy route for the entry of the IUOE into the organizational picture in western surface mining, just as utilities have done for the IBEW.

THE NEW WORK FORCE

For half a century, 1920-1970, the bituminous coal mining industry was blessed or blighted with an excess supply of labor as it reduced its work force from 640,000 to 125,000. The situation was reversed in the 1970s when the industry found itself facing a labor shortage. The first signs of that shortage appeared in 1967 when a *Coal Age* survey estimated that because of attrition in the form of retirements and resignations, approximately 30,000 new employees would be needed each year through 1970 to meet projected demands for coal.[7] Two years later, a representative of one of the nation's largest coal producers stated that "the industry faces a crisis in manpower" and will need "at least 50,000 new miners within the next five years." [8] The growth of the industry after the 1973 energy crisis, which added 100,000 new jobs in the industry between 1973 and 1980, further intensified the industry's need for new manpower.[9]

The New Worker

The industry basically has drawn on the indigenous population to meet its manpower needs in both the East and the West. In the East this has involved drawing back or retaining individuals for whom coal mining and the UMWA are familiar, if not family, traditions. In the West, it has involved attracting individuals from other industries and occupations for whom coal mining and the UMWA are whole new ways of life. Western workers lured by the promise of high and steady wages have shown little reluctance to go to work in the mines, but, unlike their eastern coun-

---

[7] Ivan A. Given, "Manpower for Coal," *Coal Age*, May 1967, p. 60.

[8] "Coal mines need labor: face crisis," *New York Times*, August 3, 1969, p. F-13.

[9] *Coal News*, September 22, 1978, p. 76.

terparts, they have shown a clear lack of receptiveness to organization by the UMWA.

There is general agreement in the industry that the western miner is different than his eastern counterpart. In the view of many union and management representatives, the western miner is characterized by a work ethic quite different from that prevailing in the East, in that he expects and wants to work to earn an income that for many enables them to sustain a second career in farming or ranching. In addition, those miners are perceived to be a highly individualistic and independent breed with little familiarity with or affinity for unionism in general and the UMWA in particular.

The efforts of the UMWA to organize these new workers face two difficulties. The first is the resistance of new, western management to the transfer of the traditions and conditions of eastern labor relations into the western coal fields. The second is a lack of appeal to western miners, who "have little of the emotional attachment for the UMW that is handed down from father to son in the Eastern fields" and who "often regard the UMW as a capricious and unruly union." [10] Thus far, these difficulties have severely limited the organizational effectiveness of the UMWA in the West to the point that

> the union has only about 20 mines under contract in the West compared with more than 2,000 in the East and out of its membership of about 170,000 only about 13,000 are in the West. While in the East it wins about half of the elections it enters, it goes down to defeat almost every time in the West.[11]

The UMWA is not unconcerned about its weakness in the West or unaware of the problems it faces in overcoming that weakness. One of those problems, in the words of a UMWA organizer, is that "except for pockets scattered throughout the region where the UMWA fought and won sometimes violent and bloody early century organizing battles, historic and family derived union traditions and support are few." [12] Thus, "workers have little or no idea of what the union can do for them," making it necessary "to

---

[10] Thomas Petzinger, Jr., "The organizer: union official in West wins over few miners in struggle to recruit," *Wall Street Journal*, October 8, 1979, p. 1.

[11] *Ibid.*

[12] Mike Hall, "Major Organizing Effort Getting Underway in Western Coal Fields," *United Mine Workers Journal*, August 1980, p. 12.

educate these people about the need for the union." [13] That task is not an easy one when dealing with "a kid off a ranch who has been making $3 or $4 an hour and all of the sudden he's making $11 or $12" and is made more difficult by the fact that "the western miner wants to work and one of the first questions is about . . . strikes." [14]

The Young Worker

The recruitment of a new work force in the East has produced a dramatic change in the age structure of the industry's work force and the union's membership. In 1967, well over one-half of active UMWA miners were over forty-five years of age; by 1975, however, more than half of those miners were under thirty-five years of age.[15] The younger miner in the East has proven to be as different a breed from his older counterpart as the western miner has proved to be different from his eastern counterpart.

The shift in the age structure of the work force in the East has made the UMWA servant to two masters. Retired as well as active miners are eligible to vote in elections for union office, which ensures that the union leadership will be sensitive to the desires of older miners in their conduct of union affairs. Only active miners, however, are eligible to vote on contract ratification, which requires that the union leadership be highly sensitive to the desires of younger miners in their conduct of collective bargaining with the BCOA. Those younger miners, like their younger counterparts in other industries, lack the reverence for the past accomplishments of their union held by older workers and are more prone to ask, "What have you done for me lately?" In both 1978 and 1981, the answer to that question was "not enough," judging by the failure of the rank and file to ratify tentative settlements in both of those sets of UMWA-BCOA negotiations.

The younger miner of the 1970s was "more likely to question authority, be less patient with fixed routine work, and have a keener appreciation of leisure" than his older counterparts.[16] In

---

[13] *Ibid.*

[14] *Ibid.*, pp. 12-13.

[15] President's Commission on Coal, *Coal Data Book*, p. 131.

[16] Everett M. Kassalow, "Labor-Management Relations and Coal Industry," *Monthly Labor Review*, Vol. 102, No. 5 (May 1979), p. 25.

short, he was a more independent breed, less amenable to authoritarian control and organizational discipline. The first victim of these characteristics of younger miners was the autocratic leadership of the UMWA established by John L. Lewis, which prevailed throughout the 1950s and the 1960s before it gave way to the return of democracy to the UMWA in the early 1970s —a movement which, among other things, gave the rank and file the right to ratify or to reject UMWA-BCOA contract settlements.

The second victim of the changing character of the work force was the labor peace and stability that had prevailed in the industry since 1950. In 1968, the industry experienced its first formal strike in UMWA-BCOA negotiations since 1950, and even that strike was not called or authorized by the union. Since then, there have been authorized strikes in each of the four succeeding UMWA-BCOA contract negotiations. Equally important and troublesome from the industry viewpoint was a dramatic increase after 1968 in the level of wildcat strike activity, which reached a peak during the term of the 1974 UMWA-BCOA contract, when approximately 9,000 wildcat strikes occurred.[17] The specific causes of these wildcat strikes were as varied as the strikes themselves were numerous, but one basic problem was conflict at the mine level between a "newer, more assertive mining work force" and an older, more authoritarian supervision whose "degree of professionalism . . . leaves much to be desired, especially in many of the older mines."[18] This conflict manifested itself in a growing number of grievances, most of which could not be settled informally because supervisors were unwilling or unable to compromise. The result was "growing impatience among miners" which finally led to a "rash of wildcat strikes as miners sought to bypass the ineffective local machinery."[19]

The worsening strike record of the UMWA in the East between 1968 and 1977 has been a significant handicap in its organizing efforts in the West. Beyond being a source of embarrassment in dealing with non-UMWA members, it has been a source of actual losses for existing UMWA members in the West. The rash of strikes in the East between 1974 and 1977 forced cutbacks in

---

[17] Wayne L. Horvitz, "What's Happening in Collective Bargaining?" *Labor Law Journal*, August 1978, p. 460.

[18] Kassalow, "Labor-Management Relations," p. 25.

[19] *Ibid.*

benefits from the union's trust funds financed by per-ton royalties. Those cutbacks applied to "innocent" western as well as "guilty" eastern UMWA members. The result was strong rank-and-file interest in the separation of western and eastern benefit systems which, by 1977, had grown to the point where "western miners have made it clear they do not want their pension and health benefits to be dependent on the vagaries of strike prone production in the East." [20]

The Minority Worker

Coal mining historically has been and continues to be an overwhelming blue-collar industry, although this situation is beginning to change. In 1977, production workers constituted 82 percent of the work force in coal mining as compared with 88 percent in 1960, and

> It is anticipated that the nonproduction work force, including engineers and technicians, will continue to grow more rapidly than the production worker component, although some significant increase in production workers is expected. It is also anticipated that there will be a growing demand for skilled maintenance employees, especially in underground mines.[21]

The work force of the industry in general, and its production work force in particular, is predominantly white and overwhelmingly male. Minorities and women together account for less than 10 percent of industry employment, with most minorities holding blue-collar and most women holding white-collar jobs. Statistically, these patterns have not changed in the past and are unlikely to change rapidly in the coming decade, but there have been some important developments in recent years, particularly with respect to the employment of women and native Americans, which are worthy of note.

The most striking aspect of the composition of the industry work force is the almost total absence of black workers, particularly since historically that has not always been the case, especially in the South.[22] In 1900, some 22,000 blacks were em-

---

[20] "A Separate Peace in Western Coal," *Business Week*, December 5, 1977, p. 41.

[21] Kassalow, "Labor-Management Relations," p. 24.

[22] Darold T. Barnum, "The Negro in the Bituminous Coal Mining Industry," in Herbert R. Northrup and Richard L. Rowan, eds., *Negro Employment in Southern Industry* (Philadelphia: Industrial Research Unit, The Wharton School, University of Pennsylvania, 1970), Part Four.

ployed in coal mining in the southern Appalachia states (Alabama, Kentucky, Tennessee, Virginia, and West Virginia). By 1930, that number had grown to over 44,000, representing more than 20 percent of industry employment in the region. Since 1930, the trend in black employment in the region has been downward to a level of 26,000 in 1950 and only 7,000 in 1960. Between 1930 and 1950, the percentage representation of blacks in the industry's southern work force fell by almost 50 percent, as it did again between 1950 and 1960 when blacks constituted 6.8 percent of southern coal mine employment.

Clearly, black workers in the South were the major victims of mechanization in bituminous coal mining. The reason was discrimination by employers against blacks in the upgrading of unskilled workers displaced by mechanization of coal-cutting and loading operations to the operation of mechanical coal-cutting and loading machines. The UMWA, "once the most equalitarian of unions," failed to force equality in upgrading and "stood idly by while its Negro members were displaced and not given a fair share of newly opened jobs." [23]

The bituminous coal mining industry has not been a significant focus of government equal opportunity or affirmative action efforts on behalf of blacks and has not been a significant source of new employment opportunities for blacks despite its substantial and growing demand for labor since the late 1960's. The fact that in terms of total employment coal mining was a declining industry throughout the 1960s may explain why it failed to attract either government attention or black workers. By the time the decline of the industry was halted and reversed in the 1970s, a new minority group had emerged to occupy the attention of the government and the industry—women.

The major civil rights issue facing the industry and the union during the 1970s has been the employment of women in production jobs—most notably as inside workers in underground mines. The issue of female employment in production jobs in coal mining first arose in the early 1970s and has persisted through the decade. The phenomenon of female entry into the mines was described by *Business Week* in 1979 as follows:

> For decades coal mines were off limits to women . . . but since the early 1970s the women's movement and federal emphasis on equal rights have prompted women to seek high-paying coal mining jobs.

---

[23] *Ibid.*, p. 64.

Their ranks have tripled in the past three years to more than 2,500 workers—and as their numbers increase, the women promise to have a growing impact on company policies, union politics, and perhaps even contract negotiations.[24]

The impact of the women's movement and federal regulation on company hiring policy already has become evident. In 1978, Consolidation Coal, the nation's second largest producer, agreed to a $360,000 settlement in a sex discrimination action and committed itself to hire one woman out of each four new hires with a goal of a work force that will be 32.8 percent female.[25] As a result of complaints from the Coal Employment Project, a nonprofit group established to help women get jobs in coal mining, the federal government in 1979 was investigating hiring practices at the nation's first and fourth largest coal producers.[26]

The impact of the women's movement on union politics also has already been felt. In June 1979, a "small but militant collection of female miners" met independently of the UMWA in the first "National Conference of Women Coal Miners." [27] Less than six months later, the UMWA sponsored its first "Women in the Mines" conference to "deal with the problems faced by approximately 2,500 Union sisters." [28] The significance of this new minority within the union is difficult to assess, but it may well be that, in the words of *Business Week*, the "greatest problem women pose to the UMWA is that they may become politically active" within the union. What that, in turn, might mean for union policies and programs is even more difficult to foresee. The issues discussed at the conference of women coal miners included job discrimination, sexual harassment, and sick leave for pregnancy and child care. Whether the still small but growing number of union sisters will be able to convince their union brothers to adopt such causes remains to be seen.

The western segment of the industry has its own special minority worker problems. To a limited extent, producers in the West must deal with the question of equal opportunity for Chi-

---

[24] "The Militant Women Mining the Coal Fields," *Business Week*, June 25, 1979, p. 30.

[25] *Ibid.*, p. 31.

[26] *Ibid.*

[27] *Ibid.*, p. 30.

[28] "Union Sponsors Women's Conference, First in History of UMWA," *United Mine Workers Journal*, November 1979, p. 8.

canos. A far more important issue, however, is affirmative action on behalf of native Americans. Indian tribes hold title to lands containing substantial reserves of coal. The sale of mining rights to such coal to private producers can be, and has been, linked to strong affirmative action requirements on behalf of tribal members. As a result, there are surface mines in the West that operate with predominantly native American work forces.

The significance of this development for the UMWA and the industry is unclear. There was no consensus among western union and management representatives as to whether native Americans were more or less receptive to union-organizing appeals than their fellow western miners. The UMWA, however, apparently is taking no chances in that respect, judging by the fact that at least one of its relatively limited number of full-time organizers in the West is a native American. Similarly, union and management representatives perceived no special issues, other than affirmative action itself, arising as a result of the employment of a native American work force.

CHAPTER V

The Geography of the Industry

There is a strong and widely held view among both union and management representatives in the industry that the "West is different," in terms of not only its prosperity, technology, and demography but also its labor relations. Indeed, the growth of western coal mining over the past decade does appear to have been accompanied by the evolution of a labor relations system that is organizationally and operationally different from and increasingly independent of that prevailing in the East. Specifically, paraphrasing the words of one management representative, the UMWA is not the force in the West that it is in the East and even where it is, it behaves differently than it does in the East.

THE EAST

The eastern segment of the bituminous coal mining industry is dominated organizationally by the UMWA and operationally by the UMWA National Agreement with the BCOA. There are non-UMWA mines in the region and not all UMWA mines are members of the BCOA, but those non-UMWA and non-BCOA mines are heavily dependent on the tolerance of the UMWA for what little independence they enjoy. Specifically, those mines must operate in the shadow of the union's proven willingness to inhibit continued operation or movement of coal from non-UMWA or non-BCOA mines using stranger pickets, threats of violence, and acts of violence.

Organization

The UMWA in the late 1970s represented about 75 percent of the miners in the eastern United States (Table V-1). Two other unions, the Southern Labor Union and the Progressive Mine Workers (PMW), also have organized miners in the East, but

57

TABLE V-1
*Union Organization in the Coal Industry,
the East*
(percent of total employment)

Union	Underground	Surface	Total
United Mine Workers of America	88.0	42.8	75.0
Southern Labor Union	1.3	1.0	1.1
Progressive Mine Workers	0.4	1.0	0.6
Nonunion	10.1	55.2	23.3

Source: Mine Enforcement and Safety Administration (MESA) Survey:
Union Organization in the Bituminous Coal Industry, November
1977.

together they account for less than 2 percent of total employment. The PMW was founded by UMWA dissidents in Illinois in
1932, in protest over wage cuts negotiated by the UMWA. It
once enjoyed a membership of almost 20,000, but obviously today
poses no real threat to the UMWA in the East.[1] The Southern
Labor Union was founded in 1959 to serve, in the words of the
UMWA, as a "company-oriented alternative" for mines in Kentucky, where its estimated 2,500 members are concentrated.[2]
    The major competition for the UMWA in the East comes not
from other unions but from nonunion operations, especially nonunion strip mines, which account for more than one-half of total
strip mine employment in the region. The origins of modern-day
nonunion mining in the East can be traced to 1959 and to the
coalfields of eastern Kentucky. In 1964, the *Wall Street Journal*
described those origins as follows:

> Since 1959, when its mines began bolting the UMW rather than sign
> the 1958 industry contract, Pike County (Eastern Kentucky) has
> been the heart of . . . non-union country . . . . Its mines were the
> nucleus of the National Independent Coal Operators Association,
> formed originally in an attempt to bargain with the UMW out-
> side the national contract. It now claims 5,000 member companies
> in 14 states: a few are unionized mines, but it's basically a non-
> union group.[3]

---

[1] William Miernyk, "Coal," in Gerald G. Somers, ed., *Collective Bargaining:
Contemporary American Experience* (Madison, Wis.: Industrial Relations
Research Association, 1980). p. 14.

[2] *Ibid.*, p. 15.

[3] J. Russell Boner, "Non-union coal," *Wall Street Journal*, December 11,
1964, p. 13.

The typically eastern nonunion mine in the early 1960s was a small "dog hole" operation in which coal was mined by pick and shovel. Many of the miners who worked such mines did so as independent contractors paid on a per ton basis by the owner of the mining rights to the area worked. Others worked as employees of small nonunion owner operators. In either event, such mines, with a reported "average investment per mine (of) $10,000 to $12,000 (about one-eighth the cost of even a low-priced continuous mining machine)" could not possibly compete with large unionized and mechanized mines on the basis of labor productivity.[4] They were, however, able to do so on the basis of labor cost by paying lower wages and avoiding some or all of the benefit costs imposed on unionized producers to finance the UMWA welfare fund (then $0.40 per ton). As a result, they were able to make a profit selling "coal at about $3.65 a ton against a 1962 industry average of $4.46"—a price differential large enough "to tempt such far-away buyers as Detroit Edison." [5]

The competitive success of nonunion, dog hole mines in the early 1960s, in the view of the *Wall Street Journal*, was "spearheading a trend" by "beginning to prod some big mechanized mines to go nonunion, too," as evidenced by the following development:

> Near Bayard, W. Va., North Branch Coal Co. is now hiring nonunion workers for a giant, brand-new and thoroughly mechanized mine totally unlike Pike County's "dog holes." In Perry County, Ky., the big mechanized Leatherwood No. 1 mine of the Blue Diamond Coal Co. cancelled its UMW contract last April 2 rather than sign the industry's 1964 wage agreement. A strike closed it, but it reopened last month as a non-union pit.[6]

The trend identified by the *Wall Street Journal* in 1964 has materialized and extended from its base in the dog holes of eastern Kentucky. In 1970, the *Wall Street Journal* again turned its attention to nonunion coal mining in the East and characterized the situation as follows:

> Historically, most nonunion coal concerns have been small, family-owned strip mines centered in Kentucky and Tennesseee. But as the industry has grown and the UMW's organizing efforts have slipped in recent years, large, professionally managed companies

---

[4] *Ibid.*

[5] *Ibid.*, p. 1.

[6] *Ibid.*

. . . have opened nonunion mines all across Appalachia and the Midwest.[7]

These new nonunion mines, unlike the dog holes of the 1960s, survive and thrive not on the basis of inferior wages but on the basis of superior productivity. The situation in one such mine was described by the *Wall Street Journal* as follows:

> Unfettered by restrictive UMW work rules and less vulnerable to labor disputes, (the mine's) average daily production per worker is nearly four times the rate of the average UMW underground mine—and even above the rate of the average UMW strip mine. A lucrative incentive bonus of 50 cents for each ton of coal mined, ample overtime and attraticev fringe benefits—which don't, however, include pensions—have drawn a highly motivated, skilled and loyal labor force.[8]

The new nonunion mines typically offer their employees a total compensation package equal or superior to that of UWMA mines. Basic wage rates typically are not much different, but total earnings generally are substantially higher in nonunion mines by virtue of production bonuses, more overtime, and less lost earnings due to labor disputes. (The nonunion mine looked at by the *Wall Street Journal* continued to pay its employees "when gun-wielding pickets forced management to close the mine for a three-month stretch during the recent UMW strike.")[9] Most non-union mines provide insurance and pension benefits superior to those in union mines, and at a lower cost, because they are not burdened by the cost of supporting benefits for miners once employed by operators who are no longer in business, as are BCOA operators. Some, however, provide only insurance and not pension benefits at a further substantial cost-saving vis-à-vis their BCOA counterparts. In addition, it is also often true that, as in the case of the nonunion mine studied by the *Wall Stret Journal,*

> other, less-crucial benefits abound. Miners can get interest-free loans to make down payments on a house or trailer. The company plans to build a swimming pool and tennis court for employees at the mine site next year. There are also gifts of jackets, knives, turkeys and other "tokens of appreciation" for work management considers well done. Some of the gifts are actually prizes in contests between mine sections to produce the most coal.[10]

[7] George Getschow, "Maverick mine," *Wall Street Journal,* October 23, 1978, p. 1.

[8] *Ibid.*

[9] *Ibid.,* p. 31.

[10] *Ibid.*

The generosity of the new nonunion mines in the East in providing earnings and benefits, other than possibly pension benefits, has not made the UMWA's organizing task an easy one. In the words of one UMWA organizer, "Our job used to be easy because scab operators didn't pay very well or treat their workers right. But today they're so doggone good to their men that we're having a tough time organizing them." [11] The union's response has been to stress the issues of safety and, to a lesser extent, pensions in its organizing efforts—efforts which thus far have not yielded substantially positive results. NLRB data reveal that between 1971 and 1980 the UMWA was a party to 128 representation elections in the Appalachian and midwestern coal fields involving some 10,000 workers.[12] It was victorious in 55 of those elections (43 percent), which involved about 3,300 workers. One-quarter of the elections in which it was involved were in Kentucky, where it was victorious in only 30 percent of its attempts.

Bargaining

In the East, the UMWA-BCOA bargaining relationship is, for all intents and purposes, the only game in town. No other union is sufficiently large or visible to rival the UMWA in setting a pattern for the industry. Prior to 1977, the same was true for UMWA-organized producers who did not belong to the BCOA. That situation changed in 1977 when the government sought to break a deadlock in UMWA-BCOA negotiations by achieving a settlement at Pittsburgh and Midway—a non-BCOA unionized producer. That effort was successful and the resulting agreement played a role in the government's further efforts to bring the UMWA and BCOA to a settlement, but it did not set a pattern for that settlement, as it was rejected by both Pittsburgh and Midway and BCOA miners in their respective ratification votes.

The prospect of a repeat of the prolonged deadlock in UMWA-BCOA negotiations, which idled the industry for 111 days in 1977-1978, in the 1981 UMWA-BCOA negotiations induced a number of unionized producers to attempt to settle with the UMWA independent of the BCOA. Two major producers—North American Coal and Emery Mining—attempted to defect from the BCOA in order to bargain independently in 1981, and a group of about twenty small non-BCOA operators organized the Unionized

---

[11] *Ibid.*

[12] Data in author's possession.

Coal Employers Association in hopes of doing the same.[13] The UMWA refused to acknowledge the defections from the BCOA and declined the overtures of smaller producers for separate settlement negotiations, in part because it seemed unlikely that they could set a pattern for the BCOA. Furthermore, the *Wall Street Journal* noted that "even if these small producers reached an agreement with the union and tried to resume production while the BCOA producers were still on strike, roving pickets would likely keep the small companies from going back to work." [14]

The dominant position of the UMWA-BCOA bargaining relationship in the East is enhanced by the proven willingness and ability of the union and/or its members to extend strike action against BCOA mines to non-BCOA and nonunion mines. In 1977, for example, the strike by the UMWA against the BCOA resulted in the closing not only of BCOA mines but also of approximately 50 percent of all non-BCOA mines, with most of those closed mines being located in the East (see Table V-2).

The ability of the UMWA to extend the effects of its disputes with the BCOA to encompass most or all of eastern coal production has given those disputes economic and particularly political significance far beyond that to be expected based on the coverage of the UMWA National Agreement. This was most evident in 1977 when a strike that was supposed to curtail coal production by only 50 percent and result in only minor inconvenience actually curtailed coal production by 75 percent and resulted in a "national emergency." The basis for that national emergency ostensibly was the national economic effects of the strike. In reality, however, it was the political ramifications of the adverse effects of the strike on the economies of a few major eastern coal producing states that led to the declaration of a national emergency.[15]

The economic importance of coal mining in such states as West Virginia, Pennsylvania, and Kentucky, which together account for more than 50 percent of all industry employment, has made labor relations in the coal industry the focus of great political interest and government involvement at the state level, particularly in

---

[13] Thomas Petzinger, Jr., "Several coal firms seek own UMW pacts as strike lengthens, but the union balks," *Wall Street Journal*, April 27, 1981, p. 18.

[14] *Ibid.*

[15] John A. Ackerman, "The Impact of the Coal Strike of 1977-1978," *Industrial and Labor Relations Review*, Vol. 32, No. 2 (January 1979), pp. 175-84.

TABLE V-2

The Impact of the Coal Strike on Working Mine Capacity

	Daily Productive Capacity (Tons)			Number of Mines Working		
	UMWA	Other	Total	UMWA	Other	Total
Normal Level[a]	1,867,785	1,380,867	3,248,652	1,588	3,275	4,863
December 8	66,345	925,634	991,979	7	1,853	1,860
December 15	65,779	737,632	803,411	6	1,308	1,314
December 22	66,429	740,912	807,341	8	1,275	1,283
December 29	127,263	744,916	872,179	14	1,290	1,304
January 5	94,671	845,361	940,032	15	1,375	1,390
January 12	128,721	848,171	976,892	18	1,378	1,396
January 19	125,721	862,491	988,212	17	1,381	1,398
January 26	126,221	850,916	977,137	18	1,356	1,374
February 2	125,721	866,996	992,717	17	1,429	1,446
February 9	126,346	890,268	1,016,614	20	1,456	1,476
February 16	128,996	903,048	1,032,044	20	1,488	1,508
February 23	128,771	908,968	1,037,739	19	1,501	1,520
March 2	129,011	941,000	1,070,011	21	1,573	1,594
March 9	130,146	972,285	1,102,431	22	1,632	1,654
March 16	135,861	1,062,921	1,198,782	34	1,884	1,918
March 23	137,166	1,083,696	1,220,862	34	1,954	1,988
March 30	1,609,456	1,347,327	2,956,783	1,496	3,119	4,615

Source: Mine Safety and Health Administration, *Comprehensive Overview of Winter Energy Data Bulletins*, Winter 1977-1978, Coal Supplement No. 17 (April 1978) (Washington, D.C.: U.S. Department of Energy, June 1978), pp. 3-4.

[a] The normal levels of productive capacity, number of mines, and number of employees are those levels which would have been attained if all active and producing mines had been in operation on normal shifts on March 30, 1978.

West Virginia. National politics and policies during the 1970s increasingly translated the desire of those states for labor peace in the coal fields into political problems and demands for action on the part of the federal government. The result was the involvement of the federal government in the UMWA-BCOA bargaining relationship to an extent rivaled only by its role in industry labor relations during the 1940s, when it seemed to be involved in a perpetual series of largely unsuccessful confrontations with the UMWA.

The record of government involvement during the 1970s is characterized by an obvious aversion to confrontation with the UMWA, first made evident in the treatment of the 1971 wage settlement under the controls program and last manifested in the avowedly reluctant declaration of a national emergency in the 1977 negotiations. In this context, it should be noted that both state and federal governments often have been unwilling or unable to contain the economic effects and limit the political effects of UMWA strike action by enforcing the right of non-BCOA or non-UMWA mines to operate. In 1977, the federal government made no real effort in this regard prior to the issuance of a national emergency injunction, despite reports to the Department of Justice Emergency Programs Center of some 111 "significant strike-related incidents of violence or disruption" involving two deaths, nine injuries and $4,232,820 in property loss (see Table V-3).[16]

TABLE V-3

Significant Strike-Related Incidents of Violence or Disruption,
1977-1978 Coal Strike

	Before March 5
Incidents	
Assaults, fatal	2
Assaults	2
Bombings	34
Hostages taken	1
Disruptions	72
	111
Location	
Illinois	7
Kentucky	44
Virginia	18
Pennsylvania	14
Indiana	9
Alabama	6
West Virginia	7
Tennessee	1
Ohio	5
	111
Injuries	9
Deaths	2
Property Loss	$4,232,820

Source: U.S. Department of Justice, 3/8/78.

[16] U.S. Department of Justice, "United Mine Workers Strike—Coal Industry Event Track 77-13: Incident Summary December 8, 1977, through March 5, 1978," (unpublished document).

THE WEST

The West, like the East, is heavily but not completely unionized. The UMWA is the single largest union in the industry in the West but does not dominate the organizational picture to the same extent as it does in the East. Operationally, the UMWA's collective bargaining activities on behalf of western miners attract the greatest attention, but they are far from the only game in town and are not always the leading game in town. Finally, the economic power of the UMWA in the West, unlike in the East, does not extend substantially beyond the perimeters of its established bargaining relationships.

Organization

In the late 1970s, the UMWA represented about 50 percent of all miners in the West as compared with 75 percent in the East, and that percentage undoubtedly fell below 50 by the end of the decade (see Table V-4). As in the East, the UMWA's organizational strength is concentrated in underground mining, where it represents approximately 75 percent of all miners as compared with possibly as little as 35 percent of all surface miners. The remaining 25 percent of underground miners essentially are nonunion in that they are either unorganized or organized by independent "company" unions—a figure that seems destined to grow, but only slowly, in the years ahead.

The UMWA's organizational strength in western underground mining is concentrated in the older mines of eastern BCOA

TABLE V-4

Union Organization in the Coal Industry,
the West
(percent of total employment)

Union	Underground	Surface	Total
United Mine Workers of America	73.3	35.5	50.6
Operating Engineers	—	16.9	10.2
Electrical Workers (IBEW)	—	11.5	6.9
Progressive Mine Workers	—	11.3	6.8
Other unions	7.5	5.3	6.2
Nonunion	19.1	19.5	19.3

Source: MESA Survey: *Union Organization in the Bituminous Coal Industry.*

producers, most of which are covered by the UMWA National
Agreement and have been since 1950. Newer underground mines,
most of which were opened in the last fifteen years and are
located in Colorado and Utah, are today at best 50 percent
UMWA-organized. The UMWA, thus far, has faced no real
competition from other unions in organizing underground mine
workers. The Operating Engineers, who are active in representing surface mine workers in the West, competed with the
UMWA in a representation election at an underground mine
in Colorado, but that contest was a first for that union and
more an accident than a sign of any basic organizational interest in underground mining. The UMWA, however, has often
encountered strong management resistance in its efforts to organize new underground mines on both institutional (labor
stability) and economic (labor productivity) grounds.

The typical nonunion or non-UMWA underground mine in
the West is not much different from its counterpart in the
East. Most pay at least competitive wage rates and have production bonus systems that can provide payouts as high as
$1,000-$2,000 per year for an individual employee. Most also
provide benefits that are simultaneously more generous and less
expensive than those of UMWA-BCOA mines, although some,
as in the East, have elected not to provide pension benefits. As
in the East, "other, less crucial fringe benefits" are common
and are designed to ensure a "highly motivated . . . and loyal
labor force." Finally, non-UMWA underground mines in the
West enjoy the same superior productivity vis-à-vis UMWA
mines as do their counterparts in the East.

The UMWA has had an uphill battle in organizing these
nonunion underground mines. Confronting managements committed to treating their employees well and avoiding the employee and labor relations problems that have beset the East,
the union's only obvious general organizing appeal has been
safety, although it has also used the pension issue in specific
situations that conform to the following scenario put forth
by one UMWA organizer:

> What happened is that the companies learned and started to give
> them a little more up front, but at the same time, they were taking
> things out of the back of the contract. What's happening when
> these guys get older, they say, "Man, I was had." [17]

---

[17] Mike Hall, "Major Organizing Effort Getting Underway in Western Coal
Fields," *United Mine Workers Journal*, August 1980, p. 13.

The issue of safety is not one that has been taken lightly by management of non-UMWA underground mines in the West. At least one such management has designed a safety bonus system along the lines of its production bonus system to demonstrate its commitment to safety as well as productivity. Whether other non-UMWA underground producers will follow that pattern remains to be seen, but many may be encouraged to do so by the fact that one of the UMWA's basic safety issues in western underground mining is also a basic productivity issue —the use of, in the view of the union, "unsafe and unhealthy" and, in the view of producers, "more efficient and harmless" diesel equipment in underground mines.

There is a general perception that the UMWA in the past ten years has been neither particularly active nor highly successful in organizing new underground mines in the West. Unfortunately, NLRB data do not provide a definitive basis for testing the validity of this view because they do not differentiate between deep and surface mines in reporting representation elections. The aggregate data for Colorado and Utah—the two Rocky Mountain states with the highest concentration of deep mining—for the 1971-1980 period, however, do lend some credence to that view.[18] Over that period, there were only eleven representation elections covering some 1,150 workers held in the industry in those two states in which the UMWA was a participant. The UMWA was victorious in almost one-half (five) of those elections, but all of those victories came in small units that together totalled less than 10 percent of all the 1,150 workers for whom the union sought bargaining rights.

The organizational picture in surface mining—the dominant and more rapidly growing segment of the industry—in the West is far more complex than in underground mining. The UMWA is the largest single union in western surface mining, representing about one-third of the work force, but it competes with three other major unions—the IUOE, the IBEW, and the PMW— whose combined membership totals about 40 percent of the work force. In addition, there is a substantial nonunion sector that accounts for almost 25 percent of surface mine employment in the West.

The strength of the UMWA in western surface mining is concentrated in the older mines of the large coal producers,

---

18 Data in author's possession.

many of which have strong direct (Peabody) or indirect (Pittsburgh and Midway) ties to the East and the BCOA. The organizational strength of the IUOE rests in the newer mines of regional coal producers with little or no historical or institutional ties to the East or the BCOA. The strength of the IBEW is in the captive surface mines of utilities in the West which, for the most part, have not been members of the BCOA. The strength of the PMW appears to be concentrated in Wyoming, where unionism was strong in coal mining as long ago as 1927, and where over the last decade it won 100 percent of its seven representation elections.

There is a substantial nonunion section in western surface mining that is likely to grow in the future with the entry into the industry of oil companies that are reputed to be committed to nonunion operation. Nonunion surface mines in the West generally pay a 5-10 percent wage premium above the UMWA rate. In addition, nonunion surface mine operators in the West, like their deep mine counterparts, typically make a determined effort to practice enlightened employee relations at the mine level and to build company loyalty through a variety of paternalistic benefits.

Nonunion surface mines in the West constitute a formidable organizing frontier for any union. The first organizing problem facing a union is access to employees who typically work in relative isolation at widely scattered locations within the mine site and live in equally isolated and scattered locations within a fairly large area surrounding the mine. The second organizing problem facing a union is that of substance. The willingness and ability of nonunion surface mine operators to match union wage and benefit standards has, in the words of one IUOE representative, "all but eliminated economics as an organizing issue." Furthermore, safety is not as important an issue in surface mining as it is in underground mining and, at least in the view of the IUOE, has been fairly well preempted as an organizing appeal by the combination of employer concern and government regulation. The most viable issue, in the view of the IUOE, is protection against arbitrary treatment by the employer, which it tends to stress in its organizing effort by focusing on the desirability of formal grievance and job bidding procedures.

There are five and possibly six unions that seem ready to confront the challenge of organizing nonunion surface mines in the West. The first, of course, is the UMWA, which has formally announced that a "Major Organizing Effort (is) Getting Underway in Western Coalfields." [19] The IUOE and IBEW have made no such formal declaration of their intent, but both are actively working to enhance their organizing capacities in the western coal fields. The PMW clearly has been and is likely to remain active in organizing surface miners in Wyoming. The Teamsters reputedly have plans to attempt to organize surface mines in the West, where they already represent miners in Alaska. Finally, the Oil, Chemical and Atomic Workers (OCAW) has attempted to organize workers in coal gasification plants and may be further drawn into the industry with the entry of oil companies into surface coal mining in the West.

The UMWA is the obvious front-runner in terms of organizational resources in this five-way battle to organize western surface mines. It also faces some special problems in terms of both employee receptiveness and employer resistance, however, which are not shared, at least to the same degree, by the union widely perceived to be its primary competitor, the IUOE. The IUOE is generally perceived in the western coalfields as a reasonable and responsible union, both in its own right and particularly in contrast with the UMWA. Thus, the IUOE represents an attractive alternative to the UMWA, if not to nonunion operation, in the eyes of a number of employers, some of whom have chosen to invite organization by the IUOE by relying on it in recruiting a work force. The IBEW may well enjoy a similar potential advantage in attempting to organize miners in captive mines of some utility companies.

Neither the UMWA nor the IUOE have been highly active in organizing surface miners in the West over the past decade, judging by the number of representation elections in the industry in which they were involved. Between 1971 and 1980, the UMWA was involved in only nine representation elections in the key surface mining states of Wyoming and New Mexico, winning eight of those elections, while the IUOE was involved in only six elections in those two states, winning four of those elections.[20] There is little doubt in the minds of industry representatives in the West that the level of representation election activity involving the IUOE and particularly the UMWA will

---

[19] Hall, "Major Organizing Effort," pp. 12-14.

[20] Data in author's possession.

rise gradually over the coming years, but equally little consensus as to the future trend in percentage of elections won, especially in the case of the UMWA.

Bargaining

The bargaining system, like the organizational situation, in the West is far more complex than it is in the East. The western system encompasses four distinct sets of contract negotiations involving three different unions. Two of the four sets of negotiations involve the UMWA and generally set a pattern or target for the parties to the other two sets of negotiations in the West—those involving the IUOE and the PMW. In this system, the UMWA wields considerable influence in the industry in the setting of terms and conditions of employment, but not the absolute control that it wields in the east because it lacks both the economic power and institutional stature to impose its will on non-UMWA mines.

The UMWA in the West is party to two distinct sets of contract negotiations with western producers. The first, and historically most important, set of negotiations is the UMWA-BCOA National Agreement negotiations, which directly or indirectly involve UMWA-organized underground mines in the West as well as the East. Thus, a strike by the UMWA against the BCOA results in the closing of most or all UMWA-organized deep mines in the West. Unlike in the East, however, such strike action is unlikely to extend beyond the mines in question, as western miners and law enforcement officials have shown little proclivity to be sympathetic toward or intimidated by stranger picketing and related activities on the part of any union, including the UMWA. The second and recently more salient set of negotiations is the UMWA-western surface mine agreement negotiations conducted on a company-by-company basis with about a dozen major western surface mine operators.

The UMWA's dual bargaining relationships in the West have made it servant to two masters—national and regional interests. Prior to 1977, national interests prevailed in that western agreement negotiations and settlements were extended until an agreement was reached in UMWA-BCOA negotiations in the East, which then provided a pattern for UMWA agreements in the West. Western UMWA surface mine operators made a concerted and determined effort, under the leadership of Peabody Coal, to break that pattern in 1974 but were unsuccessful in doing so even after a two-month strike. What western surface mine operators failed to achieve by concerted militancy in 1974 they achieved by individual accommodation in 1977 when Pittsburgh and Midway reached an agreement in its western negotiations on the eve of what proved to be a 111-day strike by the UMWA against the BCOA. That separation was carried one step further in 1981 when Pittsburgh and Midway was able to reach an agreement with the UMWA in the West almost two months prior to the expiration of the UMWA National Agreement with the BCOA.

The UMWA's western surface mine agreement negotiations, unlike their National Agreement negotiations, are conducted on a company-by-company basis. Since 1974, when Peabody Coal attempted to unify the signatories to those agreements, there has been little or no coordination among signatory companies in the conduct of contract negotiations and considerable competition among some of them for the honor of settling first and setting the pattern for the other signatories and, in very general terms, the rest of the industry in the West. The two major participants in that competition have been Peabody and Pittsburgh and Midway, both of which also have to deal with the UMWA in the East—Peabody as the largest member of the BCOA and Pittsburgh and Midway as a nonmember signatory to the UMWA-BCOA National Agreement. Thus, in terms of both timing and participants, the western tail of the industry is in a position to wag the eastern dog of the industry, as it appears to have done in the 1981 UMWA-BCOA negotiations.

The newly found independence of the UMWA in the conduct of western surface mine agreement negotiations both reflects and magnifies the effects of competitive unionism in the West. The competitive linkages among employers and employees have long required that the UMWA conduct its western negotiations with "one eye on the Operating Engineers, the Progressive Mine Workers and nonunion mines." What that eye saw in 1981 was that "miners at several Western companies that are nonunion or organized by other unions already earn higher wages and pensions than UMW members," leading it to insist on "an expensive package that it thinks will improve its chances to organize in the West." [21]

---

[21] "A High-Stakes Strike at Peabody Coal," *Business Week*, February 2, 1981, p. 18.

Contract negotiations involving the IUOE and the PMW typically are relatively low-key, local operations that attract little public attention. Negotiations are conducted on a mine-by-mine basis by local personnel. Expiration dates vary but generally tend to lag behind the expiration date of the UMWA's western surface mine agreement, leaving the unions free to "second guess" the UMWA. The IUOE's strategy in Colorado has been to have its coal contracts expire a year after the UMWA contract expires and to negotiate three-year agreements with a reopener in the third year in order to accommodate any major developments in UMWA negotiations.

There is considerable variability among these "other agreements." In general, however, they have provided for wage rates equivalent to those of the UMWA and for benefit packages superior to those of the UMWA, primarily because these units were not burdened by the high benefit costs that shaped eastern settlements and depressed western UMWA benefits. The PMW, in particular, pressed this advantage in the pension area, resulting in a benefit differential that by 1981 approached $8 per month per year of service—a differential that the UMWA reportedly felt compelled to narrow or eliminate in order to improve its prospects for organizing in the West.[22]

----

[22] *Ibid.*

CHAPTER VI

The Economics of Industrywide Bargaining

The National Bituminous Coal Wage Agreement of 1950 marked "the beginning of a new era in collective bargaining in coal." [1] The foundation of that new era was the fact that "with the formation of the Bituminous Coal Operators Association, the UMWA had for the first time successfully negotiated an industrywide contract . . . one of the goals sought since the days of John Mitchell." [2]

The UMWA's longstanding interest in industrywide bargaining is not difficult to explain. The basic goal of the UMWA, as is the case for any union, has been to "take labor out of competition." The fact that the bituminous coal mining industry historically has been characterized by small production units, chronic overcapacity, and intense competition created a formidable challenge to the union in achieving its ultimate goal. The response of the UMWA to that challenge was a series of efforts to build a system of industrywide bargaining through which it might establish the industrywide labor standards required to insulate labor from the competitive pressures of the market for bituminous coal.

The desire of the UMWA to establish industrywide bargaining and standards has not been unwelcome to management, which also has long sought a measure of stability and protection against "ruinous competition." Nor was it unwelcome to the federal government which early and repeatedly has shown an interest in promoting competitive stability in the coal industry. Thus, the potential for a cooperative or collusive relationship between labor and management with the implicit or

---

[1] William H. Miernyk, "Coal," in Gerald G. Somers, ed., *Collective Bargaining: Contemporary American Experience* (Madison, Wis.: Industrial Relations Research Association, 1980). p. 25.

[2] *Ibid.*, p. 28.

explicit support of the government has existed throughout the almost 100-year history of the UMWA. The union has been successful in exploiting this potential in the form of multiemployer bargaining three times, each of which constituted a "new era in collective bargaining in coal." The first ended with a collapse of multiemployer bargaining as a result of interregional competition in the industry. The second ended with a consolidation of regional multiemployer bargaining into industrywide bargaining. The fate of the third now hangs precariously between the fates of its predecessors.

THE RISE OF INDUSTRYWIDE BARGAINING

Unionism in the coal mining industry dates from 1849, when a small local union of anthracite miners was organized in Pennsylvania. The first national union of coal miners, the American Miners Association, was formed in 1861 and survived until the panic of 1873. It was not until 1883 that a truly durable organization of miners emerged with the formation of the Amalgamated Miners of the United States, an organization destined ultimately to become the United Mine Workers of America. The Amalgamated Miners achieved the first interstate union-management agreement in the 1880s when "successive price wars accompanied by wage reductions led the operators and miners of Illinois, Indiana, Ohio, western Pennsylvania, and West Virginia to call the interstate conference of 1886."[3] That conference produced an agreement on wage scales which remained in force for one year. At the end of that year, operators in West Virginia withdrew, followed one year later by operators in Illinois and another year later by operators in Indiana, by which time "the first attempt to regulate wages and conditions on an interstate basis failed."[4]

In December 1888, the Amalgamated Miners, now the National Federation of Miners and Mine Laborers, voted to seek affiliation with the American Federation of Labor. Several independent local unions joined this effort and a new organization, the National Progressive Union, was formed. On January 25, 1890, that union was admitted to the American Federation of Labor

---

[3] Waldo E. Fisher, *Collective Bargaining in the Bituminous Coal Industry: An Appraisal* (Philadelphia: University of Pennsylvania Press, 1948), p. 3.

[4] *Ibid.*

as the United Mine Workers of America with a membership of some 24,000.

By 1900, the UMWA had established itself as a major force within the industry primarily as a result of its success in once again establishing an interstate bargaining relationship with operators in the Midwest. As a result of that success, the union in 1901 claimed a membership of 200,000 as compared with only 33,000 in 1898, the year in which it concluded its first Central Competitive Field Compact with operators in the Midwest.[5]

The Central Competitive Field Compacts

The collapse of the interstate agreement initiated in 1886 fostered a new succession of price wars and wage reductions which culminated in a general strike involving some 100,000 coal miners in 1897. Following that strike, "the operators and miners, convinced of the futility of operating under competing bargaining units, again turned to an interstate agreement." [6] The result was the Central Competitive Field Compact of 1898 covering operators and miners in Illinois, Indiana, Ohio, and western Pennsylvania, but not West Virginia. That compact established two basic principles of labor relations which were to survive for almost thirty years: (1) the acceptance of collective bargaining; and (2) the acceptance of standardized earnings.

The Central Competitive Field Joint Conference proved to be a durable, if not always successful, mechanism for wage negotiations from 1898 to 1927. In most cases over that period, the Joint Conference produced new agreements based on the principle of "competitive equality" and the practice of "competitive wage differentials." In 1906, 1910, 1914, 1922, and 1927, however, the Joint Conference failed to produce an agreement on a regional basis leaving agreements to be worked out at the district level.[7]

The failure of the Joint Conference of 1922 was the beginning of the end of that multiemployer system of collective bargaining. The problem in 1922 was a reluctance on the part of operators in Ohio and western Pennsylvania to continue to be party to the Conference and Compact. That reluctance reflected their realization that, with the decline in the demand for coal which fol-

---

[5] Justin McCarthy, "A Brief History of the United Mine Workers of America," *United Mine Workers Journal*, Special Report, p. 6.

[6] Fisher, *Collective Bargaining in the Bituminous Coal Industry*, p. 3.

[7] *Ibid.*

lowed the end of World War I, their major competitive problem was not operators in Indiana or Illinois but "nonunion" operators in West Virginia and Kentucky who were paying lower wages.

Despite its problems in 1922, the Joint Conference system survived for another five years. The union was able to prevent wage reductions "when business fell away drastically in the depression year of 1922," [8] and two years later it was able to secure a sizable wage increase in its "Jacksonville Agreement" of 1924, which resulted in a daily wage of $7.50, well in excess of the daily wage of southern nonunion miners.[9] The competitive effects of that settlement were quickly felt and the union was forced to settle for no wage increase in its 1925 Joint Conference.

The demise of the Central Competitive Field Joint Conference came in 1927 when the operators refused to renew their compact. When a strike proved unsuccessful in coercing the operators to yield, the union was forced to abandon its cause and to permit each of its districts to do the best it could on its own. The result was the virtual elimination of the Union-Nonunion wage differential, and annihilation of the union, which by 1929 claimed a membership of only 80,000 as compared with 375,000 in 1920.[10] Thus, even before the onset of the depression, hard times and nonunion competition had destroyed multiemployer bargaining in the coal mining industry.

Both the union and the industry reached their nadir in 1932 and were revitalized by the passage of the National Industrial Recovery Act, which provided the union with a new basis for organizing and management with a new basis for stabilizing the industry. Both were quick to avail themselves of this new opportunity to be rid of the plague of "ruinous competition." The result was the rapid reorganization of coalminers and reemergence of a multistate, multiemployer bargaining system, which produced the first Appalachian agreements in 1933.[11]

---

[8] *Ibid.,* p. 5.

[9] Morton S. Baratz, *The Union and the Coal Industry* (New Haven, Conn.: Yale University Press, 1955), pp. 59-60.

[10] Arthur E. Suffern, *The Coal Miners' Struggle for Industrial Status* (New York: The Macmillian Company, 1926), p. 450.

[11] "Wage Chronology No. 4: Bituminous Coal Mines, 1933-48," *Monthly Labor Review,* Vol. 68, No. 3 (March 1949), p. 303.

The Appalachian Agreements

The Appalachian agreements represented a new interstate bargaining structure which was more consistent with competitive realities in the product market. They encompassed unionized operators in Ohio, Pennsylvania, eastern Kentucky, northern Tennessee, West Virginia and Virginia. Producers in Indiana and Illinois were not parties to the agreements but typically followed the pattern they set.

The Appalachian interstate multiemployer bargaining system provided the union with a mechanism through which it could again attempt to bring stability to the industry, a goal shared in broader perspective by both management and the government. Stability, from the viewpoint of the union, required the elimination of regional wage differentials. The organizing success of the union coupled with the gradual growth of the industry and the persistent interest of the government in the industry in the late 1930s finally provided a hospitable environment for a full-scale union assault on north-south wage differentials. In 1941, the UMWA demanded and, with the aid of a strike and government intervention, achieved the elimination of those differentials.

The union's assault on regional wage differentials produced a formal split on the management side between nothern and southern coal operators. That split, coupled with the separate status of captive mine operators (steel companies), forced the union to bargain with three distinct adversaries during the 1940s. The fragmentation of the industry caused no real problems for the UMWA during the war years and actually worked to its advantage when the industry returned to free collective bargaining after the end of the war. Throughout the war years, the UMWA showed little reluctance to flex its economic muscle against the industry and the government. That militancy combined with government timidity permitted the union not only to suppress any centrifugal forces within the industry but also to win from the industry, courtesy of the government, some very substantial concessions. The most notable of those concessions was the establishment of the UMWA welfare and retirement fund financed by a royalty payment on each ton of coal mined.

The postwar period was one of considerable turbulence in labor relations in the coal industry. The UMWA, which had showed no reluctance to flex its muscles during the war, proved no less reluctant to do the same against the power of both private industry and public interest after the war. The industry proved as vulnerable as had been the government to union militancy. Specifically, the industry's fragmented bargaining structure made it vulnerable to whipsawing by the union. The questionable cooperation, coordination, and solidarity that characterized the industry following the war gave way to a new management resolve and unity in 1949 in the face of weakened demand for both steel and coal. The result was a protracted set of negotiations which began in 1949 and were not concluded until March 1950, and then only after a strike, an unsuccessful Taft-Hartley injunction, and a Presidential request for statutory authority to seize the mines. The last of these actions forced the union and its three major industry adversaries into joint agreement on the fundamental principles of what was to become the National Bituminous Coal Wage Agreement of 1950.

The National Agreements

Since 1950, collective bargaining in the East has been conducted essentially on an industrywide basis. The 1950 National Wage Agreement set the stage for the formation of the Bituminous Coal Operators Association to supplant the three existing multiemployer groups in the bargaining context, a step previously advocated by the head of the nation's then largest coal company —Consolidation.[12]

The BCOA was and is a multiemployer association created for the purpose of conducting negotiations with the UMWA over "amendments" to the National Bituminous Coal Wage Agreement of 1950. Initially, it represented simply a confederation of the three previously independent multiemployer bargaining groups— the Appalachian, southern, and captive mine operators. Those three groups maintained their separate identities and signed separate and, in some cases, slightly different agreements for about fifteen years. Over the past fifteen years, however, these historically geographical and operational identities and distinctions have faded and are no longer institutionally manifest in the national agreement bargaining system.

The National Wage Agreement of 1950 and the formation of the BCOA laid the groundwork for a new era of peace and stability in labor relations in the industry which lasted for almost two decades. That new era was remarkable not only by contrast

---

12 Miernyk, "Coal," p. 24.

to the turbulent labor relations of the 1940s, but also because it coincided with a period of declining demand for coal—a trend which historically had produced intense competition and resistance to the union of sufficient magnitude to eventually undermine multiemployer bargaining.

The secret of the success of multiemployer bargaining in the 1950s as in the early 1900s was the identification of a basic economic trade-off which served the institutional interests of both the union and the industry. The union sought and secured a series of substantial wage increases. In exchange, the industry sought and secured the acquiescence of the union to the mechanization required to produce the productivity increases needed to offset the union's wage gains. This trade-off best served the interests of the larger companies and mines that were most easily able to avail themselves of new technology. Smaller firms and mines, which for economic or geologic reasons, were not able to mechanize, were not well served by this trade-off, as was evident in the dramatic drop in the number of operating mines, and particularly small mines, during the 1950s.

The new era of labor peace and stability which began in 1950 came to an end in 1970, which marked the beginning of a decade of conflict and instability in industrywide union-managment relations. The underlying causes of this new turbulence are both political and economic in nature. Economically, the wage-productivity trade-off of the 1950s and 1960s was no longer viable after passage of the Coal Mine Health and Safety Act in 1969, as evidenced by the decline in productivity which beset the industry during the 1970s. More importantly, the industry was also beset with growing National Agreement competition in the coal market, as evidenced by the decline in the percentage of total coal production accounted for by UMWA National Agreement output from 70 percent in 1970 to about 45 percent in 1980.[13]

THE DEMISE OF INDUSTRYWIDE BARGAINING

The UMWA's National Bituminous Coal Wage Agreement of 1950 effectively took labor out of competition. Since then, the union has fought a long and losing battle to keep labor out of competition against existing operators who sought to avoid National Agreement coverage. Prior to 1980, the union elected not

---

[13] "Bargaining Statement By Bituminous Coal Operators Association," *Daily Labor Report*, No. 15 (January 23, 1981), p. F-1.

to wage that battle through aggressive organizing efforts, but
chose instead to rely primarily on its contractual relationship with
the BCOA and its own financial, political, and institutional resources to contain and control nonunion competition. That strategy
has made the UMWA a frequent target of legal action by mine
operators, the most noteworthy of which is the *Pennington* case
which reached the Supreme Court in 1965.[14]

Contractual Controls

The economic pressure exerted by the national wage agreements
on mines unable to mechanize created an incentive for such mines
to seek relief from the terms of those agreements. One form of
such relief could have been union concessions based on productivity or ability to pay—the modern equivalent of the system of
competitive wage differentials espoused by the UMWA in the
early 1900s. In the 1950s, however, neither the UMWA nor the
BCOA felt its interests would be served by such concessions which
would only intensify competition in a declining industry already
beset by excess capacity, something both had reason to fear based
on their experience in the 1920s. Thus, in their 1958 negotiations,
the UMWA and BCOA reached agreement on a "protective wage
clause" which stated:

> The parties hereto agree that bituminous coal mines shall be so
> operated as not to debase or lower the standards of wages, hours,
> safety requirements and other conditions of work, established by
> this contract. The parties recognizing their obligation each as to
> the other to exercise all possible efforts and means to attain these
> objectives further agree as follows:
> A. During the period of this Contract, the United Mine Workers
> of America will not enter into, be a party to, nor will it permit any
> agreement or understanding covering any wages, hours or other
> conditions of work applicable to employees covered by this Contract
> on any basis other than those specified in this Contract or any
> applicable District Contract. The United Mine Workers of America
> will diligently perform and enforce without discrimination or favor
> the conditions of this paragraph and all other terms and conditions
> of this Contract and will use and exercise its continuing best efforts
> to obtain full compliance therewith by each and all the parties
> signatory thereto.
> B. It is recognized that when signatory operators mine, prepare,
> or procure or acquire under subcontract arrangements, bituminous
> coal mined under terms and conditions less favorable than those

---

[14] United Mineworkers of America v. James A. Pennington, 381 U.S. 657
(1965).

provided for in this contract, they deprive employees of employment opportunities, employment conditions and other benefits which these employees are entitled to have safeguarded, stabilized and protected. Accordingly, the Operators agree that all bituminous coal mined, produced, or prepared by them, or any of them, or procured or acquired by them or any of them under a subcontract arrangement, shall be or shall have been mined or produced under terms and conditions which are as favorable to the employees as those provided for in this Contract.[15]

The protective wage clause of the 1958 National Wage Agreement in theory applied only to UMWA dealings with BCOA member companies. In practice, however, it also extended to its dealings with all companies. In *Pennington*, it was alleged:

[T]he union entered into a conspiracy with the large operators to impose the agreed-upon wage and royalty scales upon the smaller, non-union operators, regardless of their ability to pay and regardless of whether or not the union represented the employees of those companies.[16]

The alleged conspiracy was not definitively proved in *Pennington*, but it is clear that the UMWA did make a determined effort to impose identical terms and conditions on all operators regardless of size or union status. The central element in this effort was not the organization of the unorganized. Instead, it was a contractual attempt to deny nonunion producers access to coal lands and coal markets by precluding organized operators from leasing coal lands to or acquiring coal from nonunion operators through the protective wage clause. However effective this contractual ban may have been, it was not sufficient to prevent nonunion operators from expanding their share of the coal market from 21 percent in 1958 to 28 percent in 1964.[17]

The protective wage clause was abandoned in 1964, but not the union's efforts to deter signatory operators from procuring or acquiring nonunion coal. The 1964 National Agreement implicitly acknowledged the right of signatories to do business with non-signatory producers but required that

on all bituminous coal procured or acquired by any signatory Operator for use or for sale, (i.e. all bituminous coal other than that

---

[15] *National Bituminous Coal Wage Agreement of 1950 as Amended December 1, 1958* (mimeographed), p. 3.

[16] United Mine Workers of America v. James A. Pennington, 381 U.S. 657 (1965).

[17] J. Russell Boner, "Nonunion coal," *Wall Street Journal*, December 11, 1964, p. 1.

produced by such signatory Operator) there shall, during the life of this Agreement, be paid into such Fund by each such Operator signatory hereto or by any subsidiary or affiliate of such Operator signatory hereto the sum of eighty cents (80¢) per ton of two thousand (2000) pounds on each ton of such bituminous coal so procured or acquired on which the afforesaid sum of forty cents (40¢) per ton had not been paid into said Fund prior to such procurement or acquisition.[18]

The double Welfare and Retirement Fund Royalty Penalty imposed on the acquisition of nonunion coal in the 1964 National Agreement remained in effect throughout the 1960s. The early 1970s produced a drop in the magnitude of the royalty penalty from 100 percent to 50 percent in the 1971 agreement to 0 percent in the 1974 agreement, which required only the payment of normal royalties on coal procured or acquired for use or sale on which such royalty had not been paid. That provision remained intact through the 1977-1978 negotiations but was challenged by the BCOA in its 1981 National Agreement negotiations when it sought and was almost successful in securing the elimination of all royalty payments on nonunion coal.

The first tentative agreement reached in the 1981 UMWA-BCOA negotiations did not include provision for royalty payments on acquired coal. That concession proved to be a major factor in the rejection of that agreement by the union rank and file, who apparently feared that it would open the way for new attempts to escape or break the union and were not persuaded by the leadership's view that:

> The major problem with the non-signatory coal provision was that it was unenforceable. Many BCOA companies had found legal ways to avoid paying the royalties, and many others, including the larger BCOA operators, indicated that if the royalty was included in the contract, the companies would do everything in their power to avoid payment.[19]

The 1981 negotiations did produce changes in another longstanding set of contractual controls over the right of BCOA operators to utilize, directly or indirectly, non-UMWA labor; article IA, "scope and coverage," of the agreement was, in the words of the union,

---

[18] *National Bituminous Coal Wage Agreement of 1950 as amended effective April 2, 1964* (mimeographed), p. 5.

[19] "Membership Rejects Tentative Agreement, Negotiators Return to Bargaining Table," *United Mine Workers Journal*, 92nd year, No. 4. (April-May 1981), p. 1.

changed to conform with National Labor Relation Board (NLRB) rulings and federal court rulings. Basically, the courts ruled, and the U.S. Supreme Court refused to hear the UMWA's petition for re-hearing, that it was not legal for the UMWA-BCOA contract to require that all work on leased, subleased, or licensed lands, and that all mine-related work be performed by UMWA members.[20]

The key sections of Article IA in question were those dealing with the contracting out of work and leasing of lands to non-union employers. Article IA(g) of the 1978 agreement stated that the "transportation of coal may be contracted out only to a contractor employing members of the UMWA under this agreement" and that repair and maintenance work, when contracted out, "shall be performed by UMWA members." Article IA(h) of the agreement stated that:

> the Employers agree that they will not lease, sublease or license out any coal lands, coal producing or coal preparation facilities where the purpose thereof is to avoid the application of this Agreement or any section, paragraph or clause thereof. Licensing out of coal mining operations on coal lands owned or held under lease or sublease by any signatory operator hereto shall not be permitted unless the work involved is performed by members of the United Mine Workers of America.[21]

AMAX Coal Company challenged the viability and legality of these and other similar union/job security provisions of Article IA when, in 1975, its Belle Ayr mine in Wyoming was struck by the UMWA to force that mine to agree to a contract containing these provisions.[22] Specifically, AMAX charged the union with violations of both sections 8(b)(3)—the obligation to bargain in good faith—and 8(b)(4)—the ban on secondary boycotts—by virtue of its strike action to force the company to accept its position on nonmandatory and/or legal subjects for bargaining. The NLRB and U.S. Court of Appeals (3rd Circuit) ruled in favor of the company with respect to these provisions of Article IA.

Those rulings left the union with little choice but to yield to industry pressure to alter the identical restrictions on contracting and leasing contained in the BCOA National Agreement in its 1981 negotiations. Such pressure indeed did emerge, creating a

---

[20] *Ibid.*

[21] *National Bituminous Coal Wage Agreement of 1978*, pp. 6-7.

[22] AMAX Coal Company v. National Labor Relations Board, 103 L.R.R.M. 2483.

"job security" issue that was not quickly or easily resolved. It was, however, resolved when the industry offered to address the basic job security, as opposed to union security, aspects of the provisions of Article IA. The result, in the words of the union were:

> New measures in the 1981-84 contract [which] protect UMWA workers from being laid off and guarantee laid-off members work when contracting is to be done. An operator cannot lease coal lands or coal operations or contract out for the transportation of coal or repair or maintenance if the leasing or contracting causes lay-offs or deprives laid-off employees of work that is normally theirs.[23]

Institutional Ingenuity

The efforts of the union to deny nonunion operators access to markets extended well beyond the reach of its contractual relations with the BCOA. The UMWA's second line of defense for itself and its BCOA bargaining partners against nonunion competition was its ingenuity in using its own considerable political power, financial resources, and physical muscle to make life difficult for nonunion operators.

In the 1950s, one of the nations largest, if not the largest, consumers of coal was the Tennessee Valley Authority (TVA), which purchased its coal in both term and spot markets on the basis of competitive bidding. Nonunion producers apparently enjoyed an advantage over union producers in securing orders from TVA in the late 1950s, as in *Pennington* it was alleged that:

> the companies and the union jointly and successfully approached the Secretary of Labor to obtain establishment under the Walsh-Healy Act . . . of a minimum wage being much higher than in other industries and making it difficult for small companies to compete in the TVA term contract market . . . thereafter four of the larger companies waged a destructive and collusive price-cutting campaign in the TVA spot market for coal.[24]

The union also used its considerable financial resources, including those of its trust funds, in its battle to contain nonunion competition. One of its more imaginative and successful uses of those sources to that end involved the West Kentucky Coal Company which

---

[23] "Contract Approved by 2-1 Margin," *United Mine Workers Journal*, 92nd year, No. 5 (June 1981), p. 4.

[24] United Mine Workers of America v. James A. Pennington, 381 U.S. 657 (1965).

until 1953 was the only non-union firm among the top ten coal producers. In 1952, the United Mine Workers of America made loans to Cyrus Eaton, who began to purchase stock in the coal company. In 1953, Eaton became Chairman of the Board of the West Kentucky Coal Company and immediately the company signed a union contract for 3,000 miners.[25]

In light of the means by which the UMWA gained entry to West Kentucky, it is not surprising that it was one of the companies alleged to be involved in the "collusive price-cutting campaign in the TVA spot market for coal." Specifically, in *Pennington* it was argued that, among the four companies that undertook that campaign, "two of the companies, West Kentucky Coal Co. and its subsidiary Nashville Coal Co., being those in which the union had large investments and over which it was in a position to exercise control." [26]

When contractual controls and institutional ingenuity failed adequately to contain or suppress nonunion competition, the union could always resort to the militancy and muscle of its membership.[27] Nonunion operators were and are a primary target for such activity, but union operators also were and are potential targets, as was alluded to by the union in its discussion of the deficiencies of its first tentative agreement with BCOA in 1981. Specifically, in that discussion the UMWA leadership noted that

> previous agreements since 1964 had never stated outright that firms could run non-signatory coal. In most cases, Local Unions used their power to prevent any such use of non-signatory coal. Under the proposed agreement, the Locals retained the same rights they had previously had.[28]

Nonunion producers of coal have long been and continue to be targets of efforts by union members to impede their production and shipment of coal, particularly but not exclusively in the context of local (unauthorized) or national (authorized) strike ac-

---

[25] J. P. David, "Earnings, Health, Safety and Welfare of Bituminous Coal Miners," Ph.D. diss., University of West Virginia, 1972, p. 213.

[26] United Mine Workers of America v. James A. Pennington, 381 U.S. 657 (1965).

[27] For a discussion of violence during the coal strikes of 1977-1978 and 1981 and of violence involving the UMWA in general, see *Union Violence: The Record and the Response by Courts, Legislatures, and the NLRB* (Philadelphia: University of Pennsylvania, The Wharton School, Industrial Research Unit), 79-118.

[28] "Membership Rejects Tentative Agreement," *United Mine Workers Journal*, p. 1.

tions. The basic tactic used is stranger picketing, backed by real
or implied threats of violence and sabotage. In 1978, the effect of
such actions was to close a substantial number of nonunion mines
during the UMWA's strike against the BCOA, compounding the
impact of that strike on coal supply to the point of creating, in the
view of President Carter, a national emergency. In 1981, the
same scenario was played out, but with a somewhat different
outcome. The *Wall Street Journal* described the situation in 1981
as follows:

> Mining towns throughout the coalfields of Virginia and eastern
> Kentucky are equally tense. For despite the ubiquitous threat of
> violence—from rock-throwings to dynamitings to shootings—asso-
> ciated with UMW strikes, an unusually large number of non-union
> mine managers are trying to keep operating. . . . The non-union
> operators apparently seek to get an edge in the marketplace by
> supplying coal where their unionized competitors can't, especially
> in the burgeoning export market.[29]

The phenomenon of violence extends into the UMWA's organizing campaigns. While the "violent and often bloody" organizing
campaigns of the late 1800s and early 1900s are for the most
part a matter of history, emotions still run high in organizing
confrontations between the UMWA and nonunion operators, as
four companies committed to nonunion operation of new mines
recently discovered. Although the companies—Shell Oil's Turris
Coal, Atlantic Richfield's ARCO Coal, Kerr-McGee Coal, and
Marco Coal—were just beginning construction in August 1981,
the UMWA had already begun protest actions which the *Wall
Street Journal* described as follows:

> Roving bands of miners, charging that Turris Coal is employing
> nonunion construction workers from outside Illinois, have picketed
> Shell gas stations near the company's mine site. And the union's
> 4,500 members in Illinois, who comprise 97% of the state's coal
> mining work force, staged an unauthorized strike last Tuesday
> to protest Kerr-McGee's use of nonunion construction workers.

> Nearly 1,000 of the striking miners descended on Kerr-McGee's
> mine site in Galatia, Illinois, and tore down an eight-foot-high,
> 2½-mile-long fence. . . . The miners also set fire to two trailers and
> a truck before they were dispersed by state troopers.[30]

---

[29] Thomas Petzinger, Jr., "Mine hazards," *Wall Street Journal*, April 24,
1981, p. 56.

[30] Carol Hymowitz, "UMW and four nonunion coal concerns prepare for
showdown in Illinois mines," *Wall Street Journal*, August 21, 1981, p. 6.

Organizing Operations

For most of the past thirty years, the UMWA has placed relatively little emphasis on organizing the unorganized as a means of eliminating nonunion competition. The basic goal of the union during the period of declining employment in the industry between 1950 and 1970 was the elimination of nonunion operators rather than the organization of their employees.

That goal was a logical byproduct of John L. Lewis's acceptance of the inevitability and desirability of concentrating production in large, mechanized, unionized mines. In that context, the union's organizing agenda was limited to large nonunion mining operations such as West Kentucky Coal, and its organizing efforts, as in that case, were directed as much or more at management as at miners.

The union's overall strategy was not totally effective in preserving the virtual monopoly which it enjoyed in 1950, but it worked well enough to contain the growth of nonunion operations and prevent the return of the "ruinous competition," which had ruined the union in the late 1920s, at least prior to the 1970s. The renewed growth of the industry during the 1970s, as manifested particularly in the upward trend after 1973 in the number of operating mines, has altered that situation, as evidenced by the fact that the market share of non-BCOA mines almost doubled (from 30 to 55 percent) between 1979 and 1980.[31] That growth was facilitated by the failure of the union to alter adequately its basically defensive strategy, developed to deal with nonunion competition in a declining industry, to the offensive strategy demanded by a growing industry. Specifically, the union failed to enhance the priority given to organizing sufficiently to offset the combination of industry growth and growing limits on its contractual and institutional constraints on nonunion competition—a failure that the union set out to rectify in 1980 through a commitment to launch "an intensive campaign to bring thousands of miners and millions of tons of coal under the UMW's banner."[32]

The historical background of that commitment is evident in NLRB data on UMWA participation in representation elections during the 1970s. Those data suggest a low level of organizing

---

[31] "Bargaining Statement," *Daily Labor Review*, p. F-1.

[32] Mary A. Andrews, "Mine Workers' New President Wins Dues Increase, Right to Name VP," *Monthly Labor Review*, Vol. 103, No. 3 (March 1980), p. 49.

activity during the early 1970s, when the number of operating mines was still decreasing, in that the UMWA participated in a total of only twelve elections in 1971-1973—an average of four per year—and won about 40 percent of those elections. Over the next six years, 1974-1979, there was a clear increase in the level of the union's involvement in representation elections to an average of twenty-two per year, but not in their success rate, which was about 45 percent. Overall, the union participated in 132 elections over that six-year period and won sixty-one of those elections—the equivalent of 5 percent of the 1,250 more mines in operation in 1979 than in 1974.[33]

The geographical pattern of UMWA election activity provides further insight into the strength of its historical priorities (see Table VI-1). Of a total of 148 elections in which the union participated in the 1971-1980 period, eighty-three took place in the Appalachian field, forty-five in the Central field, and twenty in the West. The leading state in terms of election activity was Kentucky, which was the target of an intensive organizing campaign by the union in the latter half of the 1970s—a campaign that netted a 30 percent election victory rate, well below its overall victory rate of 46 percent. In 1979, *Business Week* characterized that campaign in the following terms:

> Five years ago, flush from an important organizing victory, the United Mine Workers saw itself on the brink of signing up thousands of new members in the rich, largely nonunion coalfields of eastern Kentucky. But subsequent victories were minor. A primary goal of the reformers who ousted W.A. "Tony" Boyle from the UMW's presidency in 1972 was to organize the 84% of eastern Kentucky's coal that is nonunion. And in August 1974, UMW President Arnold Miller won a bloody first conquest at the Brookside mine of Eastover Mining Co., a subsidiary of Duke Power Co., in Harlan, Kentucky. But Miller has been unable to build on this victory.[34]

Symbolic of the union's problems in eastern Kentucky was the case of the Justus mine of Blue Diamond Coal Company, in Sterns, Kentucky, where the union won recognition in 1976 and then "struck when talks toward an initial contract broke down over the union's demands for stringent safety provisions." The company continued to operate, and the union found itself forced

---

[33] Data in author's possession.

[34] "A Kentucky Dispute Bodes Ill for the UMW," *Business Week*, May 7, 1979, pp. 37-38.

TABLE VI-1
*UMWA Representation Election Activity
by State and Region,
1971-1980*

Region	State	Elections	Victories
Appalachia	Kentucky	32	10
	Pennsylvania	18	7
	Vermont	5	2
	Tennessee	4	2
	Maryland	1	1
	Alabama	19	8
	Georgia	4	0
		83	30 (36%)
Central	Wisconsin	13	9
	Oklahoma	12	5
	Ohio	9	3
	Indiana	5	3
	Illinois	4	3
	Arkansas	2	2
		45	25 (56%)
West	Colorado	8	4
	Wyoming	7	6
	Utah	3	1
	New Mexico	2	2
		20	13 (65%)
Total	17 States	148	68 (46%)

Source: NLRB Data in author's possession.

into a representation election against an independent union in 1979, which it expected to and did indeed lose. Prior to the election, however, the union reverted to historical form, as is indicated by the following *Business Week* account:

> The union felt it had one final chance for victory last fall, when Standard Oil Co. (Indiana) offered to purchase Blue Diamond. . . . Although UMW leaders have strongly criticized oil company ownership of coal producers, UMW representatives met several times with officials of Standard Oil to try to arrange a UMW contract for workers if the purchase was completed. But in March, Standard Oil withdrew its offer.[35]

———
[35] *Ibid.*, p. 38.

The union is now committed to a far larger and broader organizing effort than it was in the latter half of the 1970s. At its 1980 convention, the union approved a substantial dues increase which will provide funds to augment the budget for its organizing activities, estimated in 1980 to be approximately $500,000, and add personnel to the union's organizing staff estimated in 1980 to total about forty. The convention made no definitive decision as to the allocation of funds or assignment of staff to organizing activities, but its organizing committee "recommended that specific funds be earmarked for the organizing department" and "called for an increase in the number of organizers from about 40 to about 150." [36] One year later, the union had made substantial progress toward that goal, according to the *Wall Street Journal*, which in August 1981 reported that "the union recently increased its total organizing staff to eighty organizers from thirty." [37]

The key target of the union's new commitment to organization is to be the West, where UMWA president Church told the convention that he proposed to add fifty organizers to the existing staff of nine, warning the delegates that " 'big money' will be needed to help organize the rich West." [38] Despite that proposal and commitment, industry personnel indicated that most of the early additions to the union's organizing staff were in the East rather than the West, as might have been anticipated, given the historical roots and current strength of the union. What will happen in the future remains to be seen, but the incursion of four major nonunion producers into Illinois where the union reportedly has only four organizers and feels it is "still running thin" may well constitute a real problem for the union in launching its announced "major organizing effort" in the West.[39] The problem may further be compounded by other incursions of nonunion producers into other parts of the heartland of the UMWA, at least one of which is currently in the planning stage.

The survival of the UMWA may well depend on its success in fulfilling its new commitment to organizing nonunion mines and miners. Its first two lines of defense against nonunion competi-

---

[36] Andrews, "Mine Workers' New President Wins Dues Increase," p. 49.

[37] Hymowitz, "UMW and four nonunion coal concerns," p. 6.

[38] Andrews, "Mine Workers' New President Wins Dues Increase," p. 49.

[39] Mike Hall, "Major Organizing Effort Getting Underway in Western Coalfields," *United Mine Workers Journal*, No. 6, August 1980, pp. 12-13.

tion, contractual control, and institutional ingenuity have been largely stripped away by the courts and the industry, leaving the union with organization as its only recourse to take or keep labor out of competition—a situation not entirely unlike that in which the union found itself in the late 1920s and early 1930s. At that critical point in the union's history, it was able to rescue itself from oblivion with the help of a supportive government, sanguine industry, and sympathetic work force, which are notably lacking today, particularly, but not exclusively, in the West.

CHAPTER VII

The Politics of Industrywide Bargaining: The United Mine Workers of America

The basic governmental structure of the UMWA was set in 1890 and has not changed dramatically since then. Basic union policy is formulated at the convention, currently held every three years. The implementation of that policy and the conduct of national agreement negotiations are the responsibility of the national leadership—president, vice-president, and secretary-treasurer—who are elected by vote of the membership, including retirees, and of the union's international executive board, which is composed of elected representatives from each of the union's twenty-three districts. Each district also has its own elected leadership which is responsible for development and implementation of policy and for conducting negotiations at the regional level. Strictly local policy and negotiations are the responsibility of the elected leadership of the local unions of the UMWA.

THE POLITICS OF THE UMWA

The basic governmental structure of the UMWA may have remained largely constant over the past ninety years, but the way in which that structure actually works has changed dramatically on several occasions. The UMWA began as a democratic union but went through a profound transformation in the reign of John L. Lewis to become perhaps the classic example of an autocratic union in the American labor movement. Under the leadership of Arnold Miller, the union underwent a second equally profound transformation to become a classic example of a highly democratic, if not an anarchistic, union.

The Lewis Era

The Lewis era spanned a period of over forty years—from the time when John L. Lewis became the power behind the throne of an ailing John Mitchell in 1917 to the ascendency of W. A. "Tony" Boyle to the union's presidency in the election of 1963. John L. Lewis assumed the presidency of the UMWA in 1920 and held that post for forty years before he stepped aside in favor of his long time compatriot and vice-president, Thomas Kennedy, in 1960. Kennedy was in his seventies when he assumed the presidency and was to serve in that office for only three years before his death in 1963. During those three years, he served more as a caretaker than as a leader. Indeed, his ill health made it difficult for him to run the union even on a caretaker basis. Thus, most of the responsibility for running the union on a day-to-day basis was assumed by the vice-president who had been appointed to succeed Kennedy in that position when he succeeded John L. Lewis—W. A. "Tony" Boyle. Boyle, like Lewis, served as the power behind the throne for three years before ascending to the presidency on the death of the president.

When John L. Lewis assumed the presidency of the UMWA in 1920, he became the leader of a union characterized by considerable membership control and local autonomy. Effective leadership control and local influence was divided between the national union and the districts, whose leadership enjoyed both proximity to miners and latitude in concluding agreements on their behalf with mine operators. The potential for political and economic competition inherent in that situation constituted a serious threat to the union's and Lewis's goal of stabilizing the industry and taking (and keeping) labor out of competition.

John L. Lewis was convinced that centralization of control at the national level was crucial if the union was to succeed in its efforts to organize and stabilize the industry. The vehicle he used to achieve that end was his constitutional power to place districts in trusteeship. That action permitted him to appoint not only the district leaders but also district representatives on the international executive board and district delegates to the National Wage Policy Committee, whose responsibility was to "ratify" agreements reached by the international union leadership. Thus, by 1950, Lewis was able to gain virtually total control over the governmental machinery of the union and to stifle the potential for effective dissent within the union.

Lewis's autocratic control, coupled with the respect and reverence accorded him by the rank and file by virtue of his prominent stature on the national labor scene and proven willingness to confront the industry and, when necessary, the federal government during the 1930s and 1940s, left Lewis with almost total freedom in conducting the internal and external affairs of the union. He utilized that freedom to build an almost collusive bargaining relationship with the BCOA, through which he pursued his own vision of the future of the coal industry and ultimately gained quasi-managerial control over the industry. In short, when Lewis stepped down in 1960, both the union and the industry were subject to his benevolently autocratic rule.

When Tony Boyle assumed the presidency of the UMWA in 1963, he fell heir to the benevolent autocracy built by Lewis and preserved by Kennedy. At age fifty-eight, he could perceive in that autocracy the means to ensure himself the same unchallenged control and tenure as Lewis had enjoyed as president of the union. With that end in mind, Boyle sought to perpetuate the governmental system and political machinery built by John L. Lewis on the foundation of trusteeships. He proved to be highly effective in that particular undertaking, despite a suit filed by the Department of Labor in 1964 under the Landrum-Griffin Act to force the union to terminate many of its trusteeships and to permit election of officers at the district level. That suit languished for more than seven years, and as of the end of 1971, only four of the union's twenty-three districts elected their district officers and only one of those districts, District 5 in southwestern Pennsylvania, also elected its representative on the international executive board.[1]

Following the example of Lewis, Boyle perceived his political control as a basis to lead rather than to follow the membership in the formulation of union policy. Boyle, however, lacked both the personal prestige and proven performance of Lewis that had played so important a role in his ability to lead the union. Boyle was not well known, much less revered, by the rank and file. He had risen to the presidency without ever participating in a union election—all of his national union offices had been gained by appointment, beginning with his appointment as administrative assistant to Lewis in 1947, followed by his appointments to succeed Kennedy first as vice-president in 1960 and then as president

---

[1] J.P. David, "Earnings, Health, Safety and Welfare of Bituminous Coal Miners," Ph.D. diss., University of West Virginia, 1972, p. 213.

in 1963. Furthermore, Boyle's career in national office was forged in the shadow of John L. Lewis—a shadow that left him without a personal record of service to and sacrifice for the rank-and-file miner.

The fact that Tony Boyle was a relatively unknown and unproven figure when he assumed the presidency placed him in the position of having to prove himself to the membership in order to legitimize his autocratic political control of the union. Boyle proved clearly and increasingly unequal to that task during his almost ten year tenure as president of the UMWA. His inability to prove himself to the rank and file was the product of his apparent insensitivity to the wishes of the membership in two basic areas: (1) wages and benefits and (2) safety and health. Early during his term in office, Boyle failed to pursue aggressively the wage and royalty increases that had been the fruit of Lewis's negotiations with the BCOA in the 1950s. The result was a series of settlements satisfactory to the industry but not to a substantial number of active and retired miners, as was evident in the occurrence of wildcat strikes to protest the first two agreements (1964 and 1966) with the BCOA negotiated by Boyle. In the later years of his tenure as president, Boyle addressed that problem but failed to respond to the growing interest of the rank and file in safety and health issues. As a result, the union refused to press aggressively for either federal coal mine health and safety legislation or federal and state black lung legislation, much to the displeasure of a substantial body of miners, many of whom felt such legislation was sufficiently important to warrant wildcat strike action.

These failures of Boyle to anticipate and respond to the wishes of the rank and file reflected a degree of isolation from the membership quite different from the insulation from the membership that characterized Lewis's conduct of union affairs. The result was a growing perception on the part of miners that Boyle was more attuned to the interests of the industry than those of union members. That perception could only have been reinforced when Boyle told a Senate subcommittee in 1969 that "the UMWA will not abridge the rights of mine operators in running the mines. We follow the judgment of the coal operators, right or wrong." [2]

The "responsible" leadership and policies of Boyle, unlike those of Lewis, could not go unchallenged indefinitely. The fragmented

---

[2] *Ibid.*, p. 234.

and spontaneous opposition that emerged in response to the 1964 and 1966 wage agreements coalesced on the issue of safety and health in the late 1960s and produced organized opposition in the form of Miners for Democracy—a reform movement organized in 1969 by Joseph "Jock" Yablonski, the one elected district representative on the international executive board. Yablonski succeeded in mounting a campaign for the presidency of the union in opposition to Boyle in 1969—the first contested presidential election in the union in some thirty years. That campaign, however, was unsuccessful in unseating Boyle, who "won" the election easily, with 81,000 votes against 46,000 votes for Yablonski.

Yablonski filed a protest alleging election irregularities with the Department of Labor prior to the 1969 election. The Department did not investigate those allegations until after the election, when it did uncover sufficient evidence of irregularities to warrant legal action to force a new election. That action ultimately resulted in a court order for a new election issued on May 1, 1972.

The 1969 election left Boyle in control of the union but did not eliminate his political opposition, whose challenge of the 1969 election held out some hope of an early return match with the incumbent regime. The continued existence of organized opposition and the threat of a new election did not go unnoticed by those in power who sought to quell that opposition. One unfortunate step in that process was the murder of Joseph Yablonski and two members of his family—murders for which Boyle ultimately was convicted of conspiracy. A second step in that process was a new militancy on the part of the union in its 1971 negotiations with the BCOA, in which Boyle led the union in a successful fight for a very substantial increase in wages and royalties despite the existence of wage controls.

The murder of Joseph Yablonski and the new militancy of Boyle did not quell the opposition to the Boyle regime within the union. The void left by the death of Yablonski was filled by Arnold Miller, who emerged as the leader of a new reform movement. The gains won in negotiations by Boyle in 1971 obviously were insufficient to vindicate his leadership of the union, as in the court ordered presidential election held in December 1972 Boyle was defeated by Arnold Miller by 70,000 to 56,000 votes. That election brought to an end the "Lewis era" of autocratic government in the UMWA and set the stage for a new era in the governance of the union—the "Miller era."

The Miller Era

Arnold Miller gained the office of president of the UMWA as a reform candidate committed to the democratization of the union. His success in the quest for the presidency was built on this appeal to the former supporters of Yablonski and to retired and disabled miners, of whom he was one, who had not been well served by the policies of the union under Boyle. Otherwise, his credentials for the office were limited, as he had no experience at the local, district, or national level either in contract negotiations or in union administration.

The first item of business for President Arnold Miller was to fulfill his promise to return democracy to the UMWA. That was accomplished in 1973 with the adoption of changes in the union's constitution that protected the autonomy of districts, provided once again for the election of district officers and representatives to the international executive board, and established a new procedure for contract ratification. Under that procedure, national agreements henceforth had to be approved first by a bargaining council on which all affected districts were represented and then by a vote of the affected rank and file.

The second item of business confronting President Miller was the negotiation of a new national agreement with the BCOA in 1974—a task that proved to be far more difficult than democratizing the union, in no small measure because of that action. The return of democracy, coupled with the industry's now newly found prosperity and promise after the 1973 energy crisis, brought a visible expansion in the size and scope of the union's bargaining demands. Specifically, the union, reflecting the desires of its members and demands of its district officers, entered negotiations in 1974 seeking both a sizable economic package and a host of changes in work rules designed to protect the "health and safety" of miners—the union's first real challenge to management control over mine operation. The industry did not respond favorably to the union's bargaining demands, and an agreement was reached only after a twenty-four day strike. In the course of reaching that agreement, President Miller suffered his first major political setback when the bargaining council rejected his first tentative agreement with the BCOA by a vote of thirty-seven to one. His second such tentative agreement was better received by the bargaining council, which approved it by the less-than-overwhelming margin of seven votes (twenty-two to fifteen). The rank and file showed the same lack of enthusiasm in approving that second agreement by 56 to 44 percent.

The problems encountered by Arnold Miller in winning approval of a 1974 agreement were the precursors of far more serious internal political problems that were to beset his administration over the next three years.[3] Those problems began with the international executive board, on which a number of former Boyle supporters had won seats in district elections since 1972, and extended to his own staff and the two other principal elected officers of the union. The latent dissatisfaction with Miller's performance at the bargaining table and manifest criticism of his management of the union produced challengers to Miller in the union's 1977 presidential election. Miller survived that challenge to his leadership and won reelection, but with less than a majority of the votes cast. The second-place finisher challenged the results of that election in appeals to both the union's executive board and the Department of Labor. The executive board sustained Miller's victory, but only by a relatively narrow margin. The Department of Labor did the same in a ruling issued in October 1977, the month in which Arnold Miller for the second time entered negotiations with the BCOA over a new national agreement.

Arnold Miller entered negotiations with the BCOA in 1977 clearly lacking what his two predecessors had enjoyed—control of the union. He did not have the support of a clear majority of the executive board or the district leadership, among whose numbers were several of his open and active political rivals. To make matters worse, he had lost much of his staff, who had been responsible for the work behind his reasonably successful 1974 negotiations with the BCOA. He did, however, have the support of one important ally, Sam Church, whom he had appointed as his executive assistant in 1976 and who was elected vice-president in the union's 1977 election.

The political problems of Arnold Miller proved to be a major factor in the 1977 UMWA-BCOA negotiations. Those problems did not bode well for an easy or peaceful settlement in any event, but proved particularly troublesome in light of the BCOA's bar-

---

[3] For a more detailed discussion of these problems, see William H. Miernyk, "Coal," in Gerald G. Somers, ed., *Collective Bargaining: Contemporary American Experience* (Madison, Wis.: Industrial Relations Research Association, 1980), pp. 42-45; *and* Paul F. Clark, *The Miners' Fight for Democracy* (Ithaca: New York State School of Industrial and Labor Relations, Cornell University, 1981).

gaining strategy and goals. The BCOA in 1977 sought to trade a substantial economic package for significant concessions by the union in the areas of labor productivity (work rules) and labor stability (wildcat strikes). Such a trade-off might well have been manageable for a John L. Lewis and possibly a Tony Boyle, but not for an Arnold Miller, whose ability to persuade, much less lead the union, was extremely questionable.

When the BCOA proved insistent on pursuing its trade-off even after a two-month strike, President Miller was compelled to choose between accepting that trade-off or continuing the strike for an indefinite period of time. He chose the former course of action in early February 1978 and accepted a tentative settlement with the BCOA which embodied the BCOA's trade-off. That decision provoked intense criticism within the union and gave his political rivals the opportunity they sought to embarrass him, as indeed they did when the bargaining council rejected that tentative agreement by a vote of thirty-three to six.

In retrospect, the political wisdom of President Miller's decision to accept the BOCA's "final offer" in preference to no settlement is obviously questionable. The practical wisdom of that decision at the time it was made, however, is another matter. The BCOA was firmly committed to its final offer and prepared to take a very long strike in defense of that offer, as it was to demonstrate first in its refusal to return to negotiations with the UMWA after rejection of its initial tentative agreement and later in its refusal to accept an invitation to the White House to discuss ways to break the impasse. In both cases, the BCOA's resolve to defend its offer, and thereby President Miller's decision, was bent and finally broken by pressures exerted by the Carter administration on both the BCOA and some of its individual members. The result of that pressure was a second tentative agreement clearly more favorable to the union than the first, which was approved by the bargaining council by a vote of twenty-five to thirteen.

The second agreement simultaneously confirmed and assuaged the critics of Arnold Miller in the union's governing structure. At the same time, it strengthened but did not assuage the critics of Arnold Miller among the rank and file, which ultimately voted to reject the second agreement by more than a two to one margin. The approval of the rank and file waited upon the conclusion of a third agreement ten days later, which the bargaining council approved by a vote of twenty-two to seven and the membership ratified by a 57 to 43 percent margin.

The political problems of President Miller did not end with the conclusion of the 1977-1978 UMWA-BCOA contract negotiations. His conduct at the negotiations and administration of the union continued to be the focus of vocal criticism within the union at the local and district level. The result was a further deterioration in Miller's credibility within, as well as his already limited control of, the union to the point that in late 1979 he decided, however willingly or reluctantly, to step down as president of the UMWA "for reasons of ill health" in favor of his former executive assistant and running mate in 1977, Vice President Samuel Morgan Church.

When Sam Church assumed the presidency in November 1979 to fill out the remainder of Arnold Miller's six-year term in office, he was perceived to be a strong leader able to unify and solidify the union. His ability to do this, however, would have to rest on his ability to secure and retain the support of the executive board and the district leadership. The democratic reforms instituted at the outset of the Miller era remained in place, making centralized control of the type that characterized the Lewis era difficult, if not impossible.

The first test of the strength and support to be enjoyed by President Church came at the UMWA's convention in December 1979, one month after he was sworn into office. The key issue for Church at that convention was the question of whether he would be given the right to appoint his own replacement as vice president in the "Lewis tradition." Also at issue was the matter of a substantial dues increase to preserve the solvency and expand the organizing capabilities of the union. On both counts, President Church emerged triumphant with no major battle scars. The *Monthly Labor Review* summarized the outcome of the convention in the following terms:

> The United Mine Workers of America saw its new president, Samuel Morgan Church, Jr., gavel his way to victory at the union's triennial convention in Denver, Colo. In the tradition of John L. Lewis, Church won on a number of important issues, including a dues increase, a newly established strike fund, and presidential authority to appoint a vice president.[4]

---

[4] Mary A. Andrews, "Mine Workers' New President Wins Dues Increase, Right to Name VP," *Monthly Labor Review*, Vol. 103, No. 3 (March 1980), p. 48.

The key victory for Church was on the question of his right to appoint a vice president. The *Monthly Labor Review* described his victory on that question as follows:

> After a brief but spirited debate, the delegates endorsed a resolution from the floor to waive a provision of the union's constitution requiring a general election to fill the vacancy. Some of the opposing delegates argued that such a waiver was not in the spirit of the democratic process and represented a loss of autonomy for them as representatives of the rank and file. The majority, however, upheld the president's right to pick a vice president. Another consideration was a saving of about $750,000, the cost of running an election.[5]

The second major challenge facing President Church was the 1981 UMWA-BCOA National Agreement negotiations. Those negotiations formally opened in September 1980, a full six months prior to contract expiration, although serious bargaining was not anticipated to begin until January of 1981. Even before the negotiations opened, there was considerable optimism that the situation would be dramatically different in 1981 than it had been in 1977. The Bureau of Labor Statistics in its 1980 review of "Collective Bargaining in the Bituminous Coal Industry" noted that President Church, unlike his predecessor, appeared to enjoy substantial support among the members of the executive board and bargaining council and the benefit of the "growing maturity of the large body of young, inexperienced miners who entered the industry earlier in the decade and who allegedly were responsible for much of the dissidence."[6] President Church echoed that sentiment when he expressed confidence as early as nine months prior to contract expiration that he and the UMWA could and would be able to deal effectively with the BCOA's productivity issues and suggested that the union might alter its long term policy of "no contract, no work" by either extending the contract or pursuing selective strikes.[7]

The 1981 UMWA-BCOA negotiations proved to be far more difficult than anticipated by the union in the summer of 1980, primarily because the BCOA raised at least two unanticipated "institutional" issues in those negotiations. The union apparently

---

[5] *Ibid.*

[6] U.S. Department of Labor, Bureau of Labor Statistics, "Collective Bargaining in the Bituminous Coal Industry," Report 625 (Washington, D.C.: U.S. Government Printing Office, December 1980), p. 1.

[7] "Mine Workers President Hopes to Avoid Contracts Strike in 1981," *Daily Labor Report*, No. 147 (July 29, 1980), p. A-7.

was prepared to deal with "productivity" and "jurisdictional" issues but not with the BCOA's sudden interest in such "institutional" issues as the substitution of single-employer pension plans for the union's multiemployer pension fund or the easing of the union's contractual constraints on the acquisition of nonunion coal. Ultimately, those two institutional issues were resolved by a trade-off in which the UMWA agreed to lift the royalty penalty on nonunion coal in exchange for the BCOA's agreement to continue the existing multiemployer pension fund. That trade-off, unlike Arnold Miller's trade-off in 1978, proved to be acceptable to the union's bargaining council, which voted to approve the tentative agreement concluded by President Church, an act that would seem to confirm that he enjoyed the support and confidence of a majority of the union's elected district officers. That support and confidence, however, obviously did not extend to the rank and file, which, as in 1978, voted to reject the first contract submitted to them for ratification by a two-to-one margin.[8]

It took seventy-two days on strike before a second agreement could be reached and ratified in 1981, an agreement in which the BCOA once again relinquished its half of the overt trade-off made in the first agreement. As in 1978, that apparent economic victory for the union proved to be a political defeat for the president of the union. The *Wall Street Journal* described that defeat in the following terms:

> After Mr. Church negotiated a labor contract last March that allowed unionized operators more liberal use of nonunion coal and nonunion workers, he became "sellout Sam." The contract was overwhelmingly rejected by miners, who stayed on strike for 72 days. And even though a second contract won widespread approval among UMW members, many have come to regard Mr. Church as a weak leader.[9]

President Church's initial failure in the 1981 negotiations almost immediately became an issue in local and district elections and was still an issue six months later. The result, in the words of the *Wall Street Journal* in September 1981, was that "unity within the United Mine Workers union again has given way to political infighting and dissension." Specifically, the *Wall Street Journal* reported:

---

[8] For a detailed discussion of this contract rejection see William Miernyk, "The 1981 Coal Strike: A View from the Outside," in *Industrial Relations Research Association: Proceedings of the 1981 Spring Meeting* (Madison, Wis.: 1981), pp. 564-67.

[9] Carol Hymowitz, "UMW head Church's control threatened as opponents gain on executive board," *Wall Street Journal*, September 14, 1981, p. 5.

> This time the target of dissatisfaction is UMW president Samuel Church, Jr. Mr. Church's grasp of the union hierarchy began to loosen during last spring's long coal strike. But now he is threatened with losing complete control of the UMW's powerful International Executive Board, which sets union policy.
>
> Opponents of Mr. Church have won more than one-third of the board's 21 seats in recent district elections, and the remaining elections in coming weeks could give those opponents a clear majority.[10]

Sam Church's political problems, like those of Arnold Miller, did not end or abate with the conclusion of an agreement acceptable to the rank and file. Rich Trumka, a young miner-lawyer who had been among the first and most vocal critics of the first 1981 agreement, pressed his case to the point of challenging Church in the union's 1982 presidential election. After a long, hard, and often bitter campaign, Trumka emerged victorious by a dramatic two-to-one margin. It is, at this writing, too early to know what his victory will mean for the future of the UMWA, but many outside observers of the industry suspect it portends continued unrest and instability within the union and in its relations with the BCOA.

THE POLICIES OF THE UMWA

There are competing theories regarding the basic goals and behavior of unions which differ primarily with respect to what it is that unions seek to maximize—wage rate, wage bill, or working membership. The proponents of each theory have their favorite supportive examples, and it is generally the UMWA which is the favorite of those inclined to the theory of wage-rate maximization. Indeed, the UMWA is a classic case of a union that pursued a high wage strategy at the expense of working membership. That strategy was explicitly acknowledged by John L. Lewis almost forty years ago in the following words:

> We decided it's better to have half a million men working in the industry at good wages, high standard of living, than it is to have a million men working in the industry in poverty.[11]

The most formidable barrier faced by the UMWA in its quest for "good wages" and a "high standard of living" for those employed in the industry throughout much of its history has

---

[10] *Ibid.*

[11] Joseph F. Finley, *The Corrupt Kingdom* (New York: Simon and Schuster, 1972), p. 61.

been the twin devils of "excess capacity" and "ruinous competition" which made wage rates an important element in the economic viability of a mining enterprise. The union's response to that challenge was acceptance and encouragement of a process of natural selection based on productivity rather than on wages in the form of a sanguine policy regarding the mechanization of mines. The *quid pro quo* for the union's lack of resistance to mechanization was, in the words of John L. Lewis,

> that miners had a right to participate through increased wages and shorter hours and improved safety and better conditions, in the increased productive efficiency of the industry.[12]

Wage Policies

There are two fundamental principles that have guided the UMWA in its wage negotiations since the turn of the century. The first is insistence on wage increases and resistances to wage decreases. The second is pursuit of equality in wages and earnings among mine workers. These two principles have tended to be fairly absolute and only rarely have been compromised to accommodate economic conditions in the industry. The UMWA is hardly unique among unions in its policy of pursuing rising money and real wages for its members and in resisting reductions in those wages. It does, however, stand apart from other unions with respect to both its consistent short-run commitment to and conspicuous long-run success in pursuit of that policy—two factors that account for the fact that

> the United Mine Workers in the Bituminous Coal industry has the largest effect on earnings that have been estimated for any industrial union. In the mid-1950s these were estimated to be greater than 30 percent, but no more recent estimate is available.[13]

The high wage policy of the UMWA was not the creation of John L. Lewis, but the strength and consistency of the UMWA's commitment to that policy in the face of any and all economic adversity was very much his work. Between 1920 and 1960, the union's wage demands and settlements showed little sensitivity to basic economic or competitive conditions in the industry.

---

12 U.S. Congress, House of Representatives, Committee on Education and Labor, Welfare of Miners, *Hearings, 80th Congress, 1st Session, April 3, 1947* (Washington, D.C.: U.S. Government Printing Office, 1947), p. 41.

13 Albert Rees, *The Economics of Trade Unions* (Chicago: The University of Chicago Press, 1977), p. 73.

Specifically, the union's wage demands did not moderate significantly during the two decades of decline in the industry over that period—the 1920s and the 1950s. The ultimate result of that insensitivity to declining demand and growing nonunion competition in the 1920s was an unsuccessful strike in support of the union's "no step backward" policy which destroyed the union's multiemployer bargaining system and almost destroyed the union itself. The result of that same insensitivity to declining demand and growing competition in the 1950s was a loss of control and membership similar in character but not scale to that experienced in the late 1920s.

The 1950s posed a particularly difficult challenge to the union's high wage policy. Over that decade, coal production dropped by almost 20 percent, from 516 to 415 million tons, and coal employment by almost 60 percent, from 415,000 to 170,000.[14] Over that same period, the union's share of production dropped from 90 to 70 percent and its working membership dropped from over 300,000 to under 100,000.[15] Despite those adverse trends, the union was fairly well able to hold its own in terms of wages and earnings relative to such other unions as the Auto Workers and Steelworkers. In 1950, average hourly earnings in bituminous coal mining were about 10 percent higher than average hourly earnings in the auto industry and 15 percent higher than average hourly earnings in the steel industry.[16] In 1960, average hourly earnings in bituminous coal mining still exceeded those in auto and steel industries, but by a smaller percentage margin, particularly in the case of steel.[17]

The apparent insensitivity of the UMWA's wage demands and settlements to industry conditions abated when Lewis stepped down as president. The frequent and substantial wage increases negotiated by Lewis during the 1950s gave way to more sporadic and modest wage increases during the early years of Boyle's tenure as president. That period of moderation brought the first

---

[14] *1980 Keystone Coal Industry Manual* (New York: McGraw Hill, 1980), p. 691.

[15] J. Russell Boner, "More mines drop pacts with UMW to escape high wages, royalties," *Wall Street Journal*, December 11, 1964, p. 1.

[16] U.S. Department of Labor, Bureau of Labor Statistics, *Employment and Earnings, U.S., 1904-1970* (Washington, D.C.: U.S. Government Printing Office, 1970), pp. 13, 96, 232.

[17] *Ibid.*

signs of serious rank-and-file unrest in almost thirty years. That unrest, coupled with gradually growing demand for coal and coal miners, brought an end to "wage moderation" in 1968 when the union negotiated a new contract estimated to cost the industry 41 percent over three years.[18] The 1971 negotiations brought what seemed to be a return to "wage excess" when the union struck to achieve a settlement worth 39 percent over three years despite the existence of wage controls.[19] Those two lucrative settlements, however, were not sufficient to prevent the mine workers from losing their historical advantage over steel and auto workers in terms of average hourly earnings by the end of their 1971 contract.[20] Since then, the UMWA has waged an uphill and less than totally successful battle to keep up with steel and auto workers in terms of wages.

The second basic dimension of the union's wage policy has been a drive for equality of wages and earnings within the industry. Historically, that drive has been concentrated on the elimination of earning differentials between mines, but it has also extended to the reduction of earning differentials between miners. The result has been a consistent narrowing of wage differentials based on employer ability to pay and employee productivity, which has created its own set of problems for the union and the industry.

Again, the UMWA is hardly unique among industrial unions in pursuing an egalitarian wage policy. It is, however, somewhat different from other unions in the extent to which it has been willing and able to impose earnings uniformly on a diverse population of employers and employees, despite the potential for revolt among those disadvantaged by equality—most notably, smaller employers and skilled employees.

The UMWA has long advocated and actively pursued a system of wage rates that provided for equal earnings rather than equal labor costs. In the early 1900s, this involved a complex set of wage differentials between mines in wage payments per ton of coal mined to compensate for differences in output attributable

---

[18] Arnold R. Weber and Daniel J. B. Mitchell, *The Pay Board's Progress* (Washington, D.C.: The Brookings Institution, 1978), p. 149.

[19] "Developments in Industrial Relations," *Monthly Labor Review*, Vol. 95, No. 1 (January 1972), p. 82.

[20] U.S. Department of Labor, Bureau of Labor Statistics, *Employment and Earnings*, Vol. 21, No. 6 (December 1974), pp. 92, 94, 96.

to geological or technological differences among coal mines, which resulted in higher rates for miners in thin as opposed to thick vein mines and for pick miners as opposed to machine miners— differentials inversely related to the productivity of labor. In more modern times, this involved a simple set of uniform increases in hourly pay for all miners independent of the geological or technological conditions of the mine in which they were employed—increases unrelated to the productivity of labor in individual mines.

The result of these wage policies has been to give a competitive advantage to geologically (surface) or technologically (mechanized) favored mines. Thus, the union's egalitarian wage policy has encouraged both surface mining and mechanized underground mining with obvious adverse effects on employment opportunities in the industry and its own opportunities to retain and expand its working membership. Furthermore, those mines not blessed with the geological or financial resources required to accommodate the union's wage policy were forced to choose between going out of business or going nonunion. In both the 1920s and 1950s, a number of mines were forced into the former course of action, but a substantial number were willing and able to pursue the latter course of action, creating a "problem of nonunion competition" for the union and unionized operators which overwhelmed both in the 1920s and which seemingly threatens to do the same in the 1980s.

The egalitarian predilections of the UMWA also have extended to occupational wage structure. Throughout the 1950s and into the 1960s, the union sought and secured across-the-board, dollar-per-day wage increases. The result was a dramatic compression of skill differentials which ultimately necessitated a special skilled trades wage adjustment in 1966. The compression of skill differentials during the 1950s tended to encourage the substitution of skilled for unskilled labor, thereby creating a further incentive for mechanization. In the 1970s, the continued compression of skill differentials has tended to weaken worker incentives to acquire or apply skills, thereby creating problems in the manning of mechanized operations. By 1981, those problems apparently had become sufficiently troublesome to lead the BCOA to include among its list of contract provisions "which contribute nothing to the well being of the coal miner, but do stand in the way of increased productivity" those that "allow employees too much lateral and downward job bidding." [21]

Mechanization Policies

The UMWA has had to confront the issue of mechanization virtually from its inception. Throughout its history, the union's policy regarding mechanization has been one of passive acceptance, and that remains the formal policy of the UMWA today, as manifested in the provision of its 1981 national agreement which clearly recognized management's "right to install and operate new types of equipment." [22] The UMWA is not unique among unions in pursuing such a policy, but it is unique in its willingness and ability to adhere to that policy in the face of a massive loss of jobs and members as a result of technological change.

The mechanical cutting of coal began in the late 1800s and spread through the industry at a fairly rapid rate during the first quarter of this century. The union's response to this wave of technological change was a policy of nonresistance coupled with efforts to regulate the pace of change. Thus, machine rates were set lower than pick rates in the early 1900s, "but not so low as to encourage precipitous installation of machinery." [23] The view of the union, as expressed by John Mitchell in 1903, was that "the unionist believes that machinery should be introduced with the least possible friction and the least possible hardship to individuals." [24] The spread of mechanical cutting posed only a limited threat to workers in the industry because it came at a time of expanding demand for coal. The same was not true for the second wave of technological change in the industry, the mechanical loading of coal, which came when the industry was in its depressed state during the 1920s and 1930s.[25] That wave of change brought "rumblings from the ranks against mechanization, particularly during the depression of the 1930s. Those

---

[21] "Bargaining Statement By Bituminous Coal Operators Association," *Daily Labor Report,* No. 15 (February 23, 1981), p. F-3.

[22] National Bituminous Coal Wage Agreement of 1981 Article XXII, Section (1), p. 146.

[23] Morton S. Baratz, *The Union and the Coal Industry* (New Haven, Conn.: Yale University Press, 1955), p. 54.

[24] *Ibid.,* p. 53.

[25] *Ibid.*

rumblings were overruled by a union leadership that took the
position that, "rather than object to mechanization of industry
we should devote our efforts toward a shorter work day and
work week." [26]

The third wave of technological change—the continuous mining
machine—came during the 1950s, which also was a period of
declining demand for coal, hardly a time when labor-saving machinery could be introduced with a "minimum of hardship to
individuals." Nonetheless, the UMWA continued its policy of
nonresistance and, indeed, actually encouraged mechanization by
union operators both directly and indirectly through its wage
policies. The basis of that policy was John L. Lewis's conviction
that the future of the industry and of the union rested in the
concentration of production in large mechanized (and unionized)
mines that could produce coal at a cost competitive with other
fuels while providing adequate wages for their miners—a conviction he was free to pursue by virtue of his control over the
policy-making mechanisms of the union. The employment effects
of such an industry consolidation were well understood and fairly
well estimated by the union leadership, which took the position
that

> it does not make any difference whether we have 500,000 men in the
> coal mines or only 50,000 . . . they ought to be treated humanely;
> they ought to be paid a wage to protect their standard of living.[27]

The fourth wave of technological change in the industry may
be the use of longwall mining machines on a broad scale in underground mining. Thus far, the union has accepted longwall
technology on the same sanguine basis as it did continuous mining
technology and probably will continue to do so, particularly if
the long-awaited boom in the demand for coal materializes. While
the union has not opposed the introduction of longwall mining
technology, it has opposed changes in work schedules deemed
necessary by the industry to permit the most efficient use of that
technology. Specifically, the union has resisted changes in its
long-standing ban on Sunday work and provision for vacation
shutdowns and opposed the institution of swing shifts, which
the industry has sought to permit continuous operation. These
work rule/work schedule practices were an issue in both the

---

26 Miernyk, "Coal," p. 26.

27 Baratz, *The Union and the Coal Industry*, p. 142.

1977 and 1981 negotiations, when the industry included among its "hit list" of "provisions which contribute nothing to the well-being of the coal miner, but do stand in the way of increased productivity" those which "restrict full use of expensive equipment in continuous operation." [28]

One other set of provisions on the BCOA's 1981 list of provisions that stood in the way of increased productivity were those that, in its words, "encourage featherbedding." [29] Featherbedding was not an issue during the Lewis era when the union not only made no effort to inhibit mechanization but also did little to limit the efficient use of technology in the interest of mitigating employment effects. The emergence of featherbedding as an issue in 1977 and 1981 suggests some change in that policy during the Miller era. Specifically, the union in 1974 sought and secured larger crews on certain equipment on the grounds of safety. Its real motivation, however, was more to expand employment opportunities, which suggests a marked departure from the union's traditional insensitivity to employment effects. With a substantial number of its members currently unemployed, it seems unlikely that the union will return to its former policy until or unless the long-awaited boom in the demand for coal is felt in UMWA National Agreement mines.

---

[28] "Bargaining Statement," *Daily Labor Report,* p. F-3.

[29] *Ibid.,* p. F-4.

CHAPTER VIII

The Politics of Bargaining:
The Bituminous Coal Operators' Association

The BCOA is a multiemployer association, formed in 1950 for the sole purpose of negotiating with the UWMA on National Bituminous Coal Wage Agreements. In 1950, it was a virtually industrywide, multiemployer bargaining association that represented all but a small percentage of coal production capacity in the United States. By 1970, that was no longer the case, as BCOA member companies and associations accounted for only 70 percent of the coal produced in the United States—a percentage that had fallen to under 50 percent by 1980.[1] The more than 50 percent of 1980 coal production accounted for by non-BCOA mines was divided among three types of producers: (1) nonunion mines (including some belonging to BCOA members); (2) non-UMWA union mines (again including some belonging to BCOA members); and (3) nonmember UMWA mines (including some which are, in effect, nonmember signatories to the National Wage Agreement and some, like western surface mines, which are party to truly independent agreements).

The membership of the BCOA as of June 7, 1981, consisted of seventy-three coal-producing corporations, companies, and groups and six coal producers' associations representing another seventy-two coal-producing companies.[2] Included among those 145 members are ten of the fifteen largest coal-producing groups as of 1979 (see Table VIII-1). The five nonmembers among the fifteen largest are basically western surface mine operators, some of which have mines covered by the UMWA's Independent Western Surface Mine Agreement.

---

[1] "Bargaining Statement By Bituminous Coal Operators Association," *Daily Labor Report*, No. 15 (January 23, 1981), p. F-1.

[2] National Bituminous Coal Wage Agreement of 1981, pp. 172-75.

113

TABLE VIII-1
Fifteen Largest Coal Producing Groups,
1979

Group or Company	BCOA Member		1979 Tonnage		
	Yes	No	Total	% U.S.	% BCOA
Peabody Group	X		64.4M	8.4	16.9
Consolidation Group	X		50.1M	6.5	13.2
Amax Group	X		34.6M	4.5	9.1
Texas Utilities		X	25.2M		
Bland Creek Group	X		19.9M	2.6	5.2
U.S. Steel	X		15.0M	1.9	3.9
Pittston Group	X		14.7M	1.9	3.9
Nerco Group		X	14.5M		
Amer. Elec. Pwr.	X		13.3M	1.7	3.5
Peter Kiewit Group		X	13.1M		
Arch Mineral		X	12.6M		
Bethlehem Mines	X		12.5M	1.6	3.3
Western Energy		X	11.7M		
North American Group	X		11.6M	1.5	3.1
Old Ben	X		10.0M	1.3	2.6
Total	10	5	323.2M	31.9	64.7

Source: *1980 Keystone Coal Industry Manual* (New York: McGraw Hill, 1980), p. 686.

THE POLITICS OF THE BCOA

The membership of the BCOA has never been homogeneous despite the common involvement of all the members in coal mining operations. The size, location, and ownership of the member companies vary significantly, as does the type of coal they produce and the degree of their dependence on UMWA mined coal. This diversity clearly can be, and reputedly has been, the cause of a serious problem in the development of an industry consensus on bargaining positions and strategies, and in the maintenance of that consensus, particularly in the face of a potential or actual test of economic power with the UMWA.

The formal mechanism for making decisions within the BCOA is a vote of the membership. In that process, the votes of individual members are weighted by the tonnage they produce under the UMWA National Agreement. Thus, in the final analysis, the largest producers control the industry's positions and strategies in collective bargaining. Short of that point, however, ample opportunity exists for individual members to wield "disproportionate power" based on their corporate stature or status and/or the personal prestige or persuasive power of their representative in the association. In short, the consensus/decision process within the BCOA, as in most multiemployer bargaining associations, is a subtle and complex process that is not easily studied or understood by outsiders. Indeed, in this case, it is a process that even most insiders are at a loss to describe in any detail.

The Lewis Era

The very limited literature on collective bargaining in the bituminous coal mining industry in the 1950s generally suggests that the BCOA, like the UMWA, was a monolithic and autocratic institution able to engage in essentially "one-on-one" negotiations with its adversary. As one scholar described the situation, the National Agreement of 1950 set the stage for "Harry Moses, who was named head of the BCOA in September 1950, and John L. Lewis [to] hammer out agreements that would be mutually satisfactory to the operators and the union." [3] If Moses encountered problems in dealing with his constituents in that process, they are largely unknown.

There is at least fragmentary evidence of some internal consensus problems within the BCOA in the 1950s. These problems appear to have arisen along the lines of the division that existed in the industry prior to the formation of the BCOA. Specifically, it appears that in the early 1950s, captive mine operators—primarily steel companies—who were faced with strong demand for their final product—steel rather than coal—were the doves in the industry and were an important factor in the conclusion of a series of wage agreements not fully consistent with the ability of the declining coal industry to pay.[4] When those settlements encouraged the emergence of nonunion competition, coal producers asserted their interests, and the protective wage clause of 1958 resulted. That clause, however, produced another rift within the BCOA when the leader of the Southern Coal Pro-

---

[3] William H. Miernyk, "Coal," Gerald G. Somers, ed., *Collective Bargaining: Contemporary American Experience* (Madison, Wis.: Industrial Relations Research Association, 1980), p. 28.

[4] C. L. Christensen, *Economic Redevelopment in Bituminous Coal* (Cambridge: Harvard University Press, 1962), pp. 208-09.

ducers Association agreed to accept it only on behalf of those of his members who specifically authorized him to do so.[5]

The 1958 National Agreement marked the ascendency of coal interests within the BCOA, and resulted in a dramatic change in the character of settlements concluded during the 1960s. The precarious financial condition of coal companies in the late 1950s and early 1960s sufficiently dominated the industry to preclude any further amendments to the National Agreement between 1958 and 1963. It was not until Tony Boyle assumed the presidency in 1964 that the UMWA exercised the option it had possessed since 1959 to open negotiations over a new contract, and it did so then only as a result of rank-and-file pressure. The 1964 negotiations produced, among other things, the royalty penalty for nonsignatory coal acquired by signatory companies—a provision that clearly served the interests of coal companies. Apparently, however, it did not serve the interests of captive operators, whose contract did not include that provision.[6]

The four sets of negotiations (1964, 1966, 1968, and 1971) conducted by the BCOA during the tenure of Tony Boyle at the UMWA were characterized by far greater determination on the part of the industry to impose wage restraint on the union than had been the case in the 1950s. That determination encountered growing resistance from the union rank and file throughout the period, as evidenced by wildcat strikes in protest of the 1964 and 1966 settlements, an unauthorized strike when no agreement was reached prior to contract expiration in 1968, and an authorized strike under the same conditions in 1971. Those strike actions tested the resolve of the BCOA, in general, and of its "old coal" members in particular. The record of the industry in confronting that test is not particularly distinguished. An eighteen-day wildcat strike by some 18,000 miners in 1964 elicited no further concessions from the industry, but a sixteen-day wildcat strike by some 40,000 miners in 1966 did. The BCOA took a thirty-one day strike in 1968 and a fifty-seven-day strike in 1971, but was ultimately forced in both cases to accept a 40 percent package. The 1971 settlement was particularly onerous to the industry, because it called for the first increases in royalty payments to the union's welfare funds since 1958. That

---

[5] *Ibid.*, p. 269.

[6] "Wage Chronology: Bituminous Coal Mines, Supplement No. 6—1960-1966," *Monthly Labor Review*, Vol. 88, No. 4 (April 1965), p. 425.

agreement proved even more damaging when the Price Commission ruled that the industry could pass through into prices only the equivalent of a 5.5 percent settlement.[7]

The Miller Era

The questionable solidarity and resolve of the BCOA was to be even more surely tested in the 1970s than in the 1960s. The mounting militancy of miners coupled with the return of democracy to their union resulted in a further breakdown of control and self-discipline in the union's relations with the industry, and the BCOA was forced to assume the full burden of bringing economic discipline and institutional control to collective bargaining. This task has been extremely difficult for the BCOA, primarily because of the internal difficulties it has in reaching and maintaining a consensus in the face of union militancy. These problems almost led to the dissolution of the BCOA before and during its 1981 negotiations with the UMWA and may, at least in the view of one interested observer within the industry, destroy the BCOA before its 1984 negotiations with the UMWA.

The BCOA entered the Miller era as a far more diverse organization than it had been for much of the Lewis era. The long-standing "captive v. commercial" (dig to use v. dig to sell) distinction among members still existed. The equally longstanding "North v. South" distinction among commercial coal operators had lost much of its operational significance, but at least four "new" sets of distinctions had gained operational significance:

(1) Deep v. strip mine operations, which differ dramatically with respect to productivity rates and safety problems;

(2) Metallurgical v. steam coal mines which compete in very different markets with very different short-term and long-term demand outlooks;

(3) Eastern v. western companies which differ in their degree of dependence on UMWA/BCOA-mined coal for sales and profits;

(4) Energy v. coal companies which differ with respect to their degree of short-run dependence on coal mining as a source of sales and profits.

---

[7] Arnold R. Weber and Daniel J. B. Mitchell, *The Pay Board's Progress* (Washington, D.C.: The Brookings Institution, 1978), p. 152.

The problems confronting the BCOA in developing a consensus on bargaining strategies and goals among this diverse population of coal, steel, and energy companies in the highly volatile and uncertain economic environment of the 1970s have been substantial in their own right and further complicated by the union's new propensity to strike, which has brought into play the inevitable differential vulnerability of member companies to a UMWA strike. Those problems appear to have overwhelmed the BCOA in 1974 when the settlement it reached was a costly combination of special industry interests. That settlement established new pension and welfare funds to be funded on the basis of hours worked rather than tonnage mined—a change which benefitted strip mine operators such as Peabody Coal. It also provided a substantial increase in compensation, which could not have been welcomed by deep mine operators, given their declining productivity, and which would have been unacceptable had deep-mined metallurgical coal not been in short supply, making steel companies and some coal companies more amenable to a large settlement.

The industry spent the following three years slowly repenting the agreement it had hastily concluded in 1974. The coal boom, anticipated at the time of the contract and expected to ease the economic burden of its concessions, failed to materialize. Then, the demand for metallurgical coal weakened to the point of impending surplus, thus worsening matters. Finally, the industry was beset by a rash of wildcat strikes during the term of the 1974 agreement on a scale unprecedented in the history of the BCOA. The response of the BCOA to its fate under the 1974 agreement was a determined, if ultimately unsuccessful, effort to take a solid, unwavering stand in its 1977 negotiations with the UMWA.

The initiative and/or blame for the BCOA's new-found resolve has been attributed to its steel company members, in general, and to the United States Steel Company, in particular. However true that attribution, U.S. Steel clearly did play an important role in the conduct of the BCOA's 1977 negotiations with the UMWA—a role out of proportion to its position as the fifth largest BCOA coal producer. One legacy of the Lewis era of labor peace and union control of industry labor relations was a lack of labor relations staff and expertise among most member companies and in the industry as a whole. The most notable exceptions were the steel companies, setting the stage for one of them to play a disproportionately influential role when the BCOA finally was compelled to attempt more than simple accedence to the union's vision of what was good for the industry and/or its members—a predilection reputed to beset the Chief Executive Officers (CEOs) who represent many of the "old coal" companies within the BCOA.

The united front of the BCOA in 1977 had to be built in the face of what the director of the Federal Mediation and Conciliation Service (FMCS) later characterized as the "economic factionalism" of the association.[8] That factionalism involved three groups with different motives: (1) old coal operators interested in efficiency; (2) captive operators interested in cost; and (3) energy companies interested in return on investment. The "common ground" on which all three could join forces, in the view of the FMCS, was "the question of wildcat strikes."[9] Having thus joined forces, the BCOA named a twelve-member executive committee, composed of representatives of five coal companies, four energy companies, and three steel companies, to guide its 1977 negotiations with the UMWA.

The 1977 BCOA-UMWA negotiations formally opened in September and failed to produce an agreement prior to expiration of the contract on December 8, at which time the union struck all BCOA mines. In mid-January, the executive committee named a five-man subcommittee to assume direct control of negotiations. The subcommittee consisted of one representative each from Peabody (who was later replaced by a representative of Island Creek after committing certain indiscretions in bargaining), Consolidation, U.S. Steel, Pittston, and Westmoreland—six companies (including both Peabody and Island Creek) which reportedly controlled 85 percent of the votes on the BCOA's board.[10] At the same time, the BCOA also changed its chief negotiator in the first of a series of what *Business Week* characterized as a "bewildering change of industry leaders in negotiations" and which it attributed to disagreements brought about by the fact that "the BCOA—like the UMW—has been buffeted by the conflicting interests of its members."[11]

---

[8] Wayne L. Horvitz, "What's Happening in Collective Bargaining," *Labor Law Journal*, August 1978, p. 459.

[9] *Ibid.*, p. 460.

[10] "Coal's Bungled Negotiations," *Business Week*, March 6, 1978, p. 95.

[11] *Ibid.*

There are many differing perceptions within the industry of the internal politics of the BCOA during its tortuous six-month, three-agreement pursuit of a final settlement with the UMWA. The basic thrust of those perceptions, abstracting from questions of personality and pursuit of special interest, is that the industry did divide into hawks and doves, but not as early in the process as outside observers suspected. The industry entered negotiations with a solid front and maintained that solidity through five months of negotiations, including two months of strike, until an initial tentative agreement was reached in early February 1978. When that agreement was rejected by the UMWA, the BCOA remained unified in a determination to defend that agreement by refusing to return to negotiations or to make additional concessions. That unity and determination was broken less by the union's continuing strike than by the pressure of government on the industry for further negotiations and concessions—pressure which began with the secretary of labor and quickly escalated to the level of the president and which involved intensive mediation, an end-play using a nonmember company, arm-twisting, and finally a threat to declare an impasse so that individual members could quit the association to bargain on their own.[12]

The combination of political and economic pressure eventually did divide the BCOA into hawks and doves. The old coal companies were the doves and played the role of hero, in the eyes of the government and the union, in negotiating the final settlement. The steel and energy companies were generally perceived as the hawks and in the 1977-1978 negotiation scenario by both the government and the union and even by some of the old coal companies, one of whose representatives ventured to speculate that those companies were determined ultimately to break the union.

There was considerable dissatisfaction on the part of individual BCOA members, both hawks and doves, with the process and results of the 1977 negotiations. One manifestation of that dissatisfaction was in some strong personal animosities. A second and far more significant manifestation was a growing skepticism on the part of some major companies regarding the extent to which continued BCOA membership would serve their interests. Overt criticism of the settlement and of the BCOA was rare, but the *New York Times* reported that

---

[12] "Operators' Offer of Arbitration Being Weighed by Mine Workers," *Daily Labor Report*, No. 36 (February 22, 1978), p. A-16.

after last year's 111-day miners' strike, there were reports that some major coal operators were thinking about breaking away from the association and returning to separate contract talks because of the union's repeated failure to get members to ratify proposed settlements.[13]

The first major operator to formally take that step was Consolidation Coal, the company whose leadership had been instrumental in the formation of the BCOA in 1950. On Friday, May 25, 1979, Consolidation Coal announced its intention to withdraw from the BCOA to bargain independently with the UMWA in 1981. In announcing that decision, the company stated:

> The many problems faced by the coal industry during the 1978 negotiations have convinced Consolidation that it should negotiate future collective bargaining agreements directly [with the UMWA].[14]

The lesson of history is that industrywide and/or multiemployer bargaining in bituminous coal mining is at best a fragile creature which can survive only under the protection of a strong, well-disciplined union—which the UMWA was not in 1978. Consolidation's announced withdrawal from the BCOA brought the fragile nature of the industry's bargaining structure dramatically into focus. At the time of that announcement, the *Wall Street Journal* reported that many union and company officials conceded that "without Consolidation . . . collective-bargaining in coal on a national basis [would be] very much in doubt." [15]

The withdrawal of Consolidation was followed by a demand on the part of the steel companies, led by U.S. Steel, for the BCOA to be restructured in a way that would give them greater influence. That demand was backed by at least an implicit threat of joining Consolidation in withdrawing from the association. The demand of the steel industry led to an unpublicized meeting of "executives of the nation's largest steel and coal companies [in late September 1979] to discuss a plan by the steel companies

---

[13] Ben A. Franklin, "Future coal talks clouded by pullout," *New York Times,* May 27, 1979, p. 15.

[14] Thomas Petzinger, Jr., "Continental Oil unit's break with BCOA clouds future of nationwide coal talks," *Wall Street Journal,* May 29, 1979, p. 15.

[15] Thomas Petzinger, Jr., "Anxiety is growing in the coal industry," *Wall Street Journal,* March 27, 1980, p. 15.

that would significantly boost their control over the coal industry's contract talks with the United Mine Workers union." [16]

Apparently, there was considerable division of opinion within the industry at the time of that meeting regarding the seriousness of the threat of a steel industry withdrawal from the BCOA. In light of the industry's unfortunate experience in 1978, when the government's use of a nonmember company to set a pattern to which the BCOA ultimately was forced to conform by the government, there was little doubt that the prospect of entering negotiations in 1981 without the nation's second (Consolidation), sixth (U.S. Steel), and possibly its twelfth (Bethlehem) largest coal producers as BCOA members was not a pleasant prospect for the association. One industry executive was quoted as describing the situation in the following blunt terms: " A splintering is taking place, and this pluralism is going to screw the entire coal industry." [17]

The BCOA's response to this invidious threat of pluralism came in mid-March 1980 when it announced a new organization for the conduct of its 1981 negotiations with the UMWA.[18] The new organization was a more streamlined and exclusive version of the organization, which had evolved in the conduct of the 1977-1978 negotiations, in which both Consolidation and U.S. Steel had played dominant roles. The new organization, announced by the BCOA on March 19, 1980, was a three-tier structure involving executive, negotiating, and support committees, all of which were to be under the clear control of the largest members of the association.

Under the BCOA's announced organization, the overall direction of its 1981 negotiations was to be entrusted to a "chief executive officer committee" to be composed of the chief executive officers of the nine companies or parent companies with the largest production under the National Agreement. The actual conduct of negotiations was to be the responsibility of a three-person "negotiating committee" appointed by the two largest BCOA producers and its steel industry members (acting together, in effect, as the third largest BCOA producer) and authorized to

---

[16] Thomas Petzinger, Jr., "Steel firms may quit coal-labor group unless demands for more power are met," *Wall Street Jounral*, October 1, 1979, p. 16.

[17] *Ibid.*

[18] "Resumption of Coal Talks is Possible this Weekend," *Daily Labor Report*, No. 53 (March 19, 1980), p. A-9.

select its own chairman and to plan, conduct, and conclude all negotiations on behalf of member companies. The negotiating committee was to be assisted by a support committee composed of staff representatives of the companies holding seats on the chief executive officer committee which was to provide technical assistance to the negotiating committee and serve as liaison for members not represented on the chief executive officer committee.

This restructuring met most of the demands of the steel industry members, who remained in the association for the 1981 negotiations. The restructuring also offered Consolidation, as the nation's second largest coal producer, the prospect of wielding considerable control over the conduct of negotiations if it rejoined the BCOA, which it did in late March 1980.[19] As expected, the two largest producers and the steel company members appointed their own personnel to the negotiating committee, which then elected Bobby R. Brown, president of Consolidation, as chairman and chief negotiator.

The restructuring of the BCOA and the reentry of Consolidation were not met with great enthusiasm by smaller, independent coal producers. Some of these producers questioned whether the chief executive officers of oil and steel companies understood coal mining sufficiently to set realistic bargaining goals, echoing a refrain heard at the end of the 1977-1978 negotiations.[20] In addition, independent producers were reported to be

> concerned that the stronger financial position of the large producers—some of which are believed to be willing to "pay" for changes in certain productivity-inhibiting contract work rules—may result in a settlement that smaller producers can't afford in today's weak market.[21]

The primary concern of the independent producers was that the larger producers would lead the BCOA into another strike, a strike which they could ill afford. That concern was based on the apparent determination of the larger producers to pursue again their "unrealistic" productivity and stability initiatives of 1977 and buoyed, in the case of some independents, by the private perception that the oil companies were determined to weaken and ultimately to eliminate the UMWA. In that context, the appoint-

---

[19] "Major Coal Producer Rejoins Industry's Bargaining Group," *Daily Labor Report*, No. 59 (March 25, 1980), p. A-5.

[20] Petzinger, "Anxiety is growing in the coal industry," p. 15.

[21] *Ibid.*

ment of Bobby R. Brown as chief negotiator for the BCOA offered independents little solace, as Brown was reputed to be a tough negotiator and his company to be committed to a "get tough" policy in its own day-to-day relations with the UMWA.[22] Despite those fears and suspicions, only one independent producer—American Coal, the nation's fourteenth largest producer— attempted to withdraw from the BCOA prior to the beginning of serious negotiations in January 1981, an attempt in which it was rebuffed by the union.[23]

The negotiations, which began in January 1981 and culminated in a strike by the UMWA when the contract expired on March 27, proved more difficult than either the industry or the union rank and file had anticipated. The difficulty arose out of the BCOA's interest in addressing three institutionally sensitive issues: (1) the jurisdiction/subcontracting provisions of the contract ruled unlawful by the courts; (2) the basic multiemployer structure of the union's pension system which created substantial potential liabilities for operators under the Employee Retirement Income Security Act (ERISA); and (3) the payment of royalties on nonunion coal by signatory operators. The first two of these issues were successfully, although not easily, resolved. The third, the elimination of royalty payments on nonsignatory coal, became the final sticking point in the negotiations prior to contract expiration. On March 20, 1981, UMWA President Church held a news conference in which he indicated that the BCOA's insistence on that concession was part of a broader BCOA strategy to "keep the talks bogged down and unproductive," which was leading to a strike that "could very possibly be even longer than the 111-day strike the last time around." [24] He attributed that strategy and the resulting strike to the fact that

> the big coal operators wanted a strike because their masters in big oil want a strike. They want a strike to break the union. They want a strike to break the smaller coal operators. And they want a strike to give them the opportunity to pick up the pieces of a fragmented and bankrupt coal industry.
>
> The oil firms can, and probably will, wait while their so-called partners in the BCOA, those firms which make the largest portion of

---

[22] *Ibid.*

[23] Thomas Petzinger, Jr., "Several coal firms seek own pacts as strike lengthens, but the union balks," *Wall Street Journal*, April 27, 1981, p. 18.

[24] "Mine Workers President Blames Oil Companies for Bargaining Stalemate," *Daily Labor Report*, No. 54 (March 20, 1981), p. A-11.

their earnings from coal alone, quietly slip into bankruptcy, unable to carry assets any longer. These dying enterprises can then be easily bought up by the oil interests.[25]

The emotion of March 20 quickly gave way to accommodation as the parties reached a tentative agreement on March 23, in which the union acceded to the BCOA's demand for elimination of royalty payments on nonsignatory coal. That agreement was ratified by the UMWA's bargaining council on March 24, but rejected by its rank and file on March 31, four days after the union, pursuant to its traditional policy of no contract, no work, struck the industry. Rejection of the contract by the rank and file turned what had been expected to be a short strike into what ultimately proved to be a seventy-two-day strike over the BCOA's "attempt to break the union" by eliminating royalties on nonunion coal.

The economic pressure of the strike did fall with particular weight on independents and smaller producers. One major independent producer, Emery Mining, reacted by withdrawing from the BCOA in the hope of negotiating a separate peace along the lines of Pittsburgh and Midway's agreement in 1978. Several others might have been tempted to follow that course had not the UMWA refused to deal separately with Emery or North American.[26] A number of small, nonmember, unionized producers also sought to sue for a separate peace, but also were rebuffed by the UMWA. The *Wall Street Journal* characterized these fragmentations in the industry in April 1981 as follows:

> The small producers—and a few larger independent mining companies—appear ready to give the union much to end the strike against their operations. Unlike the generally large, well-capitalized members of the BCOA, many of which are owned by financially secure oil, steel and utility companies, these outsiders say they can't long survive the losses that are piling up while the UMW is on strike.[27]

The BCOA survived the centrifugal forces created by the 1981 strike as much by the union's refusal to accommodate those forces as by its own internal cohesion. The rich (energy)/poor (coal) dichotomy within the association and the industry has not and

---

[25] *Ibid.*, pp. A-12, A-13.

[26] Petzinger, "Several coal firms seek own pacts," p. 10.

[27] *Ibid.*

will not disappear, and it remains to be seen what that dichotomy will mean for the future of multiemployer bargaining and of the BCOA and the UMWA. The possibility of continuing conflict and militancy in National Agreement negotiations puts forth a powerful incentive for independent producers to consider withdrawing from the BCOA in the hope of removing themselves from the line of fire. Should they be unable to extricate themselves effectively from UMWA-BCOA battles by withdrawal from multiemployer bargaining, their only alternative may be to extricate themselves from both the BCOA and the UMWA by nonunion operation. A return to the pervasive labor peace of the 1950s would obviate the need to contemplate either of these alternatives, but the present politics of neither the industry nor the union appear to favor such a fortuitous development in the near future.

THE POLICIES OF THE BCOA

In theory, multiemployer bargaining associations, like unions, may elect to maximize one of three variables—profit margins, profit total, or profit makers. In practice, the BCOA, like the UMWA, appears consistently to have opted for a basic policy of preserving profit rates at the expense of profit earners. Specifically, those in control of the BCOA have been willing to tolerate attrition in the population of producers and members in order to preserve the earnings of the remaining producers and members. Historically, the primary target of that predatory policy was nonunion producers—a target it shared with the union. More recently, however, the union and at least some operators believe that unionized independent producers have become the predatory target of those in control of the BCOA—a target avowedly not shared by the UMWA.

The predatory, "survival of the fittest" policy of the BCOA is not difficult to understand, given the industry's history of chronic overcapacity and ruinous competition. The economic conditions and institutional context under which that policy has been pursued, however, have changed dramatically in the past thirty years. Between 1950 and 1970, coal was a declining industry competing for a shrinking share of the nation's energy market. For most of that period, the UMWA was blessed with sufficient internal discipline and external control to permit it to practice "economic unionism" and to constrain and channel the predatory predelictions of the industry.[28] Since 1970, coal has been a growing industry, expected to compete for a growing share of the nation's and the world's energy market. The union has lost much of its internal discipline and external control over the same period, forcing the industry to assume the burden of dealing with product market competition and the union to practice "resistance unionism." [29]

The shift from economic to resistance unionism over the past decade has produced a dramatic escalation in conflict within both the UMWA and the BCOA, and in the UMWA-BCOA relationship. Interestingly, that conflict, at least on the management side, has not centered on wages to the extent that might be expected in an increasingly competitive industry. Instead, it has focused on two other issues—labor stability and labor productivity. These issues historically have been substituted for wages as the basis for keeping UMWA labor and mines competitive, but the union lost effective control over them when its internal discipline and external control diminished.

Labor Stability

One basic *quid pro quo* long sought by the BCOA for its economic concessions to the UMWA is "labor stability," or more precisely "labor peace," in both contract negotiations and contract administration. Labor peace was essential to the industry during the 1950s in its competitive struggle with alternative energy sources. During the 1970s, labor peace became equally essential to the members of the BCOA as they struggled to compete with non-UMWA producers in the growing and increasingly competitive domestic and international coal markets.

The birthright of the BCOA was a most undistinguished strike record. Prior to the formation of the BCOA, the industry had experienced strikes in contract negotiations on the average of once every eighteen months for the past thirteen years. Wildcat strikes, a longstanding tradition in the industry, had become sufficiently common and troublesome in the late 1940s to lead management to raise them as an issue in 1949 at the outset of the negotiations which ultimately culminated, after a series of job actions, in the 1950 National Agreement.

---

[28] Daniel J. B. Mitchell, "Union Wage Policy: The Ross-Dunlop Debate Revisited," *Industrial Relations*, Vol. II, No. 1 (February 1972), pp. 46-61.

[29] *Ibid.*

John L. Lewis proved both willing and able to accommodate the industry's interest in labor peace and stability. The thirteen years following formation of the BCOA produced no strikes in contract negotiations and a dramtic decline in the level of wildcat strike activity. The 1950 National Agreement contained no contractual relief from the problem of wildcat strikes, but relief proved to be forthcoming from the union's own actions. In the early 1950s, the union began "bearing down on any unauthorized strikes with fines and threats of expulsion of individual members." [30] The result was a clear downward trend in percent of working time lost due to strikes from 0.9 in 1951 to 0.2 in 1961.[31] The two exceptions to this were 1952, the year of a protest strike against a Wage Stabilization Board ruling disallowing part of a negotiated wage increase, and 1959, Lewis' last year in office. Excluding those two years, the mean percent of working time lost due to strikes from 1951 to 1961 was less than 0.5.

Tony Boyle proved far less able to accommodate the BCOA's interest in labor peace and stability. The Boyle era was one of gradual deterioration in the strike record of the industry, manifested most obviously in the fifty-seven-day strike during the 1971 UMWA-BCOA contract negotiations—the first authorized "industrywide" strike since 1950. The ten years preceding that strike had also produced a discernible upward trend in the level of wildcat strike activity. The percent of time lost due to strikes, which reached its postwar low at 0.2 in 1961, climbed steadily upward to a high of 3.0 in 1968 and 1969 before dropping back to about 1.5 by 1973.[32] Overall, the mean percent of time lost due to strikes between 1963 and 1973, excluding 1971, was 1.4, about three times the average for the last ten years of the Lewis era.

The Miller era opened with a new aura of hope for labor stability. A strike did take place in the 1974 contract negotiations, but it was fairly short and "notably lacking in rancor" by historical standards.[33] The settlement, which was generous by almost any standard, was not regarded as oppressive by the in-

---

[30] Richard A. Lester, *As Unions Mature* (Princeton, N.J.: Princeton University Press, 1958), p. 102.

[31] U.S. Department of Labor, Bureau of Labor Statistics, "Collective Bargaining in the Bituminous Coal Industry," Report 514 (Washington, D.C.: U.S. Government Printing Office, November 1977), p. 5.

[32] *Ibid.*

[33] Miernyk, "Coal," p. 32.

dustry which expected growing demand for coal and growing cooperation from the union in the expeditious handling of day-to-day problems. Unfortunately, the anticipated growth occurred in neither demand nor cooperation during the life of the 1974 agreement. The number of man-days lost to strikes, which had been running at about 1.5 percent of working time under the 1971 agreement, rose to 3.0 percent in 1975 and 3.7 percent in 1976.[34] At BCOA mines, the rise was even more dramatic, going from less than three days per 100 man-days in 1972 and 1973 to about six days in 1975, seven days in 1976, and ten days in the first eight months of 1977.[35]

The BCOA entered its 1977 contract negotiations with a resolution to restore labor stability to the industry and a willingness to pay for that stability with a generous economic settlement. The specific devices proposed by the BCOA to restore stability were an all-encompassing no-strike pledge and a pay-back provision, requiring miners to compensate the industry pension and welfare funds for production lost due to their wildcat strike actions. Both proposals were resisted by the union, but when the BCOA agreed to drop its no-strike proposal, the union reluctantly accepted the pay-back proposal as part of its initial, tentative agreement. The UMWA Bargaining Council, however, refused to approve that agreement, in large part because of the pay-back provision. That provision was one of the more important casualties of the BCOA's battles with the union and the government in route to the final agreement reached with the UMWA in 1978 after an 111-day strike.

The BCOA, in general, and its "old coal" members, in particular, emerged from the 1977-1978 negotiations with considerable optimism that the industry was about to enter a new era of labor peace and stability. For example, the chairman of the executive committee of the BCOA, speaking in December 1978, stated that the United States coal industry had entered an era of "improved relations," although he added, on a more cautious note, that the next two years would reveal whether the industry would realize its "sought after stability of the workforce." [36] Developments

---

[34] U.S. Department of Labor, *Collective Bargaining in the Bituminous Coal Industry*, p. 5.

[35] BCOA, *Will the United Mine Workers Play a Major Role*, p. 6.

[36] *Coal News*, September 22, 1978, p. 6.

during those two years appear to have at least partially justified the optimism of the BCOA chairman, as the BCOA acknowledged in 1981 when it formally stated that "Fortunately, during the term of the present agreement, the wildcat strike situation has improved," but also felt compelled to point out that, "as positive as this improvement has been . . . the fact remains that the wildcat strike problem is still with us" and that "UMWA-represented miners still lead the nation's industries in strikes." [37]

The same optimism that characterized at least some segments of the BCOA after 1978 regarding the future of their individual day-to-day relations with the union extended to their view of the future of their collective contract negotiation relationship with the union. The view of many in the BCOA was that the 1981 UMWA-BCOA National Agreement negotiations would be a simple "matter of money." Obviously, subsequent developments have proven quite the contrary. Labor stability was not an issue in the 1981 negotiations, but the fact that those negotiations involved a seventy-two-day strike—making the industry "four for four" over the past decade—has created a new labor stability issue for the industry. The competitive disadvantage bestowed on UMWA producers by virtue of their exposure to wildcat strikes can also be associated with their recurrent exposure to strikes in contract negotations given the growing number of non-UMWA alternative sources of coal. One firm which learned this lesson in 1981 was U.S. Fuel Company which

> recently secured one of the first export contracts ever awarded to a coal company in the Western U.S. Deliveries to Taiwan and Japan were to have begun this month, but the company has had to plead an inability to honor the obligations.
>
> What most worries U.S. Fuel is whether it will be able to secure export contracts for the planned production of a new mine in which the company already has invested about $5 million. 'If we can't fulfill our current commitments, how can we expect to sign a contract for future commitments? [38]

Labor Productivity

The second *quid pro quo* consistently expected and recently sought by the BCOA for its economic concessions to the UMWA has been improved productivity. In the 1950s improved productivity and stable unit labor cost were essential in the industry's

---

[37] "Bargaining Statement," *Daily Labor Report*, p. F-4.

[38] Petzinger, "Several coal firms seek own pacts," p. 18.

competitive war of attrition against alternative energy sources. In the 1960s, productivity became a major factor in the competitive battle between UMWA producers and non-UMWA producers, who had lower hourly labor costs in a relatively stable coal market. In the 1970s, productivity became the key factor in the survival and growth of the National Agreement segment of the industry, which was facing competition from increasingly efficient non-UMWA mines in what is still a slowly growing and highly competitive market for coal. In the view of the BCOA, in 1981

> the biggest reason for the failure of the UMWA-National Agreement segment of the industry to participate in the growth of the total coal market is the heavy cost burden that low productivity imposes on coal produced under the UMWA-National Agreement. Unless corrective steps are taken now to reduce this cost, coal mined under the UMWA-National Agreement cannot compete effectively in the coal market.[39]

The impressive productivity gains recorded by the industry during the 1950s, without resistance from the union and with the encouragement of its leader, clearly were not sufficient to enable the industry to hold its own against other fuel sources, although they did keep the industry alive. Those gains also were not sufficient to offset the cost advantages available to producers who could escape or avoid UMWA National Agreement coverage. The single most important such cost advantage was avoidance of tonnage royalty payments to the unions' welfare funds, as was implicitly acknowledged in 1964 with the negotiation of the double royalty on nonsignatory coal. The virtue of the royalty system from the union standpoint was that it automatically enabled workers to claim a share of the economic benefits of technological change and, indeed, labor stability. The vice of that system from the BCOA standpoint was that it could not claim the same share of such economic benefits as could nonunion producers.

The industry's continuing productivity gains during the 1960s, coupled with its successful resistance to any increase in royalty rates and the existence of the royalty penalty on nonunion coal, enabled the BCOA to hold its own fairly well against nonunion coal producers. That situation changed in the early 1970s as a result of three developments: (1) the passage of the Coal Mine Health and Safety Act in 1969 which halted and reversed the twenty-year upward trend in labor productivity in the industry;

---

[39] "Bargaining Statement," *Daily Labor Report*, p. F-2.

(2) the negotiation of a National Agreement in 1971 which not only provided for a substantial wage increase but also called for a doubling of royalty payments, the first such increase in over a decade; and (3) the negotiation of a National Agreement in 1974 which continued the trend set in 1971 and included "certain contractual changes . . . which increased employment, but did not result in more coal being mined." [40] The cumulative result of these three developments was a 300 percent increase in labor cost per ton of coal between 1969 and 1977.[41]

When it entered its 1977 National Agreement negotiations, the BCOA was resolved to secure changes in work rules in order to facilitate improvement in productivity, and it was willing to pay for those changes with a generous economic settlement, just as the case had been with wildcat strikes. As in the case for its labor stability initiative, the BCOA won an early battle for its productivity issues but ultimately lost the war for its dual stability and productivity initiatives. As a result, by 1981 the BCOA found that

> productivity levels of coal miners in the non-UMWA deep mines segment of the industry are 39% higher than UMWA-National Agreement miners—14.2 tons per man-day, compared to only 10.2 tons. In surface mining, the disparity is even greater. Productivity of non-National Agreement miners in surface mines is 55% higher than surface mines covered by the agreement—30.1 tons per man-day, against 19.4 tons.[42]

As it entered the 1981 negotiations, the BCOA was determined to try again to gain changes in work rules to facilitate improved productivity. That determination was weakened little by the fact that "recently, there has been some small improvement in UMWA-National Agreement productivity," because in the view of the association, "several reasons indicate that even this slight improvement may be only short term," leaving the parties to face the fact that "generally improved productivity must continue if our segment of the industry is to survive under the UMWA-National Agreement." [43] The UMWA, again, viewed the situation in more optimistic terms, stating:

---

[40] BCOA, *Will the United Mine Workers Play a Major Role*, p. 9.

[41] *Ibid.*

[42] "Bargaining Statement," *Daily Labor Report*, p. F-3.

[43] *Ibid.*

The union is heartened, as the BCOA must be, to see the upturn in productivity that is now occurring in the mines covered by the UMWA-BCOA collective bargaining agreement. Our analysis of the data on production and hours of work in BCOA-member mines indicates that output per hour in the year ending June 30, 1980, was 7.7 percent above the corresponding 12 months which ended one year earlier.[44]

---

[44] "Statement of United Mine Workers President Church," p. E-1.

CHAPTER IX

The Political Economics
of Industrywide Bargaining:
The Government

The federal government has a long and undistinguished record, now spanning more than four decades, of involvement in the labor relations of the bituminous coal industry. The government has based its involvement on a real or imagined "public interest" in either the substantive (settlement) or procedural (nonsettlement) outcome of UMWA "national negotiations." These efforts by the government to influence or control the substantive or procedural results of such negotiations, in the final analysis, ultimately have placed the government, however willingly or reluctantly, in the role of adversary to the UMWA. The result has been a series of confrontations between the government and the union in which the government, without exception, has fared badly.

The bulk of the government's undistinguished record of involvement in labor relations in the coal industry was built in the turbulent decade of the 1940s—first under wartime wage controls and later as a result of postwar economic emergencies. The remainder of the record was built in the almost equally trying decade of the 1970s—first under peacetime wage controls and then as a result of postcontrol energy emergencies. The obvious symmetry between those two decades with respect to the reasons for government involvement in coal industry labor relations is paralleled by an equally obvious symmetry in the results of such intervention—results which typically have been highly favorable to the union, unfavorable to the industry, and embarrassing to the government.

WAGE CONTROLS

Wage price controls have been imposed three times since 1940: in 1941 (World War I), in 1951 (the Korean War), and in 1971 (the war on inflation). In each instance, the UMWA proved to be a painful and almost fatal thorn in the foot of the lion of government. Specifically, in each case the UMWA proved both willing and anxious to challenge the government's wage standards and was not hesitant to back that challenge with an implicit or explicit threat of strike action. In the final analysis, the government, virtually without exception, has backed away from these tests of its institutional power, leaving the union in possession of the ground on which its battle was supposed to have been or actually was fought—the traditional definition of military victory.

The War Years

Wage controls were imposed during both World War II and the Korean War. The control agency in the former case was the War Labor Board (WLB) and in the latter case the Wage Stabilization Board (WSB). The directives of the WLB and rulings of the WSB generally were not enthusiastically received by unions, but few unions rivalled the UMWA in that lack of enthusiasm, and none rivalled the UMWA in the extent of its refusal to accede to those directives and rulings.

The UMWA's displeasure with wartime wage controls was first manifested in 1943 when it called and conducted an industrywide strike in support of its demands for wages increases in excess of those deemed acceptable by the WLB. That strike was ended only when the government seized the mines under the "general powers" of the president on the grounds of "noncompliance . . . with a directive order of the NWLB II." [1] That seizure placed the government in the role of the union's adversary at the bargaining table —a position it was to occupy three more times before World War II controls ended in 1947. In each of those four cases, the government learned to practice the art of constructive compromise in the interest of peaceful accommodation and productive operation.

The UMWA's 1943 strike was an important factor in the passage of the War Labor Disputes Act of 1943 (the Smith-Connally Act), which provided specific statutory authority for government seizure in the event of labor disputes and made a

---

[1] John L. Blackman, Jr., *Presidential Seizure in Labor Disputes* (Cambridge, Mass.: Harvard University Press, 1967), p. 263.

strike in a seized mine, plant, or other facility a crime.[2] Despite that law, the UMWA not only called but conducted three large-scale strikes in the industry between the time the act was passed in 1943 and the time it expired in 1947. The strikes took place in November 1943, April 1945, and May 1946; and in each case, the government seized the industry only to find itself without a work force until it could reach an accommodation with John L. Lewis on terms and conditions of employment. The union and its leadership were not prosecuted for violation of the War Labor Disputes Act in any of these cases because

> the adroit John L. Lewis soon found a way around this new restriction with the apparent acquiescence of President Roosevelt and Attorney General Biddle, and later also of President Truman and Attorney General Clark.[3]

The technique utilized by the UMWA to circumvent the strike prohibitions of the War Labor Disputes Act was the "preseizure" strike order. While the industry was still in private hands, and such a call was technically legal, the union would call a strike for some future date and then let events run their course, despite government seizure, with no overt action to either encourage or discourage compliance with the earlier strike call. The "legality" of this tactic rested on interpretation of the proviso of the statute that: "no individual shall be deemed to have violated the provisions of this section by reason only of his having ceased work or having refused to continue to work or to accept employment"— a proviso which the Justice Department interpreted as

> protecting the strikers and union officers during government possession and operation of war plants so long as they did not engage in speeches, meetings, or other overt actions intended to encourage the strike.[4]

The UMWA was not the only union to use the loophole of the preseizure strike call. A number of other unions used the same tactic with equal success in avoiding criminal prosecution. None, however, enjoyed the same success as the UMWA in employing that tactic not only to escape prosecution for strike action but also to capture the economic gains sought from such action. Specifically, by virtue of skillful use of the preseizure strike call,

---

[2] *Ibid.*, p. 28.

[3] *Ibid.*

[4] *Ibid.*, p. 29.

Lewis not only avoided prosecution during the continuance of the prearranged strikes but negotiated outstanding wage gains with the government under the pressures of the stoppages. Under these pressures, the government either made extensive concessions to the miners in the interim terms of employment—to be effective during government operations—or gave assistance in the negotiation of a final settlement with the owners. In either circumstance, the mine owners were required to make the approved concessions in order to get their mines back.[5]

The most significant of the concessions wrested from the government by John L. Lewis and the UMWA was the creation of its welfare and retirement fund. In early 1946, the UMWA called an industrywide strike to which the government responded with seizure of the industry. Seizure was followed by negotiations between Julius A. Krug, secretary of the interior, and John L. Lewis over interim terms of employment. These negotiations culminated in the now famous "Krug-Lewis Agreement" of May 1946, in which the government acceded to the union's request for establishment of a jointly administered, industrywide welfare and pension fund for miners to be financed by employer royalty payments on each ton of coal mined—a royalty initially set at $0.05 per ton.

The union, gratified but not satisfied by its victory in May 1946, continued to press the government for further concessions, particularly on wages. To enhance its bargaining power, the union announced November 20, 1946, as the effective date of contract termination and called for strike action on that date using code words such as "no contract" or "contract dishonored" as signals to miners to practice the union's tradition of no contract, no work. The use of this tactic was necessitated by the fact that the mines were still under government control, precluding an open strike call. The response of the government to this strike was quite different from its response to strikes and strike calls inherited upon seizure. President Truman, aware that the union's strike action could not be construed legally or politically as something other than a strike against the government and possibly sensitive to the fact that "the move was timed to embarrass him politically on the eve of new congressional elections," responded to the union's strike call with the threat of a "fight to the finish."[6]

---

[5] *Ibid.*

[6] *Ibid.*, pp. 33-34.

The central element in the government's fight to the finish was an appeal to the courts for a ruling that the union's action constituted an illegal strike call and for an order requiring withdrawal of that call. That appeal was successful insofar as the court found that the union's announcement constituted a call to cease work and ordered it rescinded. The union, as it had done in the case of preseizure strike calls, took no action and, as expected, miners ceased work on November 20, 1946. On December 3, John L. Lewis and the UMWA were found guilty of civil and criminal contempt and on December 4, Lewis was fined $10,000 and the UMWA $3,500,000.[7] On December 7, 1946, Lewis ordered the miners back to work until March 31, 1947, pending the outcome of an appeal to the Supreme Court.

The Supreme Court upheld the ruling of the lower court and ordered a complete retraction of the implicit strike call for March 31, 1947, which if forthcoming would result in a substantial reduction in the fines levied by the lower court against the union. The union took advantage of that opportunity and complied with the order of the Supreme Court. In one final gesture of defiance, however, the union designated the week of April 1 through 6, 1947, as a "memorial period" or "week of mourning" for miners killed in a recent mine explosion in Illinois—another code word for job action designed more to embarrass than to harass the government.[8]

The mines were returned to private ownership on June 30, 1947, when the government's seizure authority under the War Labor Disputes Act expired. With that transfer of control went transfer of the contractual concessions and labor relations problems of the past four years, including those of 1946-1947, from the government to private operators. For the next five years, the government continued to be a highly active participant in, but not a direct party to, the industry's efforts to resolve its labor relations problems through collective bargaining.

The imposition of wage controls during the Korean War once again brought the government into labor relations in the industry as a direct party to and adversary of the UMWA in the determination of terms and conditions of employment in a case which served both as epilogue to what had happened in the 1940s and as a prologue to what was to happen in the 1970s. In September

---

[7] *Ibid.,* pp. 34-35.

[8] *Ibid.*

1952, the UMWA and the BCOA reached agreement on an amendment to the 1950 National Wage Agreement that called, among
other things, for an increase in compensation averaging $1.90
per day. As required by law, that agreement was submitted to
the WSB for approval. Before the WSB issued a ruling on the
agreement, a strike began on October 13, 1952, which spread to
include approximately 100,000 miners by October 16. On October
18, the WSB ruled that only $1.50 of the $1.90 per day negotiated
increase was permissible under established regulations, and by
October 20, the strike had spread to industrywide proportions.

This unauthorized strike against the WSB and the government
ended on October 27, 1952, when the miners returned to work at
the request of their union to await the results of a further review
of the WSB ruling as promised by the president of the United
States. That further review produced the following result:

> On December 3, 1952, the President of the United States directed
> the economic stabilization Administrator to approve the full amount
> of the general wage increase; on the next day, the Administrator
> notified the parties to the agreement of such approval.[9]

The 1971 Negotiations

The wage-price freeze of August 14, 1971, and its successor,
Phase II, announced on October 7, 1971, once again placed the
government, this time embodied in the Pay Board, in the position
of having to rule on the acceptability of a negotiated UMWA-
BCOA settlement. Indeed, that settlement proved to be the first
major "problem" confronting the Pay Board after its struggle
to develop the basic standards governing acceptable compensation
increases, which were promulgated on November 9, 1971. This
problem would ultimately overwhelm the system, much as had
been the case in 1952.[10]

From its outset, the Wage-Price Control Program, initiated in
August 1971, created problems for the industry in the collective
bargaining arena. Negotiations over a new contract to replace
the one due to expire on September 30, 1971, were already underway when the freeze was announced, although little real progress

---

[9] "Wage Chronology No. 4: Bituminous Coal Mines, Supplement No. 2,"
Mnothly Labor Review, Vol. 76, No. 9 (March 1953), p. 961.

[10] These problems are extensively documented in Arnold R. Weber and
Daniel J. B. Mitchell, *The Pay Board's Progress* (Washington, D.C.: The
Brookings Institution, 1978), pp. 139-52.

toward an agreement had yet been made. Thus, the UMWA and BCOA found themselves, as of August 15, confronting the task of concluding an agreement which could not legally go into effect until such time as the freeze was lifted, and then only to the extent deemed acceptable by the government under wage standards yet to be devised. An added complicating factor from the BCOA standpoint was that the cost of any new agreement could not legally be passed through into prices until the freeze was lifted, and then only to the extent permitted by the government under standards yet to be formulated.

The uncertainties introduced into contract negotiations by controls, coupled with the removal of incentive to conclude an agreement by September 30, 1971, independent of all the other problems facing the parties, all but assured that no settlement could or would be reached before the old contract expired. That indeed was the case, and when no agreement was reached by September 30, the UMWA, true to its tradition of no contract, no work, called a strike of its 105,000 members at BCOA mines. That strike produced tension within the executive branch between the custodians of labor peace, in this case the secretary of labor, who reportedly sought "preliminary assurance from the Cost of Living Council (CLC) that any agreement concluded by the UMW and BCOA would receive a favorable ruling by the CLC" on the grounds that such assurance "was necessary to facilitate an end of the strike," and the custodians of cost/price stability, in this case the Cost of Living Council which rejected the secretary's request on the grounds that the settlement was a matter for review "by the appropriate Phase II agency." [11]

The strike lasted officially until an agreement was finally reached on November 13, 1971—the last day of the freeze— although a number of miners refused to return to work at that time. The agreement called for first-year wage increases averaging $0.55 per hour, changes in shift differentials, holidays, and vacations estimated to cost another $0.06 per hour, and a $0.20 per ton increase in royalty payments estimated to cost about $0.45 per hour. The overall first-year cost of the agreement was placed at $1.06 per hour or 17.5 percent, two-to-three times the Pay Board's recently anounced 5.5 to 7.2 percent wage standard.[12]

---

[11] *Ibid.*, p. 142.

[12] *Ibid.*, p. 145.

The Pay Board reviewed the settlement on November 18, 1971. In the course of that review, the union urged full approval of the settlement, citing a tandem relationship to steel, productivity gains, catch-up, and the special problems of the welfare and retirement fund, and alluding to the possible militant reaction of the rank and file to having to accept anything less than had been agreed to in negotiations. The BCOA also urged full approval, citing the same arguments as the union and adding that of labor shortage. Finally, the governor of West Virginia, a republican who had become identified with the settlement by virtue of his role as mediator in the final stages of negotiations and who faced a strong democratic challenge in his forthcoming bid for reelection, also urged full approval on the grounds that it would help "poor people." [13]

The public members of the Pay Board took the position that the settlement was excessive and should be reduced based on an "analysis of the substantive issues and a political judgment of what actions might be acceptable to the parties while signalling the resolve of the Pay Board to the public at large." [14] On that basis, the public members settled on a reduction of the 17.5 percent first year increase to 12.5 percent, including 5.5 percent for basic wage adjustment, 2.9 percent for tandem wage adjustment, and 4.1 percent to alleviate the special problems of the welfare and retirement funds.

The public members of the Pay Board received no support from either the labor or business members in their attempt to reduce the settlement. The position of the labor members is not hard to explain, but that of the business members is, particularly in light of their earlier tough stand on the general pay standard. The most plausible explanation for the soft stance of the business members would seem to be either their own concern or the concern of the White House over the economic and/or political consequences of a possibly long and bitter confrontation with the UMWA at the outset of Phase II. Whatever the reason, the business members joined the labor members of the board in voting approval of the full 17.5 percent first-year increase negotiated by the UMWA and BCOA—an action that had to raise serious questions about the credibility of the program and might have destroyed it had not the public members succeeded in lobbying

13 *Ibid.*, p. 148.

14 *Ibid.*, p. 149.

the Price Commission to limit cost pass-through to the equivalent of a 5.5 percent settlement not only in the case of coal but as a general rule.[15]

The union's victory over both the BCOA and, more importantly, the government under mandatory controls in 1971 did not bode well for the effectiveness of the "voluntary" wage restraints or guidelines under which UMWA-BCOA negotiations were to be conducted over the remainder of the 1970s. Indeed, both of the UMWA-BCOA settlements negotiated under such voluntary controls, 1974 and 1977, showed the same manifest disdain for governmentally imposed wage restraint as had been evident in 1971—a disdain encouraged in both cases, as it may have been in 1971, by a lack of resolve on the part of a government torn by UMWA militancy between labor peace and price stability.

The UMWA-BCOA negotiations in 1974 and 1977 followed a remarkably similar scenario. In both cases, a strike occurred en route to achieving a tentative settlement. In both cases, that tentative settlement was rejected by the UMWA Bargaining Council, threatening a prolonged strike. In both cases, that prospect created tension within the executive branch between the custodian of labor peace (the secretary of labor) and the custodian of price stability (the Council on Wage and Price Stability). In 1974 and 1977, as in 1971, that tension was resolved in favor of the expediency of labor peace, as evidenced by the immediate involvement of the secretary of labor in intensive mediation in response to, in 1974, and in anticipation of, in 1978, the Bargaining Council's rejection of an initial tentative agreement. In 1978, this mediation escalated to the level of overt presidential arm-twisting.

The outcome of both sets of negotiations was an agreement which increased labor costs in the industry by 35 to 45 percent over three years. The Council on Wage and Price Stability estimated the wage gains realized by miners as a result of the 1974 agreement as 35 percent and the wage and benefit gains won by miners as a result of that agreement as 45 percent over the life of the contract.[16] The council estimated the cost of the 1978 wage and benefit settlement as $4.65 per hour or 36.8 percent over the life of the contract and judged that to be "costly and inflationary" based, in part, on its projection that it would raise the price of

---

[15] *Ibid.*, p. 152.

[16] "An Analysis of the Coal Settlement," *Council on Wage and Price Stability News Release,* June 1, 1978, p. 2.

electricity by 1.2 to 1.9 percent and the cost of steel by $3.85 per ton by 1980.[17] The Department of Energy estimated the cost of the 1978 settlement at $4.90 per hour or 39.1 percent increase and projected its impact on the cost per ton of coal mined as $4.15 (38.4 percent) for deep-mined coal and $2.05 (37.7 percent) for surface-mined coal.[18]

NATIONAL EMERGENCIES

The national emergency disputes procedures of the Taft-Hartley Act, like wage controls, have been applied to the coal mining industry on three occasions, twice in the immediate postwar period and once in the 1970s. The government's record in the application of those procedures in the industry, as in the case of wage controls, has been undistinguished and, if anything, has worsened over time. In none of the three cases has the government been able to secure voluntary compliance by miners with a Taft-Hartley Section 208 injunction. In the case of the first such unsuccessful injunction, the union was found to be in contempt for the refusal to return to work. In the case of the second injunction, the government was unable to prove the union responsible for the miners' refusal to return to work. In the case of the third injunction, the government was not even able to support a motion for an extension of a temporary restraining order to which miners had refused to yield.

The Post-War Years

The emergency disputes procedures of the Taft-Hartley Act were used early and often in the coal mining industry in the years immediately following passage of that act in 1947. Prior to the successful conclusion of the 1950 National Wage Agreement the procedures were invoked three times: twice in 1948 in two separate disputes and once in 1950. Restraining orders were sought by the government in the first of the two 1948 disputes, but not the second, and in the 1950 dispute.[19]

---

[17] Council on Wage and Price Stability, *Quarterly Report*, Second Quarter 1978 (Washington, D.C.: U.S. Government Printing Office, 1978), pp. 6-7.

[18] U.S. Department of Energy, "Estimated Impact of the 1978 UMWA Contracts on the Costs of Mining Coal," *Analysis Memorandum* (AM/ES/78-10,) June 1978, p. 3.

[19] "Statement by President Announcing Intention to Invoke Emergency Back-to-Work Provisions of Taft-Hartley Act, and Related Materials," reprinted in *Daily Labor Report*, No. 44 (March 6, 1978), pp. X-2, X-3.

The first use of the emergency disputes procedures in coal came in the spring of 1948. On March 15, 1948, miners walked out to protest the "dilatory tactics" of the operators in negotiations over the administration and distribution of the monies in the welfare and retirement fund set up under the Krug-Lewis Agreement of 1946. The proximate cause of the strike was the resignation of the impartial trustee of the fund and the inability of the union and industry trustees to agree on a replacement. On March 23, President Truman appointed a Board of Inquiry which made its report on March 31. A restraining order was sought and secured by the government on April 3, but was not obeyed by miners. The government pursued contempt proceedings against the union and its president, and it prevailed when, on April 19, both the UMWA and John L. Lewis were found in contempt and fined. An injunction was issued on April 21 which was obeyed by the miners; and an agreement on an impartial trustee and plan of distribution was reached shortly thereafter.

At the same time that the welfare and pension fund issues were in dispute, the UMWA was in the process of attempting to negotiate new contracts with the various groups of operators. Those negotiations were not progressing well and threatened to lead to yet another strike in the coalfields in the summer or fall of 1948. In response to that threat, coming as it did on the heels of a month of lost production in March and April, the president appointed a second Board of Inquiry on June 19, 1948. That board made its report on June 26, by which time an agreement had been reached between the UMWA and the operators of commercial mines, obviating the need for further government action, in general, and for action to obtain a restraining order, in particular.

The agreement negotiated in 1948 expired on June 20, 1949. When no new agreement had been reached by that date, the union elected not to call a strike, but to impose a "stabilization period" during which miners would work only a three-day week— the same partial strike option utilized by some other unions earlier in the 1940s to evade the War Labor Disputes Act ban on strikes under government seizure. Negotiations continued without substantial progress through the summer and into the fall against a background of growing restlessness among miners. The restlessness took the form of a growing number of sporadic, spontaneous strikes which by early October involved some 300,000 members. Those strikes continued until the union ordered miners back to work in November.

Negotiations continued without notable progress until February 6, 1950, when an industrywide walkout took place involving almost 400,000 miners. On that same day, the president appointed a Board of Inquiry which made its report on February 11, whereupon the government immediately sought and quickly was granted a restraining order against the strike. The miners refused to obey that order, despite a formal request to return to work made by John L. Lewis on February 11 and repeated on February 20. A show cause order was issued against the union at the request of the government. A hearing was held on March 2, in which the union, relying on John L. Lewis' back-to-work requests, was able to show cause and thwart the government's efforts to prove contempt to the satisfaction of the court. On March 3, President Truman asked Congress for legislation authorizing government seizure of the mines, but such legislation proved unnecessary when the union and the industry reached their historic National Wage Agreement two days later on March 5, 1950.

The 1950 National Wage Agreement brought to an end a decade of both extensive conflict and intensive government involvement in collective bargaining in the bituminous coal mining industry and marked the beginning of two decades of peaceful labor relations and privacy for the UMWA and its new bargaining partner, the BCOA. The onset of that peace and prosperity brought with it time for scholarly reflection on the "national emergency" rationale for government involvement in the labor relations of "key industries," in general, and the "key coal industry," in particular. The result was a substantial body of scholarly literature on the myths and realities of national emergencies, most dating from the 1950s. This literature indicates that economically, such emergencies are basically more myth than reality, including the case of bituminous coal. For example, in his study of "The Economic Impact of Strikes in Key Industries," Berstein concluded that coal strikes, at worst, should be judged "marginal nonemergencies." [20] Christensen reached a similar conclusion in his more intensive study of ". . . the impact of Labor Disputes on Coal Production" in which he found that current-transfer

_____

[20] Irving Bernstein, "The Economic Impact of Strikes in Key Industries," in Irving Bernstein, Harold L. Enarson, and R. W. Fleming, eds., *Emergency Disputes and National Policy* (New York: Harper and Bros., 1955), p. 32.

(shift to nonstruck mines) and time-shift (stockpiling) off-set factors were highly effective in permitting consumers to mitigate the effects of strikes.[21]

The 1977 Negotiations

The two decades of relative labor peace that followed the 1950 National Agreement clearly obviated the need for government concern over the possible economic effects of a coal strike; and the dramatic decline of the industry as a factor in the nation's overall energy supply increasingly obviated the need for government concern even should a coal strike occur, as evidenced by the relative lack of a sense of urgency by the government to avoid or to end the strikes of thirty-one and fifty-seven days which occurred in the UMWA-BCOA negotiations in 1968 and 1971, respectively.

That situation changed somewhat after the 1973 energy crisis. The announcement of "operation independence" elevated the coal industry to a place of long-term prominence in the national energy picture, as evidenced by the government's relatively rapid response to the union's rejection of a tentative agreement reached after a fairly short strike in 1974. That subtle change in the political economics of labor relations in the industry clearly was more politically tied to the nation's long-run energy policy than it was economically linked to the nation's short-run energy needs or dependence on UMWA-BCOA mined coal to meet those needs, given the fact that coal represented only 20 percent of the nation's energy supply and that UMWA-BCOA mined coal accounted for only 60 percent of the nation's coal production.

The basic political and economic environment in which BCOA-UMWA negotiations opened on October 6, 1977, was not much different than it had been in 1974. President Carter, like his predecessor, was committed to a long-term energy policy in which coal was to play an important role, but he was also publicly committed to a short-term hands off policy with respect to collective bargaining. Coal still accounted for only 20 percent of the nation's energy supply, but the UMWA-BCOA share of U.S. coal production had fallen to about 50 percent. Thus, although few observers perceived any reason for optimism over the prospects for an easy or peaceful settlement, few saw any reason for pessimism over the effects of a possible strike on the economy or

---

[21] C. L. Christensen, "The Theory of the Offset Factor: The Impact of Labor Disputes Upon Coal Production," *American Economic Review*, Vol. 43, No. 4 (September 1953), p. 546.

foresaw the need for government intervention to avoid or end such a possible strike. The headline on a *Wall Street Journal* article which appeared on October 6, 1977, the day negotiations opened, aptly summarized the situation in stating, "Coal miners may walk out in December, but impact won't be what it used to be." [22]

The UMWA-BCOA negotiations over a new contract to replace the one due to expire on December 6, 1977, opened on October 6 and went on for three weeks, until October 27 when a deadlock over the structure of the bargaining agenda led the industry to break off the negotiations. That disturbing evidence of serious conflict and problems in negotiations did not go unnoticed by the Carter administration. On November 2, the secretary of labor was reported to have said that "he is less optimistic than he was a month ago that a nationwide coal strike can be avoided in December," but that "a walkout probably would not have a serious damaging effect on the national economy" and that:

> while [a strike] could adversely affect the economies of several major coal producing states, such as West Virginia and Kentucky . . . a walkout is not likely to create a national emergency that would force the Carter Administration to seek an injunction under the Taft-Hartley Act. Thus, in case of a coal strike . . . the Administration intends to follow its previously stated policy of nonintervention in collective bargaining disputes.[23]

The secretary's diminished optimism proved justified, as no agreement had been reached or was in sight when the 1974 agreement expired on December 6, 1977, resulting in a strike. That strike closed not only virtually all of the 1,600 UMWA-organized mines but almost one-half of the 3,200 non-UMWA mines in the nation, cutting total mine production capacity in operation to about 800,000 tons per day from a normal capacity of over 3,200,-000 tons per day.[24] Despite the extent of the impact of the strike, no public or governmental panic about the strike was evident. On December 7—the day the strike began—the *New York Times* published an editorial which suggested that the strike

---

[22] Byron E. Calome, "Coal miners may walk out in December, but impact won't be what it used to be," *Wall Street Journal*, October 6, 1977, p. 44.

[23] "Marshall Says Coal Strike Not Likely to Hurt Economy," *Daily Labor Report*, No. 212 (November 2, 1977), p. A-9.

[24] Mine Safety and Health Administration, *Comprehensive Overview of Winter Energy Bulletins*, Winter 1977-1978, Coal Supplement No. 17 (April 1978) (Washington, D.C.: U.S. Department of Energy, June 1978), pp. 3-4.

had been anticipated by consumers to the point that, "the nation is not particularly worried—indeed it is hardly even concerned." [25] That sanguine attitude was supported by government data which showed, at the time the strike began, record levels of coal stocks at electric utilities (110-day supply), coke ovens (84-day supply), and general industrial plants (52-day supply).[26]

Negotiations dragged on through December and January until they were once more broken off by the BCOA on January 30, 1978. That break-off of negotiations brought a sudden deluge of public expressions of concern about the effects of the strike. The *Daily Labor Report*, on January 30, noted that "concern is growing in some parts of the country over dwindling coal stockpiles." [27] Three days later, on February 2, the *New York Times* reported that the coal strike had "suddenly come within days or weeks, depending on the weather, of creating a disruptive regional curtailment of coal fired electrical power." [28] The U.S. Chamber of Commerce added its voice to this chorus on the following day when it warned that the coal strike "threatened to force massive layoff and plant closings in the steel industry and elsewhere by the end of the month." [29]

The public fears aroused by the break-off of negotiations on January 30, 1978, were quickly allayed when, on February 5, the UMWA and BCOA announced agreement on a tentative settlement characterized by the Secretary of Labor as "a fair contract, genuinely good for both parties." [30] Despite such high praise, the bargaining council of the UMWA quickly indicated its displeasure with the settlement and made that displeasure formal when it voted thirty-three to six to reject that settlement on February 12, 1978.[31] The outcome of that vote was foretold by

---

[25] "The coal strikers' burden," *New York Times*, December 7, 1977, p. A-28.

[26] Mine Safety and Health Administration, Coal Supplement No. 17, *Comprehensive Overview*, pp. 8-9.

[27] "Coal Talks Remain Deadlocked on Economic Issues; Progress Indicated on Strike Issue," *Daily Labor Report*, No. 20 (January 30, 1978), p. A-10.

[28] Ben A. Franklin, "Coal strike perils Ohio electric power," *New York Times*, February 2, 1978, p. A-16.

[29] "Coal Industry Talks Continue with Encouragement from President Carter," *Daily Labor Report*, No. 23 (February 3, 1978), p. A-8.

[30] "President Urges Coal Negotiators to Move Bargaining to White House," *Daily Labor Report*, No. 31 (February 14, 1978), p. AA-1.

[31] Wayne L. Horvitz, "What's Happening in Collective Bargaining?" *Labor Law Journal*, August 1978, p. 461.

an "unofficial" vote on March 10, which led the president to respond to the uncertainties of the current situation "by asking that the Secretary of Labor, working in close cooperation with the Federal Mediation and Conciliation Service to continue efforts to facilitate the collective bargaining process" pursuant to his continued belief "that the solution to the strike must be worked out in free collective bargaining by the parties." [32] At the same time, however, the president injected a sense of urgency into the situation in noting that

> [the] situation in some areas of the country has become a matter of increasing concern. Voluntary power cutbacks have become widespread in the East Central Region, centering in Ohio, and several utilities have ordered mandatory cutbacks to industrial customers. More such cutbacks will follow even if the strike is settled soon and employment impacts will be felt shortly.[33]

The president's mandate to the secretary of labor on February 11 was followed, on February 14, 1978, by a call for the parties to resume their negotiations under his auspices at a meeting at the White House. In issuing that call the president stated:

> the negotiations at the White House must be viewed as a final opportunity for the bargaining process to work. I continue to support the collective bargaining process. However, the welfare of this country must be my overriding concern.[34]

The meeting at the White House on February 14, 1978, was followed by intensive negotiations under the supervision of the secretary of labor, commencing on February 16. Those negotiations were conducted under a forty-eight-hour deadline imposed by the secretary because "the urgency of the problem—dwindling energy supplies and potential large-scale industry layoffs as a result of coal shortages—required setting some deadline on the talks." [35] The credibility of the secretary's statement and deadline, however, could not have been well served by the fact that the Department of Energy testified before Congress on that same day that "the coal problem is not critical." [36] In any event, the secretary's statement and deadline did not have the desired im-

[32] "Mine Workers Council Rejects Contract; President Orders Emergency State Aid," *Daily Labor Report*, No. 30 (February 13, 1978), pp. A-11, A-12.

[33] *Ibid.*, p. A-11.

[34] "President Urges Coal Negotiators," *Daily Labor Report*, p. AA-1.

[35] "Carter Administration Gives Coal Negotiators 48 Hours to Settle Contract Differences," *Daily Labor Report*, No. 33 (February 16, 1978), p. A-10.

[36] *Ibid.*, p. A-12.

pact on the parties, who were unable to narrow substantially their differences by February 18, forcing the secretary reluctantly to announce that he saw no basis for further efforts on his part to bring the union and the BCOA together.[37]

The failure of intensive negotiations under the auspices of the secretary of labor and, indirectly, the president left the government with few options for producing the "timely solution" through "free collective bargaining" to which the president had committed himself as recently as February 11 and February 14. The government quite obviously was reluctant to let the strike run its course in the hopes that the parties would "soften," and yet it was not inclined to invoke the Taft-Hartley Act to force the parties to "cool." With those two options precluded, the government felt compelled to gamble on an "end play" around both the BCOA and the UMWA in the form of a "strategy of getting an agreement with one small company by using members of the bargaining council to negotiate that agreement." [38]

The target chosen for that strategy was the Pittsburgh and Midway Coal Company. The choice of this company as the target of intensive mediation under the auspices of the Federal Mediation and Conciliation Service reflected three sets of considerations. First, the company was party to an independent agreement involving one of the union's more stable and influential districts. Second, the company had demonstrated its willingness to act independently by virtue of its December 1977 western agreement with the UMWA. Third, the company was likely to be sensitive to the government's desire for a quick settlement by virtue of the fact that its parent company—Gulf Oil—was in considerable legal trouble with the federal government. Whatever the reasons, the choice proved well advised, as mediation bore fruit with amazing speed. A tentative agreement was reached on February 19 and announced on February 20.

Achieving an agreement at Pittsburgh and Midway was only a first step in breaking the impasse in the UMWA-BCOA negotiations. Both the UMWA and the BCOA still had to be convinced to let Pittsburgh and Midway be the tail that wagged their respective dogs. That proved to be no great problem with respect to the Bargaining Council of the UMWA, which voted twenty-five

---

[37] Ben A. Franklin, "White House postpones any action to force an end to miners' strike," *New York Times*, February 19, 1978, p. 1.

[38] Horvitz, "What's Happening in Collective Bargaining?" p. 462.

to thirteen to approve the Pittsburgh and Midway agreement on February 20. It was, however, a problem with respect to the BCOA, which on that same date publicly rejected a request from the governor of West Virginia that it accept that settlement.[39] Thus, the first and most obvious challenge facing the government was to "persuade" the BCOA to accept the Pittsburgh and Midway agreement as the basis for its own settlement.

The process of "persuading" the BCOA to accept this agreement began privately on Monday, February 20, 1978. On Wednesday, the secretary of labor put the industry on notice publicly that the president was contemplating "stronger measures," including the possibility of declaring a bargaining impasse "which would allow individual BCOA members to pull out of multiemployer bargaining and settle on their own with the UMW" if a negotiated settlement was not reached by the end of the week.[40] On Thursday, the president called congressional leaders and coal state governors to the White House where they expressed their sense of urgency regarding the need for a settlement.[41] The "persuasion" process culminated on Friday, February 25, when the president met with the top officers of five influential BCOA member companies at the White House.[42] There are no public accounts of what was said in that meeting, but one industry observer speculated on what transpired in that meeting as follows:

> On Friday morning, February 24, President Carter met with five company chairmen—Edgar Speer (U.S. Steel), Lewis Foy (Bethlehem Steel), George Stinson (National Steel), Howard Blauvelt (Continental Oil), and Nicholas Camicia (Pittston). When he departed, Speer commented, "I think I can guarantee some kind of contract." Can you imagine the conversation inside the Oval Office?
>
> Do not lose sight of the fact that at the end Robert Strauss, our chief trade negotiator, was very involved. It can be safely assumed that matters such as steel import quotas and reference point pricing were mentioned—in a noncomplimentary fashion. Apart, several companies received hints that mining permits might not come so easily.[43]

---

[39] BCOA Press Release, February 21, 1978, p. 1.

[40] "Operators' Offer of Arbitration Being Weighed by Mine Workers," *Daily Labor Report*, No. 36 (February 22, 1978), pp. A-16 - A-17.

[41] "Clamor Grows for Swift Federal Action to End Coal Strike, Bring Back Miners," *Daily Labor Report*, No. 37 (February 23, 1978), pp. A-14 - A-15.

[42] "Tentative Settlement in Coal Strike Averts Direct Action by President," *Daily Labor Report*, No. 38 (February 24, 1978), p. AA-1.

[43] Dean Witter Reynolds, Inc., *The Coal Observer*, March 1978, p. 8.

Whatever was said, it had the desired effect, as the BCOA reluctantly agreed to accept the Pittsburgh and Midway agreement in time for the president to announce a settlement two hours before his 9:00 p.m. deadline.

The last remaining barrier to a settlement was the matter of ratification by the UMWA rank and file. The president took note of that fact in his announcement of the February 25, 1978, agreement when he stated that, "although a settlement has been reached, it will not be final until it is studied and democratically ratified by the members of the UMW." [44] In the interest of facilitating that process, the president went on to state:

> this agreement serves the national interests, as well as your own interests, and those of your families. If it is not approved without delay time will have run out for all of us and I will have to take the drastic and unsatisfactory legal action which I would have announced tonight.[45]

Despite the president's counsel and warning, the agreement was not approved. The day following the presidential announcement, the rank and file at Pittsburgh and Midway rejected their own pattern agreement. On March 5, the BCOA rank and file did the same by a margin of more than two to one. Thus, "time had run out," and "drastic and unsatisfactory legal action" was called for. That action was taken on Monday, March 6, when the president announced his intention to invoke the emergency disputes procedures of the Taft-Hartley Act on the grounds that

> the coal strike is three months old. The country cannot afford to wait any longer. Coal supplies have been reduced to a critical level throughout the Midwest. Tens of thousands of people are already out of work because factories have laid off workers to conserve fuel. Power curtailments have reached 50 percent in Indiana, 30 percent in West Virginia, and critical levels in other parts of the Midwest. One month from now, at least a million more Americans would be unemployed if the coal strike continued.[46]

The Board of Inquiry appointed by the president on March 6, 1978, held hearings on March 8, and submitted its report to the president on March 9. In that report, the board found that "the circumstances surrounding this controversy have reached alarming proportions" and advised that "it is imperative, in the na-

---

[44] "Tentative Settlement in Coal Strike," *Daily Labor Report*, p. AA-2.

[45] *Ibid.*

[46] "Statement by President," *Daily Labor Report*, p. X-1.

tional interest, the [controversy be resolved] as expeditiously as possible." [47] On the basis of that report, the president concluded that "this strike, if permitted to continue, will imperil the national health and safety" and directed the attorney general to seek an injunction against continuance of the strike under Section 208 of the Labor-Management Relations Act of 1947.[48] Such an injunction was sought and secured in the U.S. District Court for the District of Columbia on Thursday, March 9, 1978, to take effect on Friday, March 10, 1978.

The lesson of history offered little basis for hope that a Taft-Hartley injunction would work miracles in the coalfields. This was apparently recognized by the president on March 6, 1978, when in announcing his intention to invoke Taft-Hartley he indicated not only that he expected all concerned to "cooperate fully and abide completely by the law" but also that he had taken special steps to insure that "the law is obeyed, that violence is prevented and that lives and property are fully protected," [49]—steps which he previously had refused to take, despite the report to the Justice Department of some 111 significant strike-related incidents of violence or destruction designed to impede the production and/or transportation of non-UMWA coal.[50] Had such steps been taken earlier, it is conceivable that the impact of the strike would never have approached "emergency" proportions as the secretary of labor admitted indirectly in March 1978 when he claimed that one administration goal in declaring an emergency had been to "trigger a limited increase in coal production"—a goal he argued had been met in that, as of March 17, 1978

> reports indicate that over 400 coal mines were open on Wednesday which had not been open last week. Almost all of these are nonunion mines which opened because of the security provided by federal law enforcement efforts.[51]

The fact that UMWA District officials, in their testimony before the Board of Inquiry, extolled the virtues of seizure on the grounds

---

[47] "President's Letter Authorizing Petition to Secure Taft-Hartley Injunction in Coal Strike," *Daily Labor Report*, No. 47 (March 9, 1978), p. G-3.

[48] *Ibid.*, p. G-1.

[49] "Statement by President," *Daily Labor Report*, p. X-1.

[50] U.S. Department of Justice, "United Mine Workers Strike—Coal Industry Event Track 77-13: Incident Summary December 8, 1977, through March 5, 1978 (Pre Taft-Hartley)," (Unpublished report, n. d.).

[51] "Remarks by Secretary of Labor on Handling of Bituminous Coal Strike," *Daily Labor Report*, No. 53 (March 17, 1978), p. E-2.

that it would permit the "resumption of coal production under [the] 1974 contract with 1978 benefit levels" and condemned the use of Taft-Hartley on the grounds that it would impose "slave labor conditions" and create a "confrontation between miners and their government" suggested that the situation in 1978 might not be much different than it had been in 1948, as indeed proved to be the case.[52] The confrontation between miners and their government "predicted to follow invocation of Taft-Hartley" should have taken place on March 10, 1978, the effective date of the restraining order, but it was delayed by "procedural problems" in the enforcement process which delayed the delivery of court orders from Washington to the U.S. Marshals who were to serve them on union officials in the coalfields. Those problems were corrected in time for those orders to be served on Monday, March 13, when they were virtually totally ignored.

The refusal of miners to return to work during the week of March 13, 1978, placed the responsibility for ending a national emergency strike back on the president's shoulders. Fortunately, the BCOA and UMWA stepped forward to substantially lighten the burden of that responsibility when, on March 15, they announced a third tentative agreement. In light of that agreement, the only further legal action demanded of the government by virtue of its commitment to the Taft-Hartley Act was to appear in court on March 17, when the temporary restraining order issued on March 9 was to expire. Contempt proceedings for failure to comply with that order clearly were not politically necessary to achieve an early end to the strike as the parties themselves apparently had solved that problem.

The government did appear in court on March 17, 1978, to request a continuation of the court's March 9 temporary restraining order, which it argued would "facilitate the bargaining process," rather than an injunction, which it stated would "adversely affect the collective bargaining process."[53] The court, confronted with an unenthusiastic case for extending an order which was being neither obeyed nor enforced and which was admittedly no longer, strictly speaking, essential to the national health and welfare, denied the government's request. Thus, at 6:00 p.m. on Friday, March 17, the strike by miners officially no

---

[52] "Statements by Mine Workers and Coal Operators Before Board of Inquiry," *Daily Labor Report*, No. 46 (March 8, 1978), p. F-2.

[53] "Judge Cancels Order Directing Striking UMW Coal Miners to go Back to Work," *Daily Labor Report*, No. 53 (March 17, 1978), p. A-12.

longer constituted a national emergency, a status it maintained for the ten remaining days of its course until miners returned to work on Monday, March 27, 1978.[54]

The 1977-1978 coal negotiations added yet another chapter to the government's record of frustration and failure in intervention in labor disputes in the bituminous coal mining industry, despite the claims of success made by the secretary of labor in a speech before the National Press Club on March 17, 1978. The 1977-1978 coal strike raised once again the venerable question of whether a coal strike created a true national emergency of the type portrayed by the president on March 6, 1978. Finally, the decision of the court not to accede to the government's request for an extension of a Taft-Hartley restraining order raised some new questions regarding the relative roles to be played by the president and the judiciary in defining a national emergency and determining when such an emergency exists—questions previously raised only once, in the "grain millers" case in 1971.[55]

The economic effects of the 1977-1978 coal strike clearly did not approach, in nature or in magnitude, the dimensions required to meet the economist's standards for a true national emergency. More importantly, those effects did not even meet the standards the president stated at the time he declared the strike a national emergency, something first pointed out publicly when the General Accounting Office criticized the Carter administration for using overblown and misleading figures of the effects of the strike on employment in justifying its determination that the strike constituted, or threatened to constitute, a national emergency.[56] Indeed, unemployment caused by the strike barely met the "tens of thousands" level he cited on March 6 and never came close to the one million level he predicted for the end of March, despite the fact that the strike lasted until March 27. Bureau of Labor Statistics' estimates of unemployment resulting from coal shortages reveal that such unemployment peaked at 25,000 the week before invocation of the Taft-Hartley Act and fell to less than

---

[54] *Ibid.*, p. A-11.

[55] "Decision of U.S. District Court, Northern District of Illinois, in Case of U.S. v. International Longshoreman's Association, Local 418 *et al.*", *Daily Labor Report*, No. 194 (November 10, 1971), pp. D-1 - D-6.

[56] "Study Says Coal Strike was Mishandled," *Coal Age*, January 1979, p. 45.

20,000 by the last week in March when the miners returned to work.[57]

In his March 6 definition of the emergency confronting the nation as a result of the coal strike, the president cited, in addition to its indirect employment effects, dwindling coal stockpiles and power curtailments in the Midwest. The three electric power networks hardest hit by the strike were the East Central Reliability Coordination Agreement (ECAR), the Mid-America Inter-Pool Network (MAIN), and the Tennessee Valley Authority (TVA).[58] Coal stocks in these three networks were drawn down in the course of the strike, but never reached critical levels and might never have done so, given the break in the weather and increase in coal production which began in early February. (See Figure IX-1.) There were isolated local power problems, but overall power curtailments in these three networks between December and April totalled less than 10 percent of their estimated demand.

The rhetoric used by the president when he invoked the Taft-Hartley Act masked his true reason for doing so. His determination that a national emergency existed was based not on the actual or anticipated economic impact of the strike, but on the actual or anticipated political impact of permitting the strike to continue. In that context, the political impact of a coal strike is only partly a function of the fact that coal is a "basic" industry whose output is an "essential" input in production in other "basic or essential" industries, such as electric utilities and steel, in which curtailment of production might be the occasion of true "national emergency." The political impact of a coal strike is also as much and possibly more a function of its impact on the producers as opposed to the consumers of coal. The fact that coal strikes involve a major industry in several populous and politically critical states in close proximity to the nation's capital adds significantly to the "essentiality" of the industry and its production. In 1978, this dimension of the essentiality of coal production transformed

---

[57] U.S. Department of Labor, Bureau of Labor Statistics, "Special Survey on Impact of Coal Shortages on Manufacturing and Trade Employment in 11 Coal Dependent States, March 19-March 25, 1978," Press Release, March 30, 1978.

[58] "The Coal Strike of 1977-1978: Its Impact on the Electric Bulk Power Supply in North America," (Princeton, N.J.: National Electric Reliability Council, 1978), p. 1.

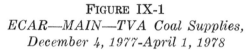

FIGURE IX-1
ECAR—MAIN—TVA Coal Supplies,
December 4, 1977-April 1, 1978

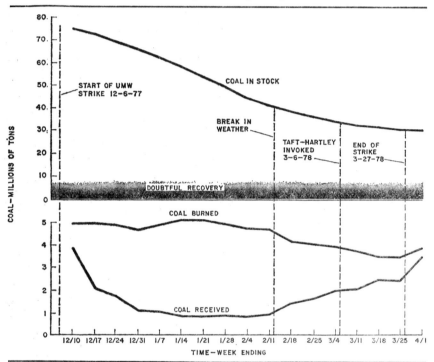

Source: "The Coal Strike of 1977-1978: Its Impact on the Electric Bulk
          Power Supply in North America," (Princeton, N.J.: National
          Electric Reliability Council, 1978), p. 4.

a regional, economic nonemergency into a national, political
emergency.

The refusal of the district court to grant the government
motion for extension of a restraining order raises questions
regarding the power of the president to utilize the Taft-Hartley
Act to deal with national, political emergencies that are not national economic emergencies as well. Indeed, the court, in reject-
ing the government's motion, suggested that economic impact,
per se, might be insufficient to warrant the finding of a threat to
"national health and safety" which would justify injunctive relief.
Thus, to the extent that the court's decision has or acquires precedential value as a general rule of law rather than as a judicial
response to a most unusual set of circumstances, one legacy of

the 1977-1978 coal strike may be to significantly constrain the government's access to Taft-Hartley injunctions. It also proved, once again, that presidential determination of the existence, or threat, of a national emergency is open to legal challenge, and it established some apparently relatively broad grounds for such challenges.

The failure of the government's ultimate weapon in the 1977 coal case raises serious questions regarding the future credibility and effectiveness of that weapon as a basis for government involvement or intervention in labor disputes. The history of compliance with Taft-Hartley injunctions in the coal industry coupled with the government's obvious ambivalence about seeking and enforcing such an injunction in the 1977 coal strike may well constitute grounds for regarding the 1977 coal experience as a "special case" with respect to voluntary compliance and enforcement problems. That same ambivalence, coupled with the fact of noncompliance and the conclusion of a third agreement which might end the strike without further government action, similarly constitute grounds for distinguishing the 1977 coal case as a "special case" with respect to judicial review of presidential declarations of national emergency. The former distinction seems quite compelling but not overwhelming; the latter distinction is less compelling given the power of precedent in judicial interpretation of the law of the land. In any event, the 1977 coal case can only have weakened the credibility and effectiveness of presidential invocation of Taft-Hartley as an ultimate weapon in government intervention in labor disputes, at least temporarily if not permanently, at a time when the public interest and government policy seem to call for a far more active and effective role for government as an independent and impartial participant in collective bargaining.

CHAPTER X

The Political Economics of
Industrywide Bargaining:
The Nonmembers

The UMWA-BCOA bargaining relationship does not encompass all coal producers. Indeed, it does not even encompass all UMWA-organized producers of coal. There is a substantial, if unknown, number of mines organized by the UMWA that are not members of the BCOA. Most, but not all, of these nonsignatory mines are small, independent operations. Historically, these non-BCOA, UMWA mines have not played a role in industrywide bargaining, but that has not been the case in recent negotiations and may not be the case in future negotiations. One nonsignatory producer, Pittsburgh and Midway, has been the central figure in the growing role of nonsignatories as a force to be reckoned with by both the BCOA and the UMWA in their national agreement negotiations.

Pittsburgh and Midway is a subsidiary of the Gulf Oil Corporation, which operates surface mines in both the East and the West. Gulf Oil is a company which has pursued a highly independent course in the conduct of its labor relations in the oil industry and has attempted to do the same in the coal industry. Philosophically, Gulf Oil is opposed to multiemployer bargaining and the loss of sovereignty that it entails and has indulged that aversion in its coal operations by electing not to join the BCOA with respect to either eastern or western operations.[1] Its eastern operations are covered by an "independent" agreement negotiated with the UMWA at the district level. Its western operations are covered

---

[1] For a recent statement of the Gulf Oil Corporation's views on multiemployer bargaining in the coal industry, see "Multiemployer Bargaining Hampers Coal Talks, Gulf Negotiator Says," *Daily Labor Report*, No. 78 (April 23, 1981), pp. A-7 - A-8.

by a separate "independent" agreement also negotiated with the
UMWA at the district level. The former agreement is part of
the national (eastern) collective bargaining system; the latter,
part of the western (surface mine) collective bargaining system
of the UMWA.

THE UPRISING IN THE EAST

There have long been non-BCOA, "independent" producers in
the East whose mine or mines were organized by the UMWA.
Although technically independent, those producers traditionally
were expected and, if necessary, compelled to follow the pattern
set by the UMWA National Agreement to the point of becoming
"non-member signatories" to that agreement. That expectation
found formal expression in the UMWA-BCOA Protective Wage
Clause of 1958 in which the union agreed that

> during the period of this Contract, the United Mine Workers of
> America will not enter into, be a party to, nor will it permit any
> agreement or understanding covering any wages, hours or other
> conditions of work applicable to employees covered by this Contract
> on any basis other than those specified in this Contract or any ap-
> plicable District Contract.[2]

The Protective Wage Clause may not have survived the test of
time and legal challenge, but the basic system of contractual
relations, in which nonmember, unionized producers were expected
to sign "the union's master work contract after it was reached
with the BCOA" remained largely intact under the watchful eye
and powerful protection of the union. Over the next decade
(1964-1974), the UMWA in the East was fairly well able to
maintain the integrity of its two-tier—member/nonmember signatory—contract system, although a few nonmembers, including
Pittsburgh and Midway, were able to conclude "independent"
agreements as opposed to simply signing the National Agreement. The theoretical significance of that distinction far out-
weighed its practical significance until 1977 when, with the encouragement and support of the government, Pittsburgh and
Midway attempted to conclude a truly independent agreement.

The 1977 Negotiations

The elevation of Pittsburgh and Midway to a position of
prominence in the eastern bargaining system in 1977 was a prod-

---

[2] National Bituminous Coal Wage Agreement of 1950 as Amended Effective
December 1, 1958, p. 3.

uct of the government's attempt to break the deadlock in UMWA-BCOA negotiations which followed rejections of the first tentative agreement by pursuing "the strategy of getting an agreement with one small company." The option of regional or company-by-company bargaining as a basis for breaking that deadlock had been mentioned by the secretary of labor in the course of his mediation efforts prior to the call for the parties to meet at the White House, but primarily as a threat to soften the position of the UMWA and particularly the BCOA. When that threat, coupled with White House intervention, failed to move the parties, the government elected to make good on its threat.

The fact that the Pittsburgh and Midway agreement proved difficult to sell to the BCOA and impossible to sell to the UMWA rank and file as a pattern dramatically pointed out the relatively limited latitude for independent action by nonsignatories in the East. It also made manifest the potential threat of such action to the control of the UMWA and the BCOA over their own destiny in their National Agreement bargaining relationship. The government elected to stress that threat in its efforts to end the deadlock and strike after rejection of the second tentative agreement, beginning with its suggestion that one alternative to invoking the Taft-Hartley Act was to declare an impasse which would allow individual BCOA members to withdraw from multi-employer bargaining to seek their own settlements and ending with the suggestion that the failure of the Taft-Hartley Act to end the strike left regional bargaining as the only procedural alternative to achieve that end.

The possibility of regional bargaining had little appeal either to the BCOA or to the UMWA and added an unknown measure of incentive to that provided by the long strike to achieve a workable settlement. To that end, some of the "old coal" members of the BCOA took the lead by seeking a private "exploratory" meeting with the union. The union responded favorably and such a meeting took place on March 10, 1978, the day the Taft-Hartley injunction went into effect. That meeting was followed by another on Saturday, March 11, at which a new conceptual outline for a settlement was agreed upon. The following three days were spent in negotiating the details of that settlement and by Wednesday, March 14, the UMWA and BCOA were able to formally announce a new tentative agreement—one negotiated on the industry side by representatives of "old coal" or "independent coal" members and believed by at least some of those members to have been all but "inevitable" from the start.

The 1981 Negotiations

The restructuring of the BCOA prior to its 1980-1981 National Agreement negotiations could hardly have been reassuring to those old, independent coal members of the BCOA who felt that the 1977-1978 strike had been an exercise in futility instigated and/or orchestrated by "non-coal" members and might well have induced many of them to attempt to escape the BCOA and seek "independent" status. The combination of initial success and ultimate failure of Pittsburgh and Midway's independent course in 1978 certainly did not encourage, but also did not totally discourage, such action. The aura of optimism regarding the prospects for a peaceful 1981 settlement which pervaded the industry in the summer of 1980 constituted a far more potent source of encouragement to "stick with" the BCOA, as virtually all elected to do. The only major independent to bolt the association was North American Coal—one of the firms instrumental in the negotiation of the final 1978 settlement—and it did not take that action until November 1980, after negotiations had begun and additional evidence became available as to the probable course and outcome of the 1980-1981 UMWA-BCOA National Agreement negotiations. The strike that ultimately occurred during those negotiations belied the optimism and betrayed the faith of at least some coal members, but produced only one other significant defection—Emery Mining.[3]

The avowed interest of large BCOA producers in productivity gains and their reputed willingness to pay for such gains reportedly was not well received among smaller member and, particularly, nonmember signatories to the National Agreement. The fact that productivity issues and trade-offs did not prove to be a major focus of the 1980-1981 UMWA-BCOA negotiations may have been of some comfort to such producers, but the strike that occurred in those negotiations over "non-economic" issues definitely was not. That strike produced strong interest on the part of a number of nonmember signatories and signatories of independent agreements to be permitted to pursue the same course of action as Pittsburgh and Midway had in 1978, in the

---

[3] Thomas Petzinger Jr., "Several coal firms seek own UMW pacts as strike lengthens, but the union balks," *Wall Street Journal*, April 27, 1981, p. 18.

hope of achieving an "independent" agreement that would permit a resumption of operations. The *Wall Street Journal* characterized the "uprising" among smaller operators in 1981 as follows:

> Several coal companies anxious about the effects of the month long United Mine Workers' strike are trying to shortcut coal's national collective bargaining system and secure private settlements with the union.
>
> For the most part, the companies seeking their own talks with the union say their interests aren't being represented by management bargainers at the UMW negotiations in Washington which are stalled over a number of noneconomic issues . . . ."It's like taxation without representation." [4]

The reaction of some smaller, nonmember signatory producers to such "taxation without representation" was an attempt to "organize a rival management bargaining group composed of small companies called the Unionized Coal Employers Association" in the hope that small operators

> could readily break the strike by capitulating to the union on one of the issues that stalemated the talks in Washington—a BCOA demand that the union agree to drop a $1,895 royalty that unionized operators must pay into the UMW Health and Retirement Funds for each ton of nonunion coal they purchase for resale.[5]

Those smaller producers, such as North American Coal and Emery Mining, were rebuffed by the union in their bid for separate talks and settlements on the grounds, in the case of the small producers, that they were, singly and collectively, "too small to set a pattern for the rest of the coal industry." [6]

The UMWA's refusal to pursue its option of separate "deals" with nonmember signatories and independents in 1981 preserved the basic bargaining structure and system in the East and reaffirmed the fact that UMWA-BCOA National Agreement negotiations are the "only game in town," thereby undoing whatever damage may have been done to that system by the government's end-play strategies of 1978. In the short run, the union's action clearly has strengthened its own and the BCOA's hold on labor relations in the industry in the East. In the long run, however, quite the opposite may be the case. Those producers who feel their interests are not well represented or served by the BCOA, having been denied the option of escaping the BCOA, now have

---

[4] *Ibid.*

[5] *Ibid.*

[6] *Ibid.*

only two options: (1) attempting to acquire influence and power within the BCOA; or (2) attempting to negate the influence and power of the BCOA not by escaping it, but by escaping the UMWA. Neither option is likely to be easily pursued given existing institutional arrangement in the East. The latter option, however unpalatable for many, may prove to be the only workable option for old and small coal producers if they are to survive in their competitive battle with the energy and steel giants, just as it was for smaller producers in their battle against the mechanized and unionized coal giants in the 1950s.

THE REVOLT IN THE WEST

The UMWA's presence in the western coalfields is not only more limited in scale but also more complex in structure than it is in the East. The union represents a substantial number of miners in the older, underground mining operations of BCOA members who are covered by the UMWA-BCOA National Agreement (member signatories). In addition, the UMWA represents miners in some smaller, regional operations whose contracts are patterned on the BCOA-UMWA National Agreement (nonmember signatories). Finally, the union represents a substantial number of miners in companies with extensive surface mine operations in the West, including both members and nonmembers of the BCOA, who are covered by a separate "independent" Western Surface Mine Agreement (nonmember, nonsignatories). As has already been noted, perhaps as many as 50 percent of all miners in the West are not represented by the UMWA at all.

The union's presence in the West in the form of member-signatory mines stems from its organizing successes of the 1930s and 1940s. The UMWA and its ancestors were active in organizing miners in the West as early as 100 years ago, but until the 1930s they did not enjoy the same degree of success in those efforts or in attaining employer acceptance of collective bargaining as they did in the Central Competitive Field. From the outset, western operators, particularly the Colorado Fuel and Iron Company, were not amenable to organization, a proclivity that produced a series of strikes at ten-year intervals beginning in 1883 and culminating in a particularly bitter strike in 1913 in which the "Ludlow Massacre" took place.[7] Despite those strike

---

[7] Mary Van Kleeck, *Miners and Management* (New York: Russell Sage Foundation, 1934), p. 36.

actions, the UMWA achieved only limited recognition among western operators, most notably in Wyoming, and never established the basis for a multistate, multiemployer bargaining system like that which it built in the Central Competitive Field between 1898 and 1927. The collapse of the Central Competitive Field Compact in 1927 came at the same time as a strike in the mines of northern Colorado under the leadership of the Industrial Workers of the World which virtually destroyed what limited recognition and cooperation the UMWA had been able to gain in the West. That setback in the West, as in the East, was reversed only with the passage of the National Industrial Recovery Act (NIRA) whose mandate for organization was sufficiently clear and strong that in 1933 even Colorado Fuel and Iron recognized the UMWA,[8] as virtually all other western operators did subsequently.

The UMWA's nonmember signatories in the west are primarily newer or newly acquired underground mines of smaller companies or regional producers. For the most part, they are mines opened during the 1960s and 1970s in which the UMWA acquired recognition by virtue of the organizational effort and success reflected in its NLRB representation election record. That record suggests that nonmember signatories constitute an even less significant factor in the industry bargaining structure and system in the West than in the East (see Table VI-1).

The UMWA's nonmember, nonsignatory producers in the West have become its most important nonsignatories in the conduct of its national negotiations. That group encompasses the surface mine operations of approximately a dozen companies, which employ about 5,000 miners in the Rocky Mountain states. Those companies include both national and regional operators and count among their national producers both BCOA members, such as Peabody Coal, and non-BCOA members, such as Pittsburgh and Midway. The fact that all of the companies in question are heavily engaged in surface mining in the West subjects them to the competitive pressure of nonunion competition—their western economic constraint. The fact that some of the larger or more prominent companies in question also are actively engaged in eastern surface mining under the jurisdiction, if not the explicit coverage, of the UMWA's National Agreement subjects

---

[8] *Ibid.*, pp. 324-25.

them to the institutional imperative for intraunion equality—their eastern political constraint.

The origins of the UMWA Western Surface Mine Agreement lie buried in the paucity of external attention paid to collective bargaining in the industry in the West and the abundance of turnover among those engaged in that function in the West. Searching the scholarly literature and probing the memories of industry representatives produced descriptions only of how the system worked prior to 1974, not descriptions of how it initially evolved. It must have begun with the insistence of some western surface mine operator for an "independent" agreement, which later arrivals emulated; as in the case of AMAX, which when it "opened a surface mine in Wyoming, with respect to which it did not join the BCOA, [it] and the union negotiated a separate collective bargaining contract. . . ." [9] In any event, the Western Surface Mine Agreement bargaining system grew into a company-by-company negotiation system as opposed to a multiemployer system. In that context, the historical pattern was set by the UMWA's National Agreement. That, at least, was the situation prior to the industry's 1974 negotiations, which produced the first rumblings of a revolt on the western front of the UMWA's industrywide bargaining system.

The 1974 Negotiations

Historically, the UMWA's Western Surface Mine Agreements expired on the same date as its National Agreement and the schedule of negotiations for the West also coincided with that of the East. In fact, however, negotiations in the West typically lagged behind those in the East by thirty to sixty days, owing to the tradition of extending the existing contract for that period of time in order to await the outcome of the UMWA-BCOA bargaining. Negotiations in the West would focus on mine/company issues until such time as the BCOA reached an agreement that then would serve as the basis for a settlement with one and ultimately all signatories to Western Surface Mine Agreements.

In 1974, the signatories of the UMWA Western Surface Mine Agreement for the first time made a determined but unsuccessful effort to break their contractual link to the BCOA by attempting to engage the union in a full-scale discussion of regional problems

[9] NLRB v. Amax Coal Co., 101 S.Ct. 2789 (1981).

and negotiation of a truly regional agreement. That effort was made under the leadership of Peabody Coal and it involved the first extensive informal coordination among the western signatories in the conduct of their individual company negotiations with the UMWA, resulting in the emergence of what was termed "the Peabody Group."

The 1974 western negotiations opened, as usual, on a company-by-company basis when BCOA negotiations got underway, languishing until the BCOA reached an agreement in late November. Prior to contract expiration on November 12, 1974, the 1971 contract was extended for sixty days. Serious negotiations began only after an agreement was reached in the East on November 24 and continued into January 1975, when the union struck the signatory companies in an attempt "to compel the mine owners to establish a multi-employer bargaining unit and to agree to a new collective contract proposed by the union." [10]

The basic cause of the 1975 impasse in the West was the concerted effort by management to break the link between the national and western agreements and to achieve a truly "independent" agreement responsive to regional conditions. Specifically, the dispute centered on management resistance to the union's demands for an economic package identical to that agreed to by the BCOA, particularly with respect to royalty payments; for added restrictions on subcontracting in the form of the same "jurisdictional" guarantees designed to protect or expand the union's representational territory as it enjoyed in the East; and on management insistence on attention to regional problems and an expiration date significantly different from that of the BCOA contract. The issue of a multiemployer bargaining unit arose as a union response to the coordination and cooperation among the companies and became and remained a factor in the dispute until AMAX filed an unfair labor practice complaint and the UMWA found itself "threatened with a complaint from the National Labor Relations Board Regional Counsel for illegally attempting to coerce the employer into a multiemployer bargaining unit." [11] That same company complaint also challenged the legality of the union's "jurisdictional" demands and ultimately resulted in an adverse ruling against the union, which forced it to accept

[10] *Ibid.*

[11] *Ibid.*

changes in Article I of its BCOA contract in its 1981 National Agreement negotiations.

The 1975 strike lasted for over two months and was the first "long" non-BCOA strike in the West since 1950. The settlement that ended the strike did not provide the break sought by the companies between national and western agreements in terms of benefit system or expiration date. The companies, however, could take solace in the fact that in the course of the negotiations leading to that settlement, the issue of separating the West from the East with respect to benefit systems had been raised and discussed and the possibility of multiemployer bargaining had been rebuffed.

That management failed in its initial attempt to break the East-West contract link and to engage the union in purely regional negotiations is hardly surprising. The issue might well have been settled for a number of years, had it not been kept alive by developments in the East over the next three years, which forced a dramatic change in the union's position on that highly sensitive institutional issue. Specifically, what the Western Surface Mine Agreement signatories had been unable to accomplish in 1974 by their united front and two-month strike, the employees in BCOA eastern underground mines accomplished with their rash of wildcat strikes during the term of the 1974 National Agreement.

The signatories to the Western Surface Mine Agreement were not afflicted by the labor instability that beset the signatories to the National Agreement between 1975 and 1977. Their employees, however, were subjected to the cutbacks in welfare benefits made necessary by the impact of BCOA labor instability in the East on royalty payments to the welfare funds—the same funds to which their employers continued to contribute and on which they continued to be dependent for benefits under the terms of the 1975 Western Surface Mine Agreement. This resulted in the emergence of a rank-and-file awareness of the potential perils of continued dependence on their eastern relations—an awareness which, as indicated previously, by 1977 had taken the form of a consensus that "Western miners . . . do not want their pension and health benefits to be dependent on the vagaries of strike-prone production in the East." [12]

---

[12] "A Separate Peace in Western Coal," *Business Week*, December 5, 1977, p. 41.

The 1977 Negotiations

In October 1977, both the National Agreement and the Western Surface Mine Agreements negotiations opened. In the West, the companies once again entered their negotiations on a truly company-by-company basis, having had their fill of the *ad hoc* coordination system tried in 1974 and the opening it had provided for the union to raise and press the issue of multiemployer bargaining. The union, in the person of its district representatives in negotiations, entered the negotiations with a greater degree of autonomy from the national union than it had previously enjoyed. In the words of one international union staff official, "This is the first time Western miners, and not the big men from the East, are negotiating Western agreements." [13]

From the outset of negotiations, the pension and benefit issue was the primary focus of attention. The union now raised the possibility of a separate, independent benefit system. The industry responded favorably as a matter of principle, and for both economic (cost) and institutional (separation) reasons, it pursued the possibility with considerable enthusiasm. This common interest paved the way for serious negotiations on a basic economic issue prior to and independent of progress on economic issues in the coincident UMWA-BCOA talks in Washington—a break with tradition that far exceeded the industry's comparatively modest autonomy goals in the 1974 negotiations.

The path to an agreement on the benefit issue was cordial, but not easy. In early November, the UMWA was reported to be negotiating details for separate multiemployer funds in the West." [14] That proposal, which was never publicly spelled out in detail, called for creation of a multiemployer fund in the West similar if not identical to the fund embodied in the National Agreement. That proposal was welcomed by the companies but not accepted by them for two reasons: (1) it was a multiemployer plan with all its attendant economic and institutional risks, and (2) it was a carbon copy of the BCOA (eastern) plan rather than a different benefit system. Those two features, particularly the first, were especially troublesome to Pittsburgh and Midway, which took the initiative in responding to the union's proposal.

The operations of Pittsburgh and Midway are characterized by the same latitude for opportunistic independence as was shown

[13] *Ibid.*

[14] *Ibid.*

by its eastern operations in 1978 and as has consistently been shown by its parent company, Gulf Oil. Not surprisingly, the philosophical aversion of Gulf to multiemployer bargaining has become labor-relations policy in Pittsburgh and Midway, in general, and in its western operations, in particular, as has its philosophical aversion to multiemployer benefit systems, because of the dilution of control and credit they entail. Thus, Pittsburgh and Midway, as much as if not more than any other western agreement signatory, had reason to perceive both opportunity and problems in the union's proposal, in addition to the latitude to attempt to exploit that opportunity and eliminate those problems.

By early November, Pittsburgh and Midway had established itself as a primary focus of union attention in western negotiations, as was indicated by a ceremonial visit to its negotiations by UMWA President Miller during a recess in national negotiations. The negotiations at Pittsburgh and Midway in Denver proceeded slowly and deliberately during November and up to the date of contract expiration on December 7. As the parties approached their deadline, it was clear that since all other economic issues had implicitly been resolved, the major stumbling block to an agreement was the union's multiemployer benefit fund proposal. At the eleventh hour, the union relented, withdrew its proposal, and accepted the company's offer to provide equivalent pension and health benefits through an individual company plan.

The "separate peace in western coal" in 1977 was the product of two compelling forces on the union side of the relationship, which facilitated, if not forced, a break with its eastern master. The first was rank-and-file pressure to divorce their benefits from those of their eastern brethren. The second was a desire on the part of the union in the West to avoid a strike in order to avoid alienating existing and/or prospective members. Directly or indirectly, both of these forces stemmed from the fact that the labor stability issue, which was such an emotional one for the UMWA in the East, was an economic and institutional embarrassment for the UMWA in the West.

The 1977 Pittsburgh and Midway Agreement achieved two of the basic goals of the industry's 1974 concerted effort to lighten the burden of the BCOA pattern. First, it broke the common chronology of eastern and western negotiations. Second, it produced a significant substantive difference in contractual content between the East and the West. Both of these "industry victories," however, turned out to be relatively transitory.

The 1977 Pittsburgh and Midway Western Agreement constituted a dramatic reversal in the traditional order of industry
settlements and a potential change in the direction of flow of the
pattern of effects within the industry. Pittsburgh and Midway,
as well as the rest of the Western Surface Mine Agreement signatories, sought to avoid any such dramatic reversal of their
traditional "followership" role in industry labor relations, opting
instead to buy out of the mantle of industry leadership by signing contracts of more than thirty-six months' duration. The Pittsburgh and Midway Agreement reached on December 6, 1977,
was a forty-month contract due to expire on April 6, 1981—four
months after the presumed contract expiration date of a new
UMWA-BCOA National Agreement. Unfortunately, the 111-day
UMWA-BCOA strike of 1977-1978 pushed that expiration date
back to March 27, 1981, and left the western producers in the
same position they had been in with respect to the contract cycle.

The 1977 Pittsburgh and Midway Agreement withdrew the
company from participation in the national pension and health
benefit funds—a major break with industry and union tradition.
That substantive victory was partially diluted when the UMWA
and BCOA subsequently agreed in their 1978 contract that "any
signatory Employer may elect to implement the above health
benefit coverage through a private insurance carrier(s)" in which
case he "shall have no further responsibilities . . . to make contributions to or otherwise be responsible for benefits provided
under the 1974 Benefit Plan and Trust." [15] The remaining portion of that victory almost disappeared in 1981 when the BCOA
raised the possibility of substituting individual company pension
plans for the existing multiemployer fund plan—a possibility
quickly rejected by the UMWA.

The 1977 Pittsburgh and Midway settlement also established
that company as a potential labor relations leader among Western
Surface Mine Agreement signatories and a challenger to Peabody
as the pattern-setter in the West. To whatever extent that fact
constituted a victory for Pittsburgh and Midway in pursuit of
independence in the conduct of its labor relations, that victory
also proved to be short-lived. Most other Western Agreement
companies followed the lead of Pittsburgh and Midway and negotiated forty-month contracts, but one did not—Peabody opted for

---

[15] National Bituminous Coal Wage Agreement of 1978, Article XX, Section
(c)(3)(ii), p. 95.

a thirty-six-month contract scheduled to expire on January 16, 1981. That shorter-duration contract placed Peabody out in front of other western agreement companies, where it once again could serve as the industry leader in the West as it did in the East. Unfortunately, because of subsequent developments, it also placed the company not only out in front of its western colleagues but also out in front of itself and its BCOA colleagues in 1981 negotiations—a position which was to prove highly uncomfortable come January 16, 1981.

The 1981 Negotiations

The UMWA entered its 1981 western negotiations with Peabody "insisting on an expensive package that it thinks will improve its chances to organize in the West." [16] Specifically, the union sought substantial wage increases to make up for the effects of inflation over the preceding three years, COLAs to protect against inflation over the next three years, and a substantial increase in pension benefits to offset the fact that "miners at several Western companies that are nonunion or organized by other unions already earn higher wages and pensions than UMWA members." [17] Overall, the cost of the union's bargaining demands was estimated at about 43 percent over the life of a three-year contract.

There was a general, if reluctant, acceptance on the part of management throughout the industry that the 1981 round of negotiations with the UMWA would result in a large economic settlement. The hope within the BCOA, in general, and among its larger members, in particular, was that the association would be able to secure some significant concessions from the UMWA on "productivity and stability" issues in exchange for such a settlement and that this would ease the impact of wage and benefit improvements on unit (per ton) labor costs, as had been the frustrated hope of the BCOA in 1977-1978. There was, however, no comparable hope in the West, where productivity and stability issues had not yet assumed the salience and importance they had in the East. The fact that there was a catch-up problem in the benefit area made obvious in the West—but not the East—by

---

[16] "A High-Stakes Strike at Peabody Coal," *Business Week*, February 2, 1981, p. 18.

[17] *Ibid.*

rival unionism further complicated the western bargaining scene in 1981.

The combination of a wage/benefit catch-up problem and a lack of a true management issue in the West placed Peabody in the position of having to give away in the West, if it was to achieve a settlement, that for which it expected to exact a price in the East, if it was to agree to a BCOA settlement with the UMWA. In its role as both a western and national leader, Peabody had little choice but to resist the union's substantial economic demands in the West for fear that "a rich settlement would jeopardize its chance and that of other producers to win a moderate contract in the Eastern coal fields." [18] That fear was recognized and addressed by the UMWA when its leadership attempted to assure Peabody and all other producers that a western settlement would "have 'nothing to do with the Eastern talks' " because of the manifest differences between western surface and eastern underground coal mining operations.[19]

The economic and institutional competitive constraints on Peabody and the UMWA in their 1981 western negotiations virtually ensured an impasse and strike in those negotiations, as indeed was the case. When that strike occurred on January 16, the company offer that was on the table was reported to total 34 percent over three years and was characterized as one that left the parties "far apart on wages" and even farther apart on pensions which reputedly were "the primary strike issue." [20] The UMWA's pension demand at that point was reported to be a more than 50 percent increase in basic pension benefits, from about fourteen dollars to twenty-two dollars per month, per year of service—a demand which it would have been costly for Peabody to meet in its western operations alone, but which would have cost the company approximately twice as much, on a per hour basis, to implement for its eastern (BCOA) labor force due to its higher age/service demographic distribution.[21]

The stalemate and strike at Peabody's Western Surface Mine Agreement operations lasted for approximately two months and might well have lasted for longer had not its impasse with the UMWA been broken by a "surprise" agreement at another com-

---

[18] *Ibid.*

[19] *Ibid.*

[20] *Ibid.*

[21] *Ibid.*

pany—once again, Pittsburgh and Midway Coal's western operations.[22] Although the Pittsburgh and Midway Western Agreement did not expire until April 6, 1981, the company and union
quietly began exploratory talks in December 1980. Those talks
went beyond "exploration" to "negotiation" even before Peabody's Western Surface Mine Agreement operations were struck
in mid-January and became even more intense after Peabody's
western operations were struck. The outcome of those exploratory discussions and impromptu negotiations was a tentative
agreement on a three-year amendment/extension of their as yet
still unexpired 1977 contract to take effect upon union ratification, which was announced on February 9, 1981—more than six
weeks before expiration of the 1978-1981 UMWA-BCOA National
Agreement.

The 1981 Pittsburgh and Midway Western Agreement dramatically reaffirmed that company's "creative independence" in the
conduct of its labor relations in the coal industry as in the oil
industry. More importantly, it reaffirmed the "effective independence" of the non-BCOA West in the conduct of its labor relations
with the UMWA. Finally, it once again placed the East in the
position of having to follow the chronological and substantive
lead of the West in the conclusion of its "National" Agreement.
That situation is unlikely to change by 1984, as the UMWA and
BCOA in 1981 signed a thirty-eight-month contract which leaves
the West chronologically ahead of the East in negotiating a new
contract.

The new-found independence of the West in the conduct of collective bargaining can be traced to the competitive burden
imposed on management and union alike by "labor instability"
in the largely non-UMWA coal mining industry in the Rocky
Mountain West. For management, that burden rests in the
impact of labor stability on their real or perceived ability to
serve as reliable suppliers of coal in a regional market dominated
by suppliers whose reliability seems unthreatened by labor problems. For the union, that burden rests in the impact of labor
stability on its real or perceived acceptability as a bargaining
representative in a region dominated by hostile employers and
skeptical employees in which it must compete with other reputedly
far more reliable/stable unions.

---

[22] Thomas Petzinger, Jr. and Carol Hymowitz, "Pittsburgh & Midway
Coal, UMW reach accord that may set pattern for west," *Wall Street Journal*,
February 10, 1981, p. 4.

The breakdown of the traditional tandem relationship of Western Surface Mine Agreements to the National Agreement has created some potentially serious problems for both the BCOA and the UMWA. Both have lost an indeterminable measure of control over their own destiny in National Agreement negotiations in the past two bargaining rounds by virtue of the existence of a "Western pattern." That was not a major problem in 1978, given the special issues and conditions in the West, but it had to be in 1981 when Pittsburgh and Midway's Western Agreement had to play about the same role in national negotiations as its Eastern Agreement had in 1978. Above and beyond that problem, BCOA member companies with western mines covered by the National Agreement now find Western Surface Mine Agreement signatories added to their list of "nonunion" competitors in the region and increasingly in both the national and international coal market. The UMWA faced an analogous problem in 1981 when it found itself with its Western Surface Mine Agreement members working under a contract they had ratified and their Western National Agreement mine members on strike over a contract offer they had voted to accept by a four-to-one margin but which their National Agreement brethren had rejected by a two-to-one margin.

The fact that the BCOA in recent negotiations has not been able to control its own destiny and set a truly national pattern in the face of the growing autonomy of its nonmembers in general and western nonmembers in particular—as personified in both cases by Pittsburgh and Midway—must raise questions regarding the value of BCOA membership from an employer's standpoint and of BCOA coverage from an employee's standpoint. The 1981 strike added a sense of urgency to such questions for western BCOA producers, as evidenced by the attempted withdrawal of Emery Mining from the BCOA. Whether competitive pressures will force other western producers to attempt to do the same before 1984, at least with respect to their western mines, remains to be seen, but it seems highly likely that should any of those producers open new western mines in the interim, they will have a new-found incentive to keep such mines nonunion, non-UMWA, and, particularly, non-BCOA.

The 1981 strike also gave western BCOA miners cause to reflect on the virtue of National Agreement coverage when they were called upon to participate in a "National Agreement strike that they personally did not want" by their "strike-happy" colleagues in the East, leading at least some "to criticize not only miners in the East but also the coal operators' association." [23] Such rank-and-file criticism seems destined to have little effect on the existing extent of UMWA organization and BCOA membership in the West, but it may well have a profound impact on the UMWA's future in the organization and representation of miners in the West as the industry grows, in that the 1981 strike was, in the words of one western UMWA local union president, "a real setback to organizing anyone" because it again raised the question of "Why would anyone who wants steady work want to join an outfit like this?" [24]

---

[23] Ben A. Franklin, "Coal miners West and East: Same pact, contrary views," *New York Times,* April 13, 1981, p. 18.

[24] *Ibid.*

CHAPTER XI

The Conduct of Multiemployer Bargaining: War and Peace, 1933–1963

The roots of the existing system of multiemployer bargaining in the bituminous coal industry rest in the Appalachian agreements concluded by the UMWA in 1933-1934. The collapse of the Central Competitive Field Joint Conference system in 1927 ended an almost thirty-year era of multiemployer bargaining and began a six-year period of chaos in labor relations in the bituminous coal mining industry. During that six-year period, average hourly earnings in the industry fell from about $0.75 to $0.50.[1] More importantly, from a labor relations standpoint, "the percentage of the total tonnage to which union contracts applied in 1933 was less than 20 per cent instead of 72 per cent, the proportion for which the union negotiated contracts at the height of its power."[2] The dramatic decline in union strength which followed the demise of multiemployer bargaining in 1927 was abruptly halted and dramatically reversed in 1933 primarily as the result of the passage of the NIRA, which gave the government's blessing to both operators and miners in the search for relief from the pressure of ruinous competition. In the words of one scholarly student of the history of labor relations in the industry:

> The National Industrial Recovery Act of 1933 . . . was a boon to the United Mine Workers. Hundreds of organizers scurried through the coal fields to carry the news that the United States Government guaranteed all workers the right to join unions of their own choosing. Union membership grew by leaps and bounds, even in the

---

[1] Waldo E. Fisher, *Collective Bargaining in the Bituminous Coal Industry: An Appraisal* (Philadelphia: University of Pennsylvania Press, 1948), p. 28.

[2] *Ibid.*, p. 26.

strongest non-union citadels. In a surprisingly short time most of the coal fields were organized. After months of protracted negotiations, the miners' union, with the help of federal agencies, negotiated wage agreements for practically the entire industry.[3]

The Appalachian agreements concluded in 1933 and 1934 were not truly industrywide in coverage. They encompassed operators in Pennsylvania, Ohio, West Virginia, Virginia, northern Tennessee, western Maryland, and eastern Kentucky, which together accounted for more than 70 percent of total coal production.[4] Operators in Illinois and Indiana were no longer party to multi-employer bargaining, "but, like those of all other outlying districts, adjusted their terms of employment to those adopted by the Appalachian (Interstate) Conference."[5] In 1941, a second major group of operators withdrew from the Appalachian Agreement System when southern coal producers—those in Virginia, southern West Virginia, northern Tennessee, and eastern Kentucky—refused to accede to an agreement calling for elimination of the North-South wage differential in the industry and formed the Southern Coal Producers Association to conduct independent multiemployer negotiations with the UMWA. A third major group of operators—captive producers—also remained formally outside of the Appalachian Agreement System.

The Appalachian Agreement System lasted for seventeen years, until it gave way to the current National Agreement System in 1950. Those seventeen years generally can be characterized as a period of growing confrontation between an increasingly militant and autocratic union under the leadership of a highly opportunistic president—John L. Lewis—and an increasingly reluctant but fragmented and vulnerable management. This conflict culminated in a major confrontation in 1950. The aftermath of that "war" was a period of "peace" which lasted for thirteen years, through the end of the Lewis era, which formally ended in 1960 when he retired as president of the UMWA but actually ended in 1963 when his chosen successor and long-time associate, Thomas Kennedy, passed away and W. A. "Tony" Boyle assumed the presidency of the UMWA.

---

[3] *Ibid.,* pp. 26-27.

[4] *Ibid.,* p. 27.

[5] *Ibid.,* p. 27.

THE OLD ORDER: 1933-1950

The history of collective bargaining under the Appalachian Agreement System between 1933 and 1950 can be divided into three distinct eras. The first extends from 1933 through 1941, when the UMWA and industry were able to engage in "free collective bargaining," albeit under the watchful and concerned eye of the federal government. The second extends from 1942 through 1946, when, for all intents and purposes, it was the federal government that was the union's adversary in contract negotiations. The third began in 1947 with the return of the mines to private control and the parties to free collective bargaining, albeit, once again, under the watchful and concerned eye of the federal government. The common theme that characterizes all of these three collective bargaining eras is an obvious aversion on the part of the federal government to a coal strike and its proven impotence in precluding strike action by the UMWA.

The Early Years

The first of the Appalachian agreements was concluded in 1933, but it was not until 1934 that an Appalachian Agreement System came into being. The last formal "Appalachian Joint Wage Agreement" was concluded on June 19, 1941, to take effect from April 1, 1941, to March 31, 1943. Overall there were four Appalachian agreements during this period—in 1934, 1935, 1937, and 1941.[6]

The first three Appalachian agreements were concluded without incident. Those three agreements resulted in an increase of $1.40 per day in the pay of coal miners ($0.40 in 1934, $0.50 in 1935, and $0.50 in 1937). The 1934 agreement established a basic seven-hour workday in lieu of the eight-hour day that had existed at no loss of daily pay, and the 1937 agreement required premium pay of time and one-half for hours in excess of seven per day and thirty-five per week. The 1934 agreement also called for an additional $0.24 per day wage increase for miners in northern West Virginia to eliminate the wage differential between them and miners in the northern Appalachian area.

The coal mining industry, like the economy, suffered a slump in 1938 which reduced coal production from almost 450 million tons in 1937 to about 350 million tons in 1938. In the face of

---

[6] "Wage Chronology No. 4: Bituminous Coal Mines, 1933-48," *Monthly Labor Review*, Vol. 6, No. 9 (March 1949), p. 304.

that slump, no contractual changes were negotiated in 1938 or 1939, apparently to the displeasure of the union rank and file, as evidenced by the first of the strike actions which by 1950 were to grow to a record of one strike every eighteen months against one or another of the various employer groups with which the union bargained.

Industry production returned to 460 million tons by 1940 and, in 1941, exceeded 500 million tons for the first time since 1929.[7] That year also saw the renegotiation of the Appalachian Joint Wage Agreement to provide a $1.00 per day wage increase and to grant paid vacations of ten consecutive calendar days to all employees with one year or more of service with vacation pay set at $20.00. That agreement also called for an additional $0.40 per day wage increase for miners in the south—Maryland, Virginia, southern West Virginia, eastern Kentucky, and northern Tennessee—to eliminate an existing North-South differential.[8]

The War Years

The strategies employed and successes enjoyed by John L. Lewis in his confrontations with the federal government during World War II have already been discussed. Those strategies and successes provide ample evidence of the opportunistic character of John L. Lewis. They also provide eloquent testimony to the militancy and discipline of the union rank and file and the impotence of the government as an adversary to a strong and willful union at the bargaining table, even when endowed with the power of the most pressing public interest. The result of that impotence was a series of concessions to the union which remain to this day a basic part of the "web of rules" that govern terms and conditions of employment in bituminous coal mining.

The collective bargaining history during the war years began with a "supplemental six-day-week agreement" reached with the industry in January 1943 and the "Krug-Lewis" agreement concluded with the government in May 1946. In the intervening three years, three other agreements were negotiated by the union with the government (in April 1943, November 1943, and April 1945), two of which (the April 1943 and April 1945 agreements), like

---

[7] *1980 Keystone Coal Industry Manual* (New York: McGraw Hill, 1980), p. 690.

[8] "Wage Chronology No. 4," pp. 304-06.

the Krug-Lewis Agreement, were to become an integral element of the contractual legacy of labor relations in bituminous coal.

The supplemental six-day-week agreement of January 1943 authorized work on a sixth day to meet the demand for coal, which in that year approached 600 million tons, with such work to be compensated at premium rates. That agreement was followed in the spring of 1943, when the 1941 Appalachian Joint Wage Agreement expired, by a new agreement that left most wage rates unchanged but increased vacation pay from $20 to $50.[9] That agreement, in turn, was followed by another reached under the threat of a strike in November 1943 which introduced "portal-to-portal" pay to the industry and the nation. Under that agreement, workers were to be paid for forty-five minutes of travel time per day at two-thirds of their regular rate, with such travel time being included in the computation of hours worked for calculation of overtime.[10]

The April 1943 "National Wage Agreement" was replaced in April 1945 by a new National Bituminous Coal Wage Agreement, which again left basic wage rates largely unchanged but introduced shift differentials and increased vacation pay from $50 to $75.[11] In addition, that agreement called for paid lunch periods, and reinstituted premium pay for all hours in excess of seven per day and thirty-five per week. These concessions, coupled with those made in 1943, raised the average hourly earnings of coal miners to about $1.20 in 1945, as compared with about $0.90 in 1941.[12]

The National Bituminous Coal Wage Agreement of April 11, 1945, was followed by the Krug-Lewis Agreement of May 29, 1946. Under that agreement the government assented on behalf of all those mines in its possession as of March 31, 1946, to a wage increase of $1.85 per day, to an increase in vacation pay from $75 to $100, and to time and one-half for work on a sixth consecutive day.[13] It also agreed that "a Welfare and Retirement Fund [should be] created and there shall be paid into said fund by the operating managers 5 cents per ton produced for use or

---

[9] "Wage Chronology No. 4," p. 306.

[10] *Ibid.*, pp. 304, 305.

[11] *Ibid.*, p. 306.

[12] Fisher, *Collective Bargaining in the Bituminous Coal Industry*, p. 28.

[13] "Krug-Lewis Agreement" (mimeographed), p. 4.

for sale" and directed that "there shall be created a medical and
hospital fund ... to be accumulated from the wage deductions
presently being made." The welfare and retirement fund was to
be managed by the tripartite board of trustees; the medical and
hospital fund by "trustees appointed by the President of the
United Mine Workers." [14]

The Krug-Lewis Agreement contained two other, less well
known provisions which have lived on and become a source of
tension in industry labor relations. The first was a provision
that "an annual vacation period shall be the rule of the industry
... a vacation period during which coal production shall cease." [15]
The second was a commitment to a "mine safety program" involving a "general mine safety code" and a "mine safety committee." Specifically, that commitment was stated as follows:

> As soon as practicable and not later than 30 days from the date of
> the making of the agreement, the Director of the Bureau of Mines
> after consultation with representatives of the United Mine Workers
> and such other persons as he deems appropriate, will issue a reason-
> able code of standards and rules pertaining to safety conditions and
> practices in the mines. The coal mines administrator will put this
> code into effect at the mines. Inspectors of the Federal Bureau of
> Mines shall make periodic investigations of the mines and report to
> the Coal Mine Administrators any violations of the Federal Safety
> Code.

> At each mine there shall be a Mine Safety Committee selected by the
> Local Union. The Mine Safety Committee may inspect any mine
> development or equipment used in producing coal .... If the Com-
> mittee believes conditions found endanger the life and bodies of the
> mine workers it shall report its findings and recommendations to
> the management. In those special instances where the Committee
> believes an immediate danger exists and the committee recommends
> that the management remove all mine workers from the unsafe
> area, the operating manager or his managerial subordinate is re-
> quired to follow the recommendations of the Committee ....[16]

The Post-War Years

The government's seizure authority under the War Labor Disputes Act expired on June 30, 1947, on which date the operation
of bituminous coal mines was returned to private control just in
time for private operators to assume responsibility for negotiation of a new agreement to succeed the Krug-Lewis Agreement of

---

14 *Ibid.*, pp. 2-3.

15 *Ibid.*, p. 4.

16 *Ibid.*, pp. 1-2.

1946. Those negotiations pitted a union emboldened by an enviable record of success of flexing its economic muscles against a management embittered by its loss of control over its own labor relations destiny but facing what was to prove a record demand for some 630 million tons of coal in 1947. The result was an agreement reached peacefully, but not easily, in July 1947, which provided for an increase in wages of $1.20 per day and for a doubling of operator contributions to the welfare and retirement fund from $0.05 to $0.10 per ton of coal mined for use or sale.[17]

The three years following conclusion of the 1947 agreement were among the most tumultuous in the industry's long and turbulent collective bargaining history. The union aggressively and militantly sought to extend the wage-and-benefit fund gains won from the government during the war. In that crusade they encountered growing resistance from coal operators, who found themselves facing declining demand as coal production dropped below 500 million tons in 1948 and to below 450 million tons in 1949. The result was a series of strikes and slowdowns beginning in March 1948 and ending in March 1950.

The negotiations over a new national agreement to replace the 1947 agreement produced two confrontations between the union and the operators, both of which resulted in invocation of Taft-Hartley. The first confrontation occurred over the issue of pension benefits, the second over wage and royalty increases. The chronology of the first confrontation has been described as follows:

> The trouble started on December 17, 1947, when, during contract negotiations, Lewis asked for a pension of $100 per month for all miners reaching age 60 after 20 years of service. A month later, T.E. Murray, the neutral trustee for the Health and Retirement Fund, resigned over the pension issue. In March 1948, miners began leaving the pits to protest the operators' "dilatory tactics" during negotiations and, on March 23, the government secured a federal court injunction against the strike under the national emergency disputes provisions of the Taft-Hartley Act.[18]

The strike was ended not by the injunction but by a compromise on the pension issue proposed by the new neutral fund trustee and accepted by Lewis in April. Resolution of the pen-

---

[17] "Wage Chronology No. 4," pp. 304-06.

[18] William H. Miernyk, "Coal," in Gerald G. Somers, ed., *Collective Bargaining: Contemporary American Experience* (Madison, Wis.: Industrial Relations Research Association, 1980), p. 23.

sion issue did not bring peace to the industry as there was still
no agreement on a new national wage agreement. "Unrest continued in the coal fields, and the Taft-Hartley national emergency
disputes provision was invoked for the second time on June 19." [19]
Shortly thereafter, agreement was reached with commercial operators on a new one-year contract calling for a wage increase of
$1.00 per day and a doubling of royalty payments from $0.10 to
$0.20 per ton. Captive mines, however, remained closed until
mid-July, when they finally reached a separate agreement with
the UMWA.[20]

The 1948 agreement was to expire on June 30, 1949. In early
June, the UMWA called for a one-week work stoppage to alleviate the problem of overproduction. When no new agreement
was reached by June 30, the union ordered miners to work a
three-day week. Negotiations continued without notable progress
through the summer and into the fall. Sporadic work stoppages
began in September and by October had spread to encompass
most union mines and miners. In November, John L. Lewis ordered the miners back to work as negotiations continued. Those
negotiations bore fruit when "in December, the first pattern-
setting agreements were reached with several Kentucky and West
Virginia companies." [21]

Those early agreements did not quickly or easily set a pattern
for the three major producer groups—northern, southern, and
captive producers. Negotiations with those groups continued into
1950. On February 6, 1950, the union again struck the industry
and the government again invoked Taft-Hartley. On February
11, an injunction was issued against the strike which was "hon-
ored" by the union but not its members. On March 3, the president asked the congress for special legislation authorizing seizure
of the mines—legislation which was rendered unnecessary when
"several hours later, representatives of the two associations and
the captive coal operators reached an agreement with Lewis on
'fundamental principles' for a new contract." [22] Those principles
were embodied in the National Bituminous Coal Wage Agreement
of 1950, signed on March 5.

---

[19] *Ibid.,* p. 24.

[20] *Ibid.*

[21] *Ibid.,* p. 24.

[22] *Ibid.,* p. 25.

The 1950 National Agreement called for a wage increase of $0.70 per day, bringing to $4.75 per day the total wage increases negotiated by the union since expiration of its 1946 agreement with the government. The agreement also called for a further increase in royalty payments from $0.20 to $0.30 per ton, bringing to $0.25 the total royalty increases negotiated since the original Krug-Lewis Agreement. Overall, the UMWA's militancy and discipline in contract negotiations after the return of the mines to private control in 1947 netted an almost 65 percent increase in daily compensation costs, from about $10.30 ($10.00 in wages and $0.30 in royalties at a production rate of five tons per man per day) to $16.85 ($14.75 in wages and $2.10 in royalties at a production rate of seven tons per man per day).

The 1950 agreement carried forward and preserved "the terms and conditions of the Appalachian Joint Wage Agreement (dated June 19, 1941) effective April 1, 1941 to March 31, 1943 . . . , the National Bituminous Coal Wage Agreement (dated April 11, 1945) effective April 1, 1945, and all the various District Agreements executed between the United Mine Workers of America and the various Operators and Coal Associations . . . as they existed on March 31, 1946," [23] except as those agreements were specifically modified by the 1950 National Agreement. Most of the modifications made by the 1950 agreement simply recodified contractual changes negotiated in 1946, 1947, and 1948. There were, however, some more fundamental modifications of prior agreements mandated by the 1950 agreement, including the following:

> any provisions in District or Local Agreements providing for the levying, assessing or collecting of fines or providing for "no strike," "indemnity" or "guarantee" clauses or provisions are hereby expressly repealed . . . [and] . . . any and all provisions in either the Appalachian Joint Wage Agreement of June 19, 1941, or the National Bituminous Coal Wage Agreement of April 11, 1945, containing "no strike" or "Penalty" clause or clauses or any clause denominated "Illegal Suspension of Work" are hereby rescinded, cancelled, abrogated, and made null and void. [24]

The repeal of all no-strike pledges was accompanied by an agreement that any and all claims, demands, or actions growing out of "disputes, stoppages, suspensions of work" would be settled "exclusively by the machinery provided in . . . this Agree-

---

[23] National Bituminous Coal Wage Agreement of 1951, p. 1.

[24] *Ibid.*, pp. 7-8.

ment; or . . . by full use of free collective bargaining as hereto-
fore known and practiced in the industry." [25] The industry's *quid
pro quo* for abandoning its contractual and legal control over
wildcat strikes was a provision that:

> The United Mine Workers of America and the Operators signatory
> hereto affirm their intention to maintain the integrity of this con-
> tract and to exercise their best efforts through available disciplinary
> measures to prevent stoppages of work by strike or lockout pending
> adjustments or adjudication of disputes and grievances in the man-
> ner provided in this agreement.[26]

THE NEW ORDER: 1950-1963

The National Bituminous Coal Wage Agreement set the stage
for more than a decade of labor peace in the industry which was
notable in its own right and remarkable by contrast to the turbulent decade which preceded it. The industry, which had experienced strikes in contract negotiations on the average of once
every eighteen months in the previous thirteen years, was not to
experience a single such strike in the following thirteen years.
The only major job action taken by miners during that period
was their strike in 1952 to protest the Wage Stabilization Board
ruling on their negotiated wage increase. Otherwise, all was
quiet on the bituminous coal labor-relations front, as the UMWA
and BCOA peacefully negotiated a series of five amendments to
the 1950 agreement—1951, 1952, 1955, 1956, and 1958.

The serenity that suddenly descended on labor relations in
bituminous coal came at a time when the industry experienced
its second decade of long-term decline in the twentieth century,
the first having been the 1920s (see Table XI-1). The experience of the 1920s indicated that hard times and the return of
ruinous competition that they brought were not conducive to
serenity and stability in labor relations. The experience of the
1950s, however, defied that historical precedent in large part because of the unique power, prestige, and philosophy that John
L. Lewis brought to the bargaining table. That power, prestige,
and philosophy enabled the UMWA and BCOA in the 1950s to
substitute a "survival of the fittest" for the 1920s "shared misery"
solution to the problem of excess capacity and ruinous competition and thereby avoid or forestall the type of confrontation that
occurred in 1927 and led to the "disorganization" of the industry.

---

[25] *Ibid.*, p. 8.

[26] *Ibid.*

TABLE XI-1
The Decline of the Industry,
1920-1932 and 1950-1962

Production (million tons)		Employment (thousand men)		Mines (thousands)	
1920-32	1950-62	1920-32	1950-62	1920-32	1950-62
569	516	640	416	8.9	9.4
416	534	664	373	8.0	8.0
422	467	688	335	9.3	7.3
565	457	705	293	9.3	6.7
484	392	620	227	7.6	6.1
520	465	488	225	7.1	7.9
573	501	594	228	7.2	8.5
518	493	594	229	7.0	8.5
501	410	522	197	6.5	8.3
535	412	503	180	6.1	7.7
468	416	493	169	5.9	7.9
382	403	450	150	5.6	7.6
310	422	406	144	5.4	7.7

Source: *1980 Keystone Coal Industry Manual* (New York: McGraw Hill, 1980), p. 690.

The Peace Process

The five amendments to the 1950 agreement negotiated during the 1950s were the product of "two-man, rational bargaining" between John L. Lewis and Harry Moses. The process through which John L. Lewis acquired his personal prestige among miners and his political power over the decision-making mechanisms of the UMWA has already been described. The route by which Harry Moses, who had in 1950 served as the representative of captive producers in negotiations, acquired similar stature and authority within the BCOA is not a matter of public record.

The process through which agreements were worked out between Lewis and Moses took the form of private discussions and surprise agreements more suggestive of collusion than conflict. In form, at least, the UMWA-BCOA bargaining relationship during the 1950s indeed gave every appearance of "collusive" rather than "genuine" collective bargaining, particularly on the union side, as negotiations generally were conducted "secretly without the use of negotiating committees" with the membership

unaware of the negotiations until "after a settlement (deal?)
has been made" and unable to vote on the resulting agreement.[27]
The "two-man, rational" approach to bargaining did not en-
counter serious resistance within the union. The only apparent
internal problems arising out of this approach came in 1956 when
"a few delegates suggested (complained is too strong a word)
that the agreement might have included provision for shorter
hours" but did not press the point as "the agreement was accepted without a dissenting vote." [28] Those suggestions, however,
seem to have been sufficiently disquieting to prompt John L.
Lewis to defend the two-man, rational approach in the following
terms:

> For six years now there have been no major stoppages in the indus-
> try, and for an indefinite period into the future that will continue,
> providing the leaders of the industry on both sides continue to
> exercise that discretion and judgement which they have now ex-
> hibited that they possess.[29]

The problems encountered by Moses in dealing with his constituents in the context of two-man, rational bargaining are virtually unknown, but generally believed to have been nonexistent.
As has been indicated, that view may be simplistic given the
somewhat different interests and problems of captive and commercial producers, most notably with respect to the phenomenon
of nonunion competition particularly after the end of the Korean
War. Nonetheless, most BCOA members undoubtedly supported
the "BCOA executive" who in 1956 was reported to have "em-
phatically" denied the allegation that "the present method of
arriving at new contract terms could not be defined as negotiations" and to have lauded that method as a mechanism for reaching settlements without strikes or strike threats and establishing
a cooperative relationship in which the union could join with
management "without reservation in all overt efforts to combat
the influence of competitive fuels, government interference and
unreasonable safety regulations." [30]

---

27 Richmond A. Lester, *As Unions Mature* (Princeton, N.J.: Princeton
University Press, 1958), pp. 69-70, 102.

28 *Ibid.*, p. 102.

29 *Ibid.*, p. 102.

30 *Ibid.*, p. 70.

The Price of Peace

The substantive, as opposed to procedural, basis of the new order in labor relations in bituminous coal in the 1950s was a trade-off of wages by the industry for labor stability and productivity from the union. The union's wage policy in the 1950s, as it had been in the 1920s, was to resist wage reductions and pursue wage increases, despite declining demand and growing potential for nonunion competition. In exchange, it offered unionized producers freedom to mechanize (productivity) and promised them union protection against rank-and-file militancy (stability)—a tradeoff that at least the larger operators who controlled the BCOA found acceptable. The price they paid for wage increases totalled $9.50 per day between 1950 and 1963; the price the union paid was a drop in industry employment from 415,582 in 1950 to 141,646 by 1963.[31]

The five amendments to the 1950 National Agreement concluded during the 1950s were primarily wage settlements. The 1951 amendment raised daily wages by $1.60; the 1952 amendment, by $1.90; the 1955 amendment, by $2.00; the 1956 amendment, by $2.00; and the 1958 amendment, by $2.00. In addition, the 1952 agreement raised the royalty rate to $0.40 per ton and the 1955, 1956, and 1958 agreements liberalized vacations from ten to fourteen calendar days and increased vacation pay from $100 to $200. Excluding vacation pay, those five agreements produced an approximately 65 percent increase in the daily wage and a 75 percent increase in daily compensation cost between 1950 and 1960 (see Table XI-2).

The economic impact of the wage and royalty settlements of the 1950s on unionized producers is not difficult to estimate. Between 1950 and 1960, direct wage and royalty costs per ton of coal mined actually declined from about $2.50 to $2.30, accounting for about the same percentage (50) of the average price per ton of coal in 1960 as in 1950 (see Table XI-3). The fluctuations in the compensation cost/selling price ratio over the 1950s suggest some interesting historical analogies to the 1920s. The fairly sizable wage settlement in 1952, which raised the cost/price ratio to 0.58, seems analogous to the Jacksonville accord of 1924, which opened a substantial North-South/union-nonunion wage differential. The 1958 agreement which restored the cost/price ratio to its 1956 and 1954 level seems vaguely

---

[31] *1980 Keystone Coal Industry Manual*, p. 690.

TABLE XI-2
Daily Wages and Compensation,
1950-1960

Year	Wage [1]	Royalty [1]	Tons/Day [2]	Royalty/Day	Cost/Day
1950	14.75	.30	6.77	2.03	16.78
1951	16.35	.30	7.04	2.11	18.46
1952	18.25	.40	7.47	2.99	21.24
1953	18.25	.40	8.17	3.27	21.52
1954	18.25	.40	9.47	3.79	22.04
1955	19.45	.40	9.84	3.94	23.39
1956	21.45	.40	10.28	4.11	25.56
1957	22.25	.40	10.59	4.24	26.49
1958	24.25	.40	11.33	4.53	28.78
1959	24.25	.40	12.22	4.89	29.14
1960	24.25	.40	12.83	5.13	29.38
Change	9.50	.10	6.06	3.10	12.60
	(64.4%)	(33.3%)	(89.8%)	(152.7%)	(75.1%)

Sources: [1] Data in author's possession; [2] *Keystone Coal Industry Manual 1980*, p. 691.

TABLE XI-3
Compensation Costs Per Ton,
1950-1960

Year	Wage/Ton	Royalty/Ton	Cost/Ton	Price/Ton	Cost-Price
1950	2.18	.30	2.48	4.84	.51
1951	2.32	.30	2.62	4.92	.53
1952	2.44	.40	2.84	4.90	.58
1953	2.23	.40	2.63	4.92	.53
1954	1.93	.40	2.33	4.52	.52
1955	1.98	.40	2.38	4.50	.53
1956	2.09	.40	2.49	4.82	.52
1957	2.10	.40	2.50	5.08	.49
1958	2.14	.40	2.54	4.86	.52
1959	1.98	.40	2.38	4.77	.50
1960	1.89	.40	2.29	4.69	.49
Change	−.29	+.10	−.19	−.15	−.02
	(−13%)	(+33%)	(−8%)	(−3%)	(−4%)

Source: Data in author's possession; 1980 Keystone Coal Industry Manual, p. 690.

reminiscent of the union's unsuccessful battle to hold the line in 1927 in the face of growing nonunion competition. Both analogies are strengthened by the fact that the two agreements in question contained provisions obviously intended to inhibit nonunion operation and competition and were followed by a period of "wage restraint" of two years when the union did not take advantage of its option to terminate the agreement after one year.

The 1952 amendment to the 1950 agreement contained a number of noneconomic provisions, including the basic seniority system, which still governs employment rights in the industry, and a basic commitment to settle disputes and claims during the life of contracts "without recourse to the courts," which is still the union's norm for acceptable managerial behavior. More importantly, however, that agreement contained two provisions designed to preclude signatory operators from attempting to escape the union and its contractual requirements under the pressure of nonunion competition. The first required signatory operators to give "proper" monthly notice to the union that required payments for the prior month had been made to the welfare and retirement fund. The second required:

> As a part of the consideration for this Agreement, the Operators signatory hereto agree that this Agreement covers the operation of all of the coal lands owned or held under lease by them, or any of them, or by any subsidiary or affiliate at the date of this Agreement, or acquired during its term which may hereafter (during the term of this agreement) be put into production. The said operators agree that they will not lease out any coal lands as a subterfuge for the purpose of avoiding the application of this Agreement.[32]

The "non-escape" language of the 1952 amendment was greatly elaborated in the Protective Wage Clause of the 1958 amendment. A Joint Industry Contract Committee, empowered to appoint Joint District Contract committees, was established to enforce the Protective Wage Clause, with each signatory operator required to certify in writing to such industry or district committee every six months "that he is in full compliance with all the terms and conditions of this contract," and each union district president was required to certify in writing to such industry or district committee every six months "a complete list of Operators and Mines engaged in the production of bituminous

---

[32] National Bituminous Coal Wage Agreement of 1950, as Amended September 29th, 1952 (mimeographed), pp. 5-6.

coal within his district whose operations are under contract with the Union." [33]

The 1958 amendment was negotiated as the industry entered a "cyclical slump" which saw coal production drop from 500 million tons in 1956 and 1957 to 400 million tons in 1958. Coal production basically continued at that depressed level for the next four years before it began to rebound in 1963. Interestingly, that period saw no further amendments to the 1950 agreements—a period of wage restraint rivaled only by that of 1927-1933 when the union was not a powerful factor in the industry. The reasons why the union decided to forego its contract termination option from November 30, 1959, until November 1963 are numerous and must include the retirement of John L. Lewis and the poor health of his successor. They must also include, however, the same real or feared resurgence of nonunion competition from smaller producers not burdened by union wage scales and royalty payments which prompted the protective wage clause and a more basic concern for the financial health of the unionized sector of the industry.[34]

The five years of wage restraint that followed the 1958 agreement obviously produced no increases in the basic daily wage from its average of $24.25 or in the basic per ton royalty from its level of $0.40. Increasing productivity, however, increased daily average compensation costs from $29.38 in 1960 to $30.58 in 1963—a 4 percent increase. That same increase in productivity also reduced average wage and royalty costs per ton of coal mined from $2.30 in 1960 to $1.95 in 1963—a drop of 15 percent. As a result, compensation (wage and royalty) cost per ton fell from about 50 percent of average selling price to under 45 percent of average selling price per ton over the period, despite the fact that average selling price fell from $4.69 per ton in 1960 to $4.39 per ton in 1963.[35]

At the risk of overdoing historical analogy, it seems that the UMWA, at the end of the Lewis era in 1963, was not in much different condition than it was in 1933 when it entered the "modern" Lewis era. Nonunion competition and declining de-

[33] National Bituminous Coal Wage Agreement of 1950 as Amended Effective December 1, 1958 (mimeographed), p. 6.

[34] *Wall Street Journal*, August 30, 1963, p. 18.

[35] *1980 Keystone Coal Industry Manual*, p. 690.

mand for coal in the late 1950s and early 1960s, as in the late 1920s and early 1930s, once again seemingly constituted a formidable challenge to the union and imposed severe constraints on its wage bargains. In terms of its working membership, the union once again had been reduced to a shadow of its former self. In terms of its bargaining presence, however, it had not, as it still controlled about 80 percent of all bituminous coal production in the United States in 1962 as compared with only 20 percent in 1932.

CHAPTER XII

The Conduct of Multiemployer Bargaining: The Gathering Storm, 1963 – 1976

The twelve years of labor peace (1951-1963) which followed the historic National Bituminous Coal Wage Agreement of 1950 and carried the industry through the end of the Lewis/Kennedy era was followed by a twelve-year period (1963-1975) of growing turbulence in labor relations which carried the industry through the Boyle era and over the threshold of the Miller era. This latter period generally was characterized by growing membership militancy and shrinking leadership control on the union side, and growing tension and tendency toward confrontation on the industry side. With respect to all but the trend of leadership control, the 1963-1975 period bears a strong resemblance to the 1937-1949 period in industry labor relations, in that both were marked by growing militancy and conflict and that both culminated in a major union-management confrontation out of which came an "historic" agreement.

The "gathering storm" between the industry's two world wars actually came in two stages. The first was between 1963 and 1969 when W. A. Boyle was in control of the UMWA, at least outwardly, and most membership militancy was directed internally against that control rather than externally against the industry. The second began after the conclusion of the 1968 negotiations when formal, organized political opposition to Boyle emerged within the UMWA, and ended with the triumph of that opposition and the negotiations of its first national agreement in late 1974.

THE 1960s

The dramatic downward trend in coal production during the 1950s was halted and replaced by gradual growth in the 1960s. The gradual growth in production, however, was not sufficient to halt the downward trend in numbers of men employed or in mines operating which characterized the 1950s Furthermore, the increase in the demand for coal, which accounted for the increase in production, was not strong enough to produce an upward trend in coal price. Thus, for the industry, times were better but still tough, as was the case for unionized operators as nonunion operators were able to hold their market share over the decade.

Just as the renewed growth of coal production brought no appreciable improvement in the economic fortunes and outlook of unionized operators, the new leadership of the union brought no appreciable change in the politics and policies of the UMWA. Tony Boyle attempted to "entrench himself in the leadership of the union, exploiting the undemocratic practices that had been defined by Lewis," but with less than Lewis's remarkable success.[1] Boyle also sought to continue the system of rational bargaining instituted by Lewis, again with less than Lewis's remarkable success. Finally, Boyle also continued to pursue Lewis's defensive strategy of "hold[ing] on to your existing operators" in dealing with the problem of nonunion competition rather than attempting an active and extensive campaign to organize nonunion mines.

The 1964 and 1966 Negotiations

The grass roots militancy of miners long controlled or stifled by John L. Lewis manifested itself once again at the outset of the presidency of Tony Boyle. In late 1963, a delegation of miners appeared in Washington to press the national union to exercise its contractual option to initiate negotiations over modification to the existing (1958) agreement—an option the union had possessed, but chosen not to exercise, since November 30, 1959. Tony Boyle heeded that call to seek improvements in the existing contract and negotiations opened with the BCOA in December 1963 over a new amendment to the National Bituminous Coal Wage Agreement of 1950. Those negotiations resulted in a new contract reached peaceably, which was signed on March 23, 1964, and provided for "gains in wages and supplemental benefits for some 80,000 miners."[2]

---

[1] Arnold R. Weber and Daniel J. B. Mitchell, *The Pay Board's Progress* (Washington, D.C.: The Brookings Institution, 1978), p. 141.

[2] "Wage Chronology: Bituminous Coal Mines, Supplement No. 6," *Monthly Labor Review*, Vol. 88, No. 4 (April 1965), p. 425.

The terms of that agreement were approved by the UMWA National Wage Policy Committee but "were protested by some workers in a series of sporadic wildcat strikes, but by mid April, almost all miners had returned to work." [3] Specifically, on March 25, two days after the agreement was signed, some 18,000 miners in six states were reported to have gone on strike to express their "dissatisfaction with the agreement approved on March 23." [4] That strike lasted approximately eighteen days and did not result in any change in the negotiated agreement.

The 1964 agreement was a two-year contract that could not be amended before March 31, 1966—a first for the industry. The UMWA did exercise its option to negotiate a new agreement in 1966. Those negotiations resulted in a new thirty-month contract reached peaceably and signed on April 8, 1966. That agreement called for a wage increase for skilled workers to take effect in 1966 and a general wage increase to take effect in 1967.

At that point, the 1964 scenario was repeated, but with one symbolically significant difference. On April 11, some 40,000 miners walked out to protest the agreement. That walkout lasted for approximately sixteen days and resulted in a renegotiation/rearrangement of the agreement to the distinct economic advantage of miners. Specifically, under the pressure of extensive wildcat strike action, the UMWA was compelled to seek, and the BCOA to accept, immediate skilled and general wage increases effective April 1, 1966. [5]

The 1968 Negotiations

The reemerging grass roots militancy manifested in 1964 and 1966 escalated significantly in 1968 as a result of three developments. First, economic conditions in general and in the industry were sufficiently good to raise the expectations of miners. Second, the work force of the industry was experiencing an influx of younger workers less awed by the union's historical accomplishments and more interested in its ability to deliver now. Third, the growing public and governmental concern over occupational safety and health in general and coal mining in particular

---

[3] *Ibid.*

[4] U.S. Department of Labor, Bureau of Labor Statistics, "Collective Bargaining in the Bituminous Coal Industry," Report 514 (November 1977), pp. 8-9.

[5] *Ibid.*, p. 9.

created a new focus for member expectations in an area that historically had been one of cooperation rather than confrontation in union-management relations.

The growing expectations of mine workers were not matched by a growing sense of affluence on the part of mine operators, who could not yet see the light at the end of the industry's tunnel. Although coal production was growing, excess capacity was still a problem, as is suggested by the continuing downward trend in the number of operating mines. Nonunion competition and competition from other energy sources also remained a problem, as is suggested by the fact that despite growing demand and shrinking capacity the average price per ton of coal in 1967 was about what it had been in 1960. Thus, by the time the 1966 agreement expired in the fall of 1968, the stage seemed set for a possible union-management confrontation.

Both the UMWA and the BCOA had no desire to see their now enviable record of labor peace brought to an end in their 1968 negotiations. Nonetheless, they were unable to reach an agreement by the time the existing contract expired on October 8, 1968, at which point the union would have been honor bound by its tradition of "no contract-no work" to call a strike. The UMWA, however, was spared the onus of such a strike by its own membership, which began to walk out when no agreement had been reached by October 1.[6] That "unauthorized" strike action eventually spread to involve approximately 65,000 miners and ultimately lasted for about one month, despite the fact that a new agreement was formally reached on October 14—an agreement subsequently valued at $2.48 per hour or 41 percent over its three-year term.[7]

The turbulence that surrounded the 1968 contract negotiations, unlike that in the 1964 and 1966 contract negotiations, did not subside when a new agreement was finally in place. The term of the 1968 agreement was marked by a "rash" of unauthorized strike activity over a wide range of issues. The problem actually began in January 1968 when some 60,000 miners in five states walked out to protest "arrests of pickets by state police at a newly certified mine in Pennsylvania," prior to the unauthorized October strike involving 66,000 miners which, in turn, was followed by another unauthorized strike involving 45,800 miners in

---

[6] "Developments in Industrial Relations," *Monthly Labor Review*, Vol. 91, No. 12 (December 1968), p. 55.

[7] Weber and Mitchell, *The Pay Board's Progress*, p. 149.

February 1969 over improved "black lung" legislation, and then by a walkout involving 54,000 miners in June 1971 to protest a federal court order directing Tony Boyle to step down as a trustee of the welfare and retirement funds.[8] Overall, including the October walkout, unauthorized strikes cost the industry approximately 2.45 percent of its total working time in the 1968-1970 period as compared with less than 1.0 percent in the preceding five years.

The Legacy of the 1960s

The UMWA under the leadership of Tony Boyle in the 1960s served more as a mediator than as a negotiator in the relations between mine workers and mine operators. Institutionally, it is difficult for even the most charismatic of labor leaders to play such a statesmanlike role for any length of time, as John L. Lewis might well have discovered had his tenure in office extended another decade, and virtually impossible for the "unannointed" labor leader to play, as Tony Boyle increasingly learned during his first six years in office. The price paid by Tony Boyle for this lesson was the emergence of open opposition to his reelection as president of the UMWA in 1969—opposition that ultimately was to oust him from office. The price the industry paid for that lesson during the 1960s, however, was relatively minor in terms of both time lost and concessions made.

The three agreements negotiated by the UMWA during the 1960s raised the basic daily wage of miners from $24.25 to $34.25, with $7 of that $10 per day basic wage increase coming as a result of the 1968 agreement. Those three agreements also raised vacation pay from $200 to ten-days' pay ($342.50). In exchange for these wage concessions, the BCOA extracted concessions on work rules/schedules, including the right to load previously mined coal on Sundays, to assign helpers to serve as operators of continuous mining machines, and to stagger vacations so as to operate mines without interruption. Perhaps the most significant concession or nonconcession won by the BCOA during the 1960s was no change in the basic per-ton royalty payment to the welfare and retirement funds, which stood at $0.40 in 1971 as it had in 1961.

The relatively large wage settlement ($7 per day) negotiated in 1968 enabled miners to more than keep pace with steel workers

---

[8] "Collective Bargaining in the Bituminous Coal Industry," pp. 10-11.

between 1960 and 1971, but it also brought the first wage-per-ton cost increases of the decade. This was due not only to the size of that wage settlement but also to the slowing and eventual halting of productivity growth (see Table XII-1). The fact that the trend of wage costs per ton, consistently declining

TABLE XII-1
Wage and Royalty Costs,
1960-1970

	Wage (Day)	Tons (Day)	Wage (Ton)	Royalty (Ton)	Cost (Ton)	Royalty (Day)	Compensation (Day)
1960	24.25	12.83	1.89	40	2.29	5.13	29.38
1961	24.25	13.87	1.75	40	2.15	5.55	29.80
1962	24.25	14.72	1.65	40	2.05	5.89	30.14
1963	24.25	15.83	1.53	40	1.93	6.33	30.58
1964	25.25	16.84	1.50	40	1.90	6.73	31.98
1965	26.25	17.52	1.50	40	1.90	7.01	33.26
1966	27.25	18.52	1.47	40	1.87	7.41	34.66
1967	27.25	19.17	1.42	40	1.82	7.67	34.92
1968	30.25	19.37	1.56	40	1.96	7.75	38.00
1969	32.25	19.90	1.58	40	1.98	7.96	40.21
1970	34.25	18.84	1.82	40	2.22	7.54	41.79

Source: Data in author's possession.

since 1958, reversed in 1968, marks the 1968 agreement as an institutional and economic turning point in the UMWA-BCOA relationship—one to be compounded by the subsequent passage of the Federal Coal Mine Health and Safety Act of 1969. In short, the 1968 agreement, in retrospect, constituted the first in what has proven to be a series of victories for rank-and-file militancy over leadership restraint and industry resistance.

The wage-cost problems for the industry that resulted from the 1968 agreement were matched by benefit-cost problems for the union resulting from the continuation of the $0.40 royalty rate—problems that had occurred once before, exactly ten years earlier. The royalty rate was first set at $0.40 in 1952, and left unchanged in the following three contracts—1955, 1956, and 1958. Over that period, royalty and investment income generally was sufficient to cover fund expenditures and to permit the growth of fund reserves from $100 million to $145 million (see Table XII-2). The sharp decline in coal production that began in 1958 and continued through 1961 produced an equally sharp drop in royalty income, with no offsetting decline in expenditures. The result was three years of deficit operation that reduced the fund surplus to $100 million and forced the trustees to reduce pension benefits from $100 to $70 effective in 1961.[9]

The gradual growth in coal production that began in 1962 coupled with the benefit reductions made in 1961 restored the solvency of fund opeartions and permitted restoration of a $100 pension in 1965, at which time the retirement age was lowered from sixty-two to fifty-five. The result was a dramatic increase of from $60 to $95 million in pension expenditures between 1965 and 1968 (see Table XII-2). Despite that increase, the funds continued to operate in the black and by 1968 showed a surplus of $180 million. That surplus, coupled with internal union politi-

TABLE XII-2

Welfare and Retirement Fund Income and Expenditures,
1952-1971
(millions of dollars)

Year	Income		Expenditures			Reserve
	Royalty	Total	Pension	Medical	Total	
1952	125.7	126.5	51.8	59.3	126.4	99.5
1953	129.7	131.5	58.9	65.6	139.0	92.0
1954	132.4	134.9	64.1	57.5	133.3	93.6
1955	127.9	129.2	69.9	42.8	119.1	103.6
1956	152.9	154.2	73.2	47.5	127.7	130.2
1957	155.3	157.1	75.0	59.6	141.9	145.3
1958	138.3	143.1	76.7	58.1	142.6	145.8
1959	131.0	132.9	78.3	57.8	144.2	134.5
1960	127.6	130.1	79.0	61.2	148.3	116.3
1961	114.5	116.7	70.0	55.0	133.1	99.8
1962	123.6	124.1	60.1	50.6	118.2	105.8
1963	123.2	124.1	59.6	50.5	117.7	113.1
1964	133.5	135.9	58.7	52.2	118.8	114.0
1965	142.6	145.1	62.1	48.8	118.9	140.2
1966	146.5	148.1	82.1	52.8	143.4	145.0
1967	159.8	164.2	85.7	45.5	139.9	169.3
1968	163.1	167.8	96.7	50.2	156.9	180.1
1969	157.5	163.2	96.0	55.1	163.8	179.5
1970	166.7	174.2	123.1	65.6	202.7	151.1
1971	174.7	181.8	121.6	83.2	220.0	112.9

Source: Annual Reports, UMWA Welfare and Retirement Fund.

9 "Wage Chronology: Bituminous Coal Mines, Supplement No. 6," p. 425.

cal pressures, led to a further liberalization of pension ($150) and medical benefits as a by-product of the 1968 negotiations. The result was a sharp increase in benefit expenditures—one that this time so exceeded the growth of royalty income that by 1971 fund reserves had declined to $113 million.

The final noteworthy facet of the agreements negotiated in the 1960s is the fact that those agreements put into place the "union security" provisions that were to prove so troublesome in 1981. As has been noted, the 1964 agreement initiated the royalty penalty on nonunion coal acquired for use or sale. The 1966 agreement asserted the jurisdiction of the union over all hauling work in or about the mine, and the 1968 agreement extended such work jurisdiction claims to repair and maintenance work and to construction of mine and mine-related facilities.

The final labor relations legacy of the 1960s was the return of labor instability (wildcat strikes) to the industry. The combination of union discipline and royalty incentives, which had been instrumental in promoting labor stability between 1950 and 1965, seemingly lost its power to maintain that stability during the latter years of the 1960s. The fact that the 1968 agreement instituted a "Christmas bonus" of $120 less $10 for "each calendar month during the immediately preceding December 1 through November 30 period in which the employee failed to work all the days he was scheduled to work that month unless his failure to work was due to good cause," also apparently had little effect in promoting labor stability during the late 1960s.

THE EARLY 1970s

No labor relations system or union-management relationship is immune to shock waves from external events, but few such systems or relationships have had to face the array of shock waves felt by the coal industry and the UMWA and BCOA in the early 1970s. The first shock came from passage of the Coal Mine Health and Safety Act of 1969 and its role in halting and reversing the favorable productivity trend that had played such an important part in facilitating the economic gains of the union. The second shock came from the imposition of controls in 1971, the timing of which, as has been indicated, could not have been worse from the standpoint of the UMWA and BCOA in terms of their 1971 negotiations. The third shock came from a federal court ruling in 1972 invalidating the UMWA's 1969 presidential election and ordering a new election—an election that produced a whole new and inexperienced union leadership to conduct the UMWA's 1974 negotiations. The final shock came from the oil embargo of 1973 and subsequent announcement of "Operation Independence" promising the industry a glowing future as it entered its 1974 negotiations.

All these external events, important as they were in the course of the UMWA-BCOA bargaining relationship during the early 1970s, did not alter or overwhelm two basic facts of life in industry labor relations. The first was the rising expectations and growing militancy of the UMWA rank and file—expectations and militancy that the 1968 negotiations had shown even the autocratic and entrenched leadership of Tony Boyle could not significatly curb or control. In that context, the election of Arnold Miller to the UMWA presidency and the democratization of the UMWA and its negotiation procedures may have been more symbolic than substantive in their implications for the industry in its 1974 negotiations. The second was the continuing unwillingness or inability of the BCOA under the control of its commercial mine members to undertake a true test of economic power with the UMWA in order to impose some semblance of the economic discipline on the substantive results of negotiations that the UMWA had provided prior to 1968.

The 1971 Negotiations

The procedural difficulties encountered by the UMWA and the BCOA—which were primarily but not necessarily exclusively owing to the imposition of controls—in reaching an agreement in their 1971 negotiations have already been discussed and need not be elaborated further. Procedurally, the most salient result of those negotiations was the fact that they involved the first authorized strike in contract negotiations by the UMWA against the BCOA since 1950. While it is easy to attribute that strike to the complications of controls, it is also possible that such a strike might well have occurred without controls. The UMWA and BCOA had been unable to reach agreement on a timely basis on their 1968 40 percent settlement and might well again have been unable to do so on another 40 percent settlement in 1971 even without controls, particularly since that settlement involved substantial labor-cost increases—only part of which the industry ultimately was permitted to pass through to consumers.

The 1971 agreement increased the basic daily wage of miners by $8.00 to $42.25 over its three-year term. That increase coincided with the first time in twenty years that there was no real prospect of offsetting productivity gains to maintain the industry's record of relatively stable per-ton wage costs. The 1971 agreement also increased the basic royalty rate from $0.40 to $0.80 and the penalty royalty rate from $0.80 to $1.20 over its term. That increase, of course, is a direct addition to per-ton production costs, independent of productivity—the very reason the industry and union avoided such increases in the late 1950s and early 1960s in the face of nonunion competition, which by 1960 and through the 1970s accounted for some 30 percent of bituminous coal production.

The 1971 wage agreement involved a significant break with union tradition with respect to wage structure. All previous amendments to the 1950 wage agreements had called for straight dollar-per-day increases to be added to rates in effect in 1950. The 1971 agreement halted that practice by recognizing six labor grades and providing different wage increases for each, thereby halting the twenty-year history of wage compression in the industry (see Table XII-3). The agreement also provided for wage differentials by labor grade between underground and surface mines (Table XII-3).

The parties also "agreed" in 1971 to some changes to be made in the benefits provided by the welfare and retirement fund. Top

TABLE XII-3
Wage Rates by Labor Grade,
Underground and Surface Mines,
1970-1973
(per day)

Labor Grade	Underground				Surface			
	1970	1971	1972	1973	1970	1971	1972	1973
1	34.25	37.00	39.75	42.25	33.85	31.35	38.85	41.25
2	34.50	37.25	40.00	42.75	34.00	36.50	39.00	41.50
3	34.50	37.45	40.45	43.25	34.50	37.00	39.50	42.00
4	35.75	38.75	41.75	44.75	34.90	37.90	40.90	43.75
5	36.75	40.25	43.75	47.25	35.50	39.00	42.50	46.00
6	37.25	41.50	45.75	50.00	38.00	42.00	46.00	50.00

Source: National Bituminous Coal Wage Agreement of 1971, pp. 61-62; Data in author's possession.

priority was to be given to institution of a sick leave plan and a long-term disability plan. Secondary priority was to be given to altering pension benefits from a flat $150 per month after twenty years of service to benefits ranging from a maximum of $225 per month at age sixty-five after thirty years of service to a minimum of $112.50 per month at age fifty-five after ten years of service.

The 1974 Negotiations

The 1974 UMWA-BCOA negotiations took place against a background of rising production and record prices in the coal industry, with the prospect of more of the same in the future under "Operation Independence." The affluent state and prospects of the industry were matched by an equally rich set of expectations on the part of the union rank and file. The *Monthly Labor Review* characterized the situation in 1974 as follows:

> Mine workers expected their new leadership to negotiate a big settlement with the Bituminous Coal Operators Association in 1974 because of high profits of coal companies and the increased importance of coal as a source of fuel in an economy in which energy demand threatened to exceed supply. Workers' expectations took on a new dimension in 1974, because, for the first time in 50 years, any agreement the union negotiated would have to be approved by a rank-and-file vote.[10]

In 1974, the BCOA had to confront more than simply high rank-and-file expectations. It also had to deal with a whole new set of expectations in the area of health and safety. Thus, in addition to demands for a substantial wage increase, cost-of-living escalation, increased royalty payments, and paid sick leave, the industry for the first time in recent history faced an extensive list of safety demands—demands that accounted for more than one-fifth of the UMWA's initial proposals and included, among other things, "full-time helpers on dangerous machinery, a company-paid safety committeeman of the union's choice, access to mines by union safety inspectors, safety education and training for new miners, and changes in the 'imminent danger' provision. . . ."[11]

The 1971 contract expired on November 12, 1974. As had been the case in 1968 and 1971, the parties were unable to reach

---

[10] "Labor and the Economy in 1974," *Monthly Labor Review*, Vol. 98, No. 1 (January 1975), p. 11.

[11] *Ibid.*, p. 11.

an agreement prior to expiration and a strike began involving some 130,000 UMWA miners. One day later, a tentative agreement was reached on a new three-year contract. Prior to 1974, that agreement would have required only the approval of the UMWA National Scale and Policy Committee to become final—a committee which "during the tenure of Lewis and Boyle . . . was not likely to include a substantial number of members whose views differed from their own." [12] Under the UMWA's new "democratic" procedures, however, to become final that agreement needed the approval first of its newly created Bargaining Council and then that of the affected rank and file. The Bargaining Council was composed of the top officers of the international union and the elected district presidents and executive board members from the eighteen districts with BCOA mines—a group guaranteed to have views of their own and to be more sensitive to their own constituents than to the international union leadership. That indeed proved to be the case in 1974 when the Bargaining Council rejected the November 13 agreement by a vote of thirty-seven to one.

At the request of the Bargaining Council, President Miller sought to reopen negotiations with the BCOA. The BCOA initially refused but later relented with the encouragement of the government. Negotiations resumed on November 23 and a second tentative agreement was reached on November 24 with the assistance of the director of the FMCS and the encouragement of the secretary of the treasury, who met with the members of the BCOA's bargaining committee—assistance and encouragement that "reflected the Administration's increasing concern over the economic impact of the walkout." [13] When that agreement was submitted to the Bargaining Council, it too was voted down, prompting President Miller to threaten to bypass the council and seek ratification by the membership without council approval of the agreement. Under that threat, the council reluctantly approved the November 24 agreement by a twenty-two to fifteen vote. Finally, on December 5, the UMWA announced membership ratification of a new contract by a vote of 44,700 to 34,700 (56 percent to 44 percent).

---

[12] William H. Miernyk, "Coal" in Gerald G. Somers, ed., *Collective Bargaining: Contemporary American Experience* (Madison, Wis.: Industrial Relations Research Association, 1980), p. 35.

[13] "Developments in Industrial Relations," *Monthly Labor Review*, Vol. 98, No. 1 (January 1975), p. 82.

The problems encountered by the UMWA and BCOA in bringing their 1974 contract negotiations to a conclusion did not end with membership ratification. As had been the case in 1968, the 1974 agreement was followed by a dramatic increase in wildcat strike activity. The number of man-days lost due to strikes in the bituminous coal industry, which had been running at about 1.5 percent of working time in 1972 and 1973, rose to 3.0 percent in 1975 and 3.7 percent in 1976.[14] BCOA mines which had lost less than three days per 100 man-days available in 1972 and 1973 due to unauthorized strikes saw that figure rise to six days in 1975, seven days in 1976, and ten days in the first eight months of 1977.[15]

The specific causes of the some 9,000 wildcat strikes that occurred in the industry between 1974 and 1977 were as varied as the strikes were numerous. Among the causes cited, directly or indirectly, were dissatisfaction with the leadership of the union, the new grievance procedure, the gasoline shortage, and the legal and contractual limitations on the right to strike. The consequences of those strikes were serious for both the UMWA and the BCOA. On the union side, the rash of wildcat strikes had a sufficiently adverse effect on employer royalty payments by early 1977 to force the funds' trustees to curtail welfare benefits and impose a deductible on medical benefits, an action that sparked yet another large-scale walkout, which further exacerbated the problem. On the industry side, the rash of strikes had serious adverse effects, not only on production but on productivity and profitability, effects that stemmed from the capital-intensive character of most BCOA mines and were made more painful by growing non-UMWA competition in a coal market whose growth fell short of the projections and expectations of 1974.

The final 1974 economic settlement was consistent with the pattern set by the previous two contracts. The agreement called for general wage increases of 10, 4, and 3 percent (the first agreement had called for increases of 9, 3, and 2 percent), provided for the first-time COLA at $0.01 for each 0.4 point change in the CPI capped at $0.98 over the life of the contract, and granted improvements in overtime and shift premiums. Overall,

---

[14] "Collective Bargaining in the Bituminous Coal Industry," p. 5.

[15] Bituminous Coal Operators' Association, "Will the United Mine Workers of America Play a Major Role in Coal's Future?" (Washington, D.C.: Bituminous Coal Operators' Association, 1977), p. 6.

these wage gains were estimated by the Council on Wage and
Price Stability to total 35 percent over three years.[16] The contract also provided for increased royalty payments and various
other benefit improvements, which brought the total estimated
cost of the package to over 45 percent over the life of the
contract.

The 1974 agreement provided for some fundamental changes
in the welfare and pension fund system. First, the existing fund
was restructured into four separate funds: (1) the 1950 pension
trust, (2) the 1950 benefit trust, (3) the 1974 pension trust, and
(4) the 1974 benefit trust. Second, funding of the 1974 trusts
was primarily based on royalties computed by hours worked
rather than tons produced—a change which benefitted surface
mine operators with their superior productivity. Specifically, the
royalty rates for the four trusts as of the final year of the contract were set as follows: (1) the 1950 pension trust—$0.554
per ton; (2) the 1950 benefit trust—$0.19 per ton; (3) the 1974
pension trust—$0.076 per ton plus $0.66 per hour; (4) the 1974
benefit trust—$0.88 per hour. Royalties on nonunion coal ac-
quired for use or sale were set at $0.554, $0.19, $0.389 and
$0.417, respectively, representing a total of 1.55 per ton as com-
pared with $0.80 under the 1971 agreement.

The agreement also called for some new and improved benefits. One of the more interesting was a one-time $80 "cost-of-
living catch-up allowance" to be paid on the payday just before
Christmas in 1974. More prosaic was the granting of five days
of paid sick/personal leave and the addition of sickness and
accident benefits as called for in the parties' 1971 joint memorandum to the fund trustees. Pension benefits for those already
retired or retiring before January 1, 1976, were raised from
$150 to $225 per month for those receiving black lung benefits
and $250 per month for those not receiving such benefits. Pen-
sions for those retiring after January 1, 1976, were to be based
on a dollar per month per year of service formula, which for
1977 retirees called for $12.50 per month for the first ten years
of service, $13.00 per month for the second ten years, $13.50 for
the third ten years, and $14.00 for each year of service after
thirty. As before, minimum eligibility for retirement was age 55
with ten years of service.

---

[16] "An Analysis of the Coal Settlement," *Council on Wage and Price
Stability News Release*, June 1, 1978, p. 2.

The 1974 contract made three noteworthy changes in the non-economic area. In the health and safety area, the contract "gives individual miners the right to leave worksites they consider dangerous, and union safety officials are guaranteed access to mines for inspections." [17] In the safety/manning area, the contract called for the "addition of two helpers on most continuous mining machines," a provision "which was expected to increase employment by 7,000." [18] Several changes were also made in the grievance/appeals procedure for the "settlement of disputes," including the elimination of one of the four steps prior to arbitration. The contract also added a new post-arbitration step, however, in the form of a trilateral "arbitration review board" to which "either party to an arbitration, upon receiving a final award by a panel arbitrator may petition . . . to appeal the decision" on one or more of the following grounds: [19]

> (i) That the decision of the panel arbitrator is in conflict with one or more decisions of the same issue of contract interpretation by other panel arbitrators.

> (ii) That the decision involves a question of contract interpretation which has not previously been decided by the Board and which in the opinion of the Board involves the interpretation of a substantial contractual issue.

> (iii) That the decision is arbitrary and capricious, or fraudulent, and therefore, must be set aside.

The "new" grievance procedure put into place in 1974 is one of the reputed "causes" of the labor relations problems which beset the UMWA and BCOA during the term of that contract.[20] As has been indicated, those problems may have been as much or more the product of personnel, politics, policies, and personalities as procedures. Nonetheless, the UMWA-BCOA grievance procedures are complex and at least potentially cumbersome, as can be judged from a diagram of those procedures provided for the President's Commission on Coal (see Figure XII-1).

---

[17] "Labor and the Economy in 1974," *Monthly Labor Review* (January 1975) p. 11.

[18] "Developments in Industrial Relations," p. 83.

[19] BCOA, "Will the United Mine Workers of America," p. 9.

[20] For a description of the underlying premise and operational problems of the Arbitration Review Board, see Robert C. Benedict, "Industrial Relations in the Coal Industry: The UMW Perspective on Industrial Relations," *Labor Law Journal*, Vol. 32, No. 8 (August 1981), pp. 561-63.

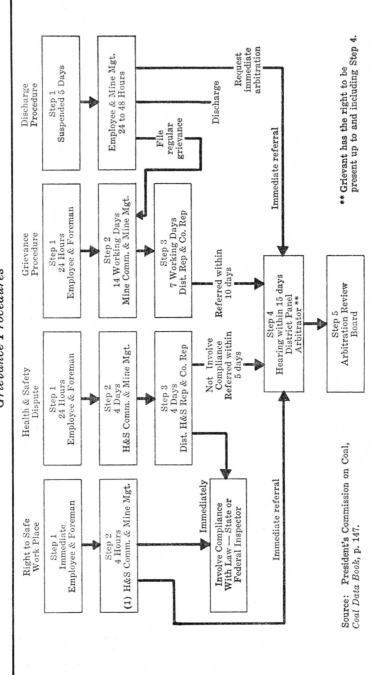

FIGURE XII-1
UMWA-BCOA
Grievance Procedures

Source: President's Commission on Coal,
Coal Data Book, p. 147.

The Legacy of the Early 1970s

The most obvious institutional change in the labor relations system of the bituminous coal industry in the early 1970s was the "democratization" of the UMWA. That change in governmental structure and style, when overlaid on the resurgent and mounting "grass roots" militancy of a "new" work force, brought a final end to any potential for restraint in negotiations on the part of the union. It also brought the onset of what has proven to be an era of distrust and second-guessing of the international union leadership with respect to its negotiated settlements with the BCOA—a delayed reaction against the two-man rational bargaining of John L. Lewis. Most importantly, however, it brought a return of labor instability on a scale reminiscent of the 1940s. The BCOA estimated that such instability cost the UMWA health and retirement funds $108 million in employer contributions during the term of the 1974 agreement [21]—losses that left the 1950 pension trust with a $6 million operating deficit for the year ending June 30, 1977, the 1950 benefit trust with a $15 million deficit for the same period, and the 1974 benefit trust with a $50 million operating deficit for that year.[22] The BCOA characterized its own losses due to such instability as follows:

> Such instability has caused Union coal to suffer competitively in terms of cost, but more importantly, has signalled major customers that UMWA mines do not represent a reliable source of coal. Thus, many of the customers have turned from UMWA coal mines to those whose employees are represented by other unions or are nonunion.[23]

A second, more subtle institutional change in the industry's labor relations system involved the return to public prominence of the UMWA-BCOA contract negotiations—in 1971 due to controls, in 1974 due to the energy crisis. That public prominence brought with it not only public attention but also government intervention, again reminiscent of the 1940s. Such intervention was based less on the fact that a coal strike created an economic emergency than on the fact that it created a political embarrassment. Indeed, the economic rationale for intervention declined over the period as national agreement tonnage slipped from 70

---

[21] *Ibid.*, p. 7.

[22] United Mine Workers of America Health and Retirement Funds, *1977 Annual Report*, pp. 7, 10, 13.

[23] BCOA, "Will the United Mine Workers of America," pp. 5-6

percent of total coal production in 1970 to 60 percent in 1974 and 50 percent in 1977.[24]

The most significant development of the early 1970s was economic, not institutional, and involved the end of two decades of cheap coal and stable coal mine labor costs (see Table XII-4).

TABLE XII-4
Wage and Royalty Costs,
1970-1976

Year	Wage (Day)	Tons (Day)	Wage (Ton)	Royalty (Ton)	Cost (Ton)	Royalty (Day)	Compensation (Day)
1970	34.25	18.84	1.82	0.40	2.22	7.54	41.79
1971	37.00	18.02	2.05	0.60	2.65	10.81	48.81
1972	39.75	17.74	2.24	0.70	2.94	12.42	52.17
1973	42.25	16.76	2.52	0.80	3.32	13.41	55.66
1974	47.03	17.58	2.68	1.20	3.88	21.10	68.13
1975	48.91	14.74	3.32	1.45	4.77	21.37	70.28
1976	50.38	14.46	3.48	1.55	5.03	22.41	72.79

Source: Data in author's possession.

One culprit in this development was a continuing decline in productivity which reduced output per man per day by over 20 percent between 1970 and 1976. A second culprit was the two substantial economic settlements negotiated during the period— settlements that raised the basic daily wage rate by almost 50 percent and the basic tonnage royalty rate by almost 300 percent. The result was an almost 100 percent increase in the wage/ royalty cost per ton of coal mined, independent of the decline in output per man day. Overall, the labor cost per ton of coal mined more than doubled between 1970 and 1976, leading the BCOA to note in 1977 that

> the pressure of declining productivity and [rising] costs where prices are set competitively has become a major problem in the segment of the industry whose employees are represented by the UMWA ... without productivity increases to offset negotiated gains, the economic position of that segment of the coal mining industry represented by the UMWA is threatened as is the bright potential which coal has in relation to other fuels.[25]

----

[24] *Ibid.*, p. 5.

[25] *Ibid.*, p. 9.

CHAPTER XIII

The Conduct of Multiemployer Bargaining: Armageddon, 1977–1978

From the outset, the 1977 UMWA-BCOA National Bituminous Coal Wage Agreement negotiations promised to prove difficult and unlikely to be concluded without a strike. The prospect of a coal strike, however, was not seen as a potential economic or political catastrophe of the magnitude to warrant "massive" federal intervention in the collective bargaining process.

The pessimism over the prospects for a peaceful coal settlement in 1977 reflected more than the general deterioration in BCOA-UMWA relations during the term of their 1974 agreement. The negotiations and negotiators were to be burdened by a particularly difficult and sensitive set of issues—labor stability and labor productivity. That set of issues would have to be resolved by a union obviously beset by internal political problems and an industry that could hardly be described as monolithic, although its internal political divisions were far less obvious to the outside observer than those of the union both prior to and during the course of the negotiations.

The optimism regarding the limited impact of a possible coal strike was the product of two factors. First, the prospects for a strike had been so good that all affected had anticipated and prepared for just such an eventuality, as confirmed by government data which showed coal stockpiles to be at record levels when the strike began on December 6.[1] Second, UMWA National Agreement production now accounted for only approximately 50 percent of total U.S. coal production.

---

[1] Mine Safety and Health Administration, *Comprehensive Overview of Winter Energy Data Bulletins*, Winter 1977-1978, Coal Supplement No. 17 (April 1978) (Washington, D.C.: U.S. Department of Energy, June 1978), pp. 8-9.

The pessimism of the prognosticators of the industry's fate proved fully justified. Their optimism regarding the impact of a strike did not. The path to a final agreement was indeed difficult, involving an 111-day strike and a series of three tentative agreements. That tortuous path was travelled for most of its length in the company, if not the custody, of the Carter administration despite that administration's basic and oft-repeated commitment to free collective bargaining and a policy of nonintervention.

THE FIRST AGREEMENT

The 1977 UMWA-BCOA negotiations opened in Washington on October 6, two months before contract expiration on December 6, 1977. The BCOA entered those negotiations committed to achieving two goals as a condition for a settlement—restoration of labor stability (control of wildcat strikes) and improvement of labor productivity (change in work rules). The UMWA entered those negotiations with its own two conditions for a settlement—recognition of the right to strike over grievances, and restoration and protection of the integrity of its welfare and retirement funds and benefits. Its first condition clearly raised an issue of principle between it and the BCOA. Its second condition also, at least in part, created an issue of principle in that wildcat strikes had been the major factor undermining the integrity of the existing fund/benefit system over the past three years. The BCOA's productivity issue, at least initially, was a matter of money rather than principle, although that was to change when an industry "buy-out" became a union "sell-out" as negotiations progressed.

The First Two Months

During the first two months of the 1977 BCOA-UMWA negotiations the parties made virtually no progress toward an agreement. This remarkable lack of progress became evident to the FMCS, which found that "when we went into the negotiations on the 28th of November, eight days before the strike deadline, there had not been one negotiation meeting of any consequence from the time they started in October." [2]

The failure of the parties to make progress prior to the strike deadline was the product of a basic impasse over procedure

---

[2] Wayne L. Horvitz, "What's Happening in Collective Bargaining?" *Labor Law Journal*, Vol. 29, No. 8 (August 1978), p. 461.

rather than substance. The BCOA entered the negotiations willing to buy relief on stability and productivity through a generous economic settlement, including the restoration and guarantee of welfare benefits. To that end, it sought to structure the negotiations in terms of a total package based on a series of trade-offs. The UMWA under the leadership of Arnold Miller, who had won reelection in 1977 by the narrowest of margins and who still faced strong political opposition and competition within the union, resisted this approach and insisted that negotiations and concessions on its two basic issues come first, independent of any and all other issues.

The central issue in the union's view at the outset of negotiations was the restoration and protection of benefits. The BCOA indicated that it was willing to discuss this issue, but only in conjunction with its proposals on productivity and particularly stability, on the grounds that it had been labor instability that had created the benefit program confronting the parties. The union refused to accept this linkage and, when the industry refused to separate the two issues, negotiations were broken off on October 27, at which point both parties felt compelled to issue public statements. The UMWA statement indicated that further negotiations were pointless because "there isn't going to be any agreement . . . without resolving the Funds question in a satisfactory manner." [3] The BCOA responded with a statement that pointed out that

> the negotiations involve many important issues all of which must be addressed. No meaningful purpose will be served by attempts of one side to separate or isolate a given problem . . . in addition to issues concerning the Health and Retirement funds, there are, at least, equally important issues concerning wildcat strikes, absenteeism and declining productivity . . . indeed, the future success of the benefits program is largely dependent on a successful resolution of those problems affecting work stability. [4]

When the negotiations resumed on November 8, the BCOA suggested that the parties turn their attention to the grievance procedure, which did not appear controversial since both sides agreed that there was a need to improve that procedure. The UMWA responded by proposing the abolition of the Arbitration Review Board and the inclusion of the "right to strike." When it pursued this latter demand seriously, the result was a second

---

[3] UMWA Press Release, October 27, 1977, p. 2.

[4] BCOA Press Release, October 27, 1977.

impasse, which prompted a second public statement by the BCOA on November 11, in which it asserted:

> The Union has demanded that the operators agreed to a right to strike proposal under which . . . [union] officers would totally abdicate their responsibility for delivering a stable workforce which is their principal guarantee to management when they sign a new wage agreement. . . . [We] urge the union to work with us in improving dispute settlement at the earliest step of the grievance procedure and to face up to the fact that unless we achieve stability in this manner the unionized sector of the coal industry will continue to decline.[5]

Negotiations continued in a desultory fashion until they were recessed for the Thanksgiving holiday. The only further developments in those negotiations came just prior to the recess and did little to narrow the differences between the parties. On Monday, November 21, the UMWA presented the BCOA and the public with a report prepared by a consulting firm which indicated that an increase of $6.89 in hourly compensation of miners was justified.[6] On the following day, the trustees of the welfare funds informed the parties that those funds would not be able to continue benefits after December 6 if a strike occurred. Arnold Miller announced that fact to the public, but with the following warning:

> I want to state emphatically that this action by the Trustees will not cause us to reduce our demands, compromise the principles we have established in these negotiations, or accept a contract that otherwise would have been unacceptable.[7]

By the time the parties recessed for Thanksgiving it was effectively too late to conclude an agreement that could be ratified prior to contract expiration. Thus, no serious attempt at further negotiation was made until after a strike began on December 6.

The Second Two Months

The FMCS, which had entered the negotiations after the Thanksgiving recess, devoted its early efforts to finding a basis on which the parties could discuss rather than debate the issues. To that end, the FMCS suggested that each side reduce its bargaining committee to four people—a suggestion which both sides

[5] BCOA Press Release, November 11, 1977, p. 2.

[6] UMWA Press Release, November 21, 1977, p. 2.

[7] UMWA Press Release, November 22, 1977, p. 2.

accepted. Negotiations between these small committees resumed in earnest on December 8. Considerable progress was made, as had been the case in 1968, 1971, and 1974, and by December 15, the BCOA felt that agreement had been reached on the outline of a possible settlement of the major issues of principle. The central elements of this outline were:

1. The UMWA would drop its "right to strike" and the BCOA would drop its "no strike" counterproposal, leaving control of wildcat strike activity to the right of operators to discipline miners for such activity under the terms of an existing arbitration award.
2. The BCOA would guarantee welfare benefits and agree to target health benefit levels, and the UMWA would agree to a requirement that miners "pay back" the funds for contributions lost due to wildcat strikes.
3. The UMWA would accept the right of individual operators to institute absenteeism control and production bonus systems at the mine level with the agreement of the local union.

This agreement in concept was, of course, conditional on reaching agreement on all other issues. Negotiations to that end proceeded slowly during the last two weeks of December and then suddenly were broken off by the BCOA on December 30 when it perceived that the UMWA was retreating from its agreement in concept on a stability package. The BCOA explained its action to the public in the following terms:

> Contract negotiations with the United Mine Workers of America broke off today when the Union began to back away from provisions to curb wildcat strikes and restore labor stability in the coal fields. . . . Unless the Union can come to a position where it is willing to stick with the hard decisions necessary to achieve labor stability there cannot be a successful resolution of these negotiations.[8]

The UMWA's reluctance to accept the agreed-upon stability package was understandable in light of the sacrosanct status of such actions among the rank and file. Its problems in accepting that package were complicated, in the view of the FMCS, by the fact that the rank and file tended to hear of and/or focus on only the restraints in the package and not on the concessions made in exchange for those restraints. Thus, the challenge facing the FMCS was to get the parties to put together a package that

---

[8] BCOA Press Release, December 30, 1977.

could hold together long enough to present the trade-offs to the membership in the ratification process.[9]

The next step in putting together such a package was taken during the second week of January 1978. The FMCS called the parties to separate meetings on January 9 and 10, and then reconvened negotiations at the FMCS offices on January 12. Some progress was made on noneconomic issues to the point where the BCOA could be induced to make a new economic offer. That offer was made on January 23 and was rejected by the UMWA, whereupon negotiations were recessed. Negotiations resumed on January 27 when the BCOA made its final offer—an offer which, in its own words, committed the industry "to wage increases clearly higher than those granted in other industries . . . [and] to guarantee all health benefits, restore the pension funds, and to provide a contract right to deal fairly on both sides with wildcat strikes." [10] Those commitments were not acceptable to the UMWA, which formally rejected the BCOA's "final offer" on January 29, at which point the BCOA concluded publically "that even after 54 days of strike, the Union is not interested in settlement on any responsible basis." [11]

The BCOA was now fully convinced that further negotiations would be futile and prepared for a prolonged recess. The FMCS, however, was not ready to admit defeat and proved both tenacious and successful in keeping the negotiations from breaking off completely. The BCOA was prevailed upon to agree to another meeting on February 1, this time between the UMWA bargaining committee and the full BCOA steering committee. That meeting failed to produce any real progress or to reveal any serious division within BCOA ranks, leaving the parties with little to do but go home, as the BCOA representatives prepared to do. Before all of them left Washington, however, the FMCS launched a final and ultimately successful "last ditch" effort to put together an agreement. That attempt began on the afternoon of Friday, February 3, and culminated on Sunday, February 5, when President Miller announced a tentative agreement which he characterized as "by far the best agreement negotiated in any major industry in the past two years." [12]

---

[9] Horvitz, "What's Happening in Collective Bargaining?" p. 461.

[10] BCOA Press Release, January 29, 1978, p. 1.

[11] *Ibid.*

[12] "Tentative Three-Year Settlement Announced by Miller in Coal Talks," *Daily Labor Report*, No. 25 (February 6, 1978), p. AA-1.

The First Agreement

The agreement announced on February 5 differed from the BCOA's last offer only in that it provided for the elimination of the black lung pension differential for 1950 pension trust retirees, the addition of one vacation day, and the addition of eye care to the health benefits program.

The agreement called for wage increases totalling $2.30 per hour ($0.90-$0.70-$0.70) over the three-year life of the contract plus a $100 bonus for miners who returned to work as scheduled and provided for the guarantee of pension and health benefits (but with a deductible for health benefits) plus reimbursement of health care expenses incurred by miners between July 1 and December 5, 1977, due to benefit cutbacks. In exchange for those economic concessions, the BCOA gained acceptance of the "pay back" principle, the right to schedule staggered starting times and Sunday work (continuous operation), and the option to institute production bonus and absenteeism control programs.

On Monday, February 6, the members of the UMWA Bargaining Council began to arrive in Washington for a meeting on the following day to review the tentative agreement. On their arrival, the members of the council began to picket UMWA headquarters to protest the agreement, which none of them had yet seen. In the course of that protest, President Miller was physically prevented from entering the building, which ultimately was taken over by the protesters.

On Tuesday, February 7, the Bargaining Council met as scheduled but adjourned without a decision. A second meeting of the council was scheduled for Friday, February 10. This meeting was disrupted by a group of about 200 miners demanding rejection of the agreement. President Miller refused to hold the meeting under such conditions and adjourned it. Most of the members, however, remained and voted "unofficially" to reject the agreement by a thirty-three to three margin. President Miller refused to accept this vote and scheduled a third, "official" meeting of the council for Sunday, February 12. At that meeting, the complete text of the agreement was distributed for the first time to the members of the council, who studied that text for less than one hour before voting thirty-three to six to reject the agreement—an action taken as much to embarrass President Miller and further the political ambitions of his rivals as to express dissatisfaction with the substance of the agreement.

THE SECOND AGREEMENT

Following rejection of the February 5 tentative agreement, President Miller wrote to the BCOA requesting a resumption of negotiations, as he had done in 1974. As had also been the case in 1974, the initial response of the BCOA was negative and couched in the following terms:

> In view of the high cost of the settlement, and its solution to many of the problems concerning both the industry and the UMWA, we find it difficult to believe that the contract has received fair and adequate consideration.
>
> We urge that the Bargaining Council now review the contract carefully and in its entirety, and we feel sure that such action will result in approval of our Agreement.[13]

The announcement and subsequent rejection of the February 5 agreement took place in an environment quite different from that in which negotiations opened or in which the strike began. Public concern over the existing and prospective effects of the coal strike, as manifested in press reports or predictions of problems, began to mount appreciably in late January and early February. The announcement of an agreement provided a welcome measure of relief for the Carter administration from the growing pressure on its nonintervention policy generated by that public concern. That relief disappeared with the rejection of the agreement on February 10 and turned into positive pain with the BCOA's refusal to resume negotiations on February 14. In short, the administration found itself faced with a choice of "standing the heat" (inaction) or "getting out of the kitchen" (intervention). Faced with mounting public concern and political pressure and the prospect of a much longer strike, the administration chose to get out of the kitchen to undertake what proved to be a long and relentless pursuit of a second negotiated agreement acceptable to the UMWA Bargaining Council.

The First Two Weeks

The second stage of negotiations began even before the first agreement was formally rejected by the Bargaining Council. On Monday, February 6, the secretary of labor requested a private meeting with the industry to discuss what might be done if the agreement was not approved. The BCOA argued that such a

---

[13] BCOA Press Release, February 14, 1978, p. 2.

meeting was premature, at best, and urged that the government's attention and efforts be directed to encouraging acceptance of the agreement. The secretary, however, was able to persuade the BCOA to meet with him at the Labor Department the following morning.

The meeting on the 7th was devoted to a review of the union's unmet demands in an effort to identify areas in which the BCOA might be willing to move. The BCOA took the position that it had moved as far as it intended to move and that it was committed to defending the agreement, through a prolonged strike if necessary. The BCOA came away from that meeting with the perception that it was now engaged in bargaining with the government on behalf of the UMWA—a perception that was only strengthened in the course of subsequent conversations with the secretary over the next five days.

The secretary of labor, acting under his presidential mandate to "facilitate the bargaining process" issued the day after the UMWA's "informal" rejection of the contract, met with the BCOA on the morning of Tuesday, February 14, to discuss a resumption of negotiations. At that meeting the BCOA informed the secretary of its negative response to the UMWA's request to reopen negotiations, which was to be announced later that day, and of its rationale for that response. The meeting was cordial and was adjourned with the BCOA under the impression that the secretary would be back for another meeting after he had a chance to meet with the union. The call to a second meeting with the secretary never came. Instead, that afternoon the president invited the parties to resume their negotiations at the White House.

The call to the White House was welcomed by the UMWA, but it came as both a surprise and a disappointment to the BCOA. The call was perceived as the first step in "politicizing" the dispute and as a major step toward undermining the concepts as well as the details of the first agreement in search of a "quick fix" for the strike problem. The BCOA's first line of defense against such a quick fix was to continue to refuse to reopen negotiations, which it did in a letter to the secretary of labor on March 15, informing the secretary that "with all deference and courtesy . . . we are obliged to decline the request." [14] The secretary of labor responded immediately and was able to "per-

---

[14] BCOA Press Release, February 15, 1978, p. 2.

suade" the BCOA to attend a meeting of the parties with the president at the White House that evening. That meeting was devoted primarily to encouraging remarks by the president and discussion of the ground rules for proceeding with negotiations under the supervision of the secretary of labor and the FMCS. The meeting was cordial and noncontroversial, despite some press reports that the industry had been read the riot act—reports that further strained industry-government relations.

The following day brought the beginning of the "intensive negotiations" under a forty-eight-hour deadline set by the secretary of labor. That day was spent primarily in meetings between the secretary and the BCOA. The next day was spent primarily in meetings between the secretary and the UMWA. The purpose of the secretary throughout these separate meetings was to identify those areas in which some movement by the BCOA was possible and would be productive from the viewpoint of the UMWA. The secretary apparently believed he had been successful in that search when, late on the 17th, he held a final meeting with the BCOA to discuss a possible new industry offer. In that meeting the BCOA was persuaded to make three changes in the agreement: (1) the pay-back provisions would be dropped, as would the benefit guarantees to which they had been linked; (2) COLAs would be reinstated for the second and third years, but with offsetting reductions in the amounts of fixed-wage increases for those years; and (3) several agreed-upon changes in scheduling would be modified or dropped.

The secretary conveyed these changes to the UMWA in the early hours of the 18th. They were not favorably received. The union bargaining committee apparently had expected that the offer would include an additional $0.05 in the first-year wage increase and would retain the benefit guarantees as well as reinstate COLA and drop pay-back. At the request of the secretary, the committee reluctantly submitted the offer to the Bargaining Council, which rejected it by a thirty-seven to zero vote. The secretary then asked the council to submit the offer to the rank and file, but that request was denied by a vote of twenty-six to eleven. The secretary made one more futile effort to explore the "possibilities for a negotiated settlement" on the 18th after which he reluctantly announced that he saw no basis for further efforts on his part to bring the union and the BCOA together.[15]

[15] Ben A. Franklin, "White House postpones any action to force an end to miner's strike," *New York Times*, February 19, 1978, p. 1.

The Second Two Weeks

On Monday, February 20, the tentative agreement between the UMWA and Pittsburgh and Midway was announced. Not surprisingly, that agreement contained all of the items that the union had expected to be in the BCOA's revised proposal on the 18th. Specifically, the agreement (1) added $0.05 to the first-year wage increase and called for COLA in the second and third years; (2) provided benefit guarantees and was silent on payback; (3) eliminated Sunday work and was silent on production bonus systems; and (4) was silent on discipline for workers who engaged in wildcat strikes.

On that same day, the governors of West Virginia, Ohio, Kentucky, and Pennsylvania publically hailed the agreement and the governor of West Virginia formally requested BCOA acceptance of that agreement in a letter to the association. In its response to that request, the BCOA clearly indicated that it did not intend simply to accept the Pittsburgh and Midway agreement. Specifically, it stated:

> [We] assure you that we are willing to return to face-to-face bargaining with the Union and that our negotiators are prepared to do so promptly . . . [so] no one is under any illusions, we plan to vigorously present our case to the Union bargainers so that true collective bargaining in good faith can be accomplished.[16]

The BCOA's "rejection" of the Pittsburgh and Midway agreement was accompanied by a public proposal for "voluntary, binding interest arbitration." On February 22, the UMWA Bargaining Council, in a meeting with the secretary of labor, voted overwhelmingly to reject that proposal and then voted twenty-five to thirteen to accept the Pittsburgh and Midway agreement as the basis for a settlement with the BCOA. That action produced a new deadlock which was not broken until the president twisted some industry arms on Friday, February 25.

Negotiations resumed immediately on the afternoon of the 25th under a 9:00 P.M. deadline imposed by the president. In those negotiations, the BCOA made one final attempt to salvage its scheduling and production bonus system gains in exchange for the added $0.05 in wages and two more holidays agreed to by Pittsburgh and Midway. That effort was not well received by the union and had to be abandoned. Finally, the BCOA "under enormous pressure" agreed to make "numerous additional conces-

---

[16] BCOA Press Release, February 21, 1978, pp. 1-2.

sions with respect to the first agreement without any corresponding concessions from the union" and accepted the Pittsburgh and Midway pattern.

The Second Agreement

The second agreement clearly constituted a major defeat for the BCOA. The productivity/stability package it had fought for and gained in the first agreement was dismantled in the second agreement. The economic *quid pro quo* originally offered by the BCOA in exchange for its productivity/stability gains, however, remained intact, although it was not substantially increased.

From the union standpoint, the second agreement proved to be a necessary but not sufficient victory to produce a final agreement. The elimination of the most politically sensitive "issues of principle"—pay-back and work rule changes—was a necessary step to appease the Bargaining Council, but not sufficient to please the rank and file. On February 26, the rank and file at Pittsburgh and Midway failed to ratify their contract, and on March 5 the BCOA rank and file did the same by a more than two to one margin, thereby demanding a third bite at the industry apple. The hunger for that third bite, in the view of the union, was a product of a combination of deprivation and democracy in action. The industry, however, perceived the rank and file's appetite to have been significantly whetted by the fact that the second bite of the industry's apple had been so large and juicy.

THE THIRD AGREEMENT

The third stage of the 1977 BCOA-UMWA contract negotiations opened on Monday, March 6, and concluded eight days later, on Wednesday, March 14, when the UMWA and BCOA announced a new tentative agreement. That agreement was approved by the UMWA Bargaining Council on March 15 by a vote of twenty-two to seven and ratified by the UMWA rank and file on March 24, by a 57 to 43 percent margin. The agreement was signed on March 25, and took effect on Monday, March 27, when over 90 percent of striking miners returned to work after 111 days on strike.

The First Four Days

Between Monday, March 6, and Friday, March 10, the BCOA and UMWA were largely preoccupied with Taft-Hartley matters.

The president announced his decision on Monday. On Wednesday the Board of Inquiry required by law held its hearings, at which both the BCOA and UMWA made statements. In its testimony, the UMWA national union denied that the strike was causing an emergency and argued that "it would be an outrage to adopt the one-sided approach of the Taft-Hartley law rather than to take other measures . . . [including] if necessary, seizing the mines." [17] District unions in West Virginia went further, condemning the use of Taft-Hartley as creating a "confrontation between miners and their government" and imposing " 'slave labor conditions' " and extolling the virtues of seizure on the grounds that it would permit "impartial evaluation of operators' financial conditions" and "resumption of coal production under 1974 contract with 1978 benefit levels." [18]

Despite the views of the union, the Board of Inquiry concluded that the national interest demanded that the dispute be resolved expeditiously in its report issued on Thursday, and the president decided to proceed with securing a Taft-Hartley injunction on that same day. Such an injunction was issued on March 9 to take effect on March 10, but was not served on local union officials until Monday, March 13, one day before a new agreement was reached.

The Second Four Days

The initiative for a resumption of negotiations after the rejection of the second agreement, unlike the first, came from the industry and from its "old coal" members. The BCOA had already lost all it could lose of any importance and had to be prepared to enter into an agreement "in the national interest, with the full recognition that the breakthrough in stability and productivity that BCOA had hoped originally to achieve may not now be realized." [19] The prospect that a Taft-Hartley injunction either would be obeyed or serve to produce such an agreement in a timely fashion was not good. Thus, to hasten the inevitable, some BCOA representatives sought an impromptu "exploratory" meeting with the union and without the government on March 9.

---

[17] "Statements by Mine Workers and Coal Operators Before Board of Inquiry," *Daily Labor Report*, No. 46 (March 8, 1978), p. F-1.

[18] *Ibid.*, p. F-2.

[19] *Ibid.*, p. F-4.

The UMWA responded favorably and an agreement was reached to begin private talks the following day.

Those private talks began on Friday, March 10, with the BCOA now represented primarily by "old coal" company personnel. By Saturday, a conceptual outline for a new settlement was agreed upon. The following two days were spent in negotiating the details of that settlement. That process proved relatively easy and was completed in time to announce a third settlement on March 14—three days before the government was due back in court to argue for an extension of its Taft-Hartley temporary restraining order, an argument that it lost on Friday, March 17.

The Third Agreement

The third agreement represented something of a victory for both sides. The union achieved some politically popular gains in the welfare and pension benefits area. In return, the industry gained the right to replace the 1974 benefit trust system with private, single-employer insurance coverage. In addition, the industry regained the option of instituting production bonus systems, for which concession the union won an additional holiday.

The wage settlement in the third agreement was identical to that in the second—$1.00-$0.40-$0.40, plus $0.30 in guaranteed COLAs in both the second and the third years. In addition, miners who returned to work as scheduled were to receive a $100 bonus, and all miners were to receive two additional paid holidays. The basic benefit package remained largely unchanged between the second and third agreements in that the industry agreed to guarantee benefits and to reimburse miners for health care deductibles paid between July 1 and December 6, 1977. The elimination of the black lung pension benefit differential, which had been the final price of the first agreement, was embodied in the third agreement. A number of liberalizations in benefits and benefit eligibilities, however, were made, including a reduction in the deductible for hospitalization, a reduction in the hours-worked eligibility requirement for pension credit, and the partial elimination of the pension benefit differential between pre- and post-1974 retirees.

THE LEGACY OF 1977

The 1978 BCOA-UMWA National Bituminous Coal Wage Agreement clearly constituted a major defeat for the BCOA—a defeat that left the industry with no concrete relief on its two major economic problems, productivity and stability. The process by which that agreement was reached seemed to confirm and extend the worsening record of union-management relations in the industry and to set the stage for a further extension of that trend by virtue of the rewards reaped by the union as a result of its militancy and intransigence. Despite those two disturbing facts, there was substantial sentiment within the BCOA that the 1977-1978 negotiations and settlement signaled the beginning of a "new era" in industry-labor relations, similar to that which followed the 1949-1950 negotiations and settlement—a view shared by at least some of the elected leaders of the UMWA.

The basis for this optimism regarding the second coming of a "new era" in labor relations was difficult to isolate. The obvious procedural and substantive similarities between 1949-1950 and 1977-1978 undoubtedly played a role. In addition, both sides seemed convinced that the other had entered negotiations "spoiling for a strike" and, having proven their resolve, should be ready to put down their swords. The fact that both sides had been severely tested both economically and institutionally by the strike and by the government's intervention increased the hope of a retreat from confrontation. Finally, both sides believed that their opposite number had received a sound and serious education in their problems and concerns and that this would lay a foundation for more reasoned approaches to issues in the future.

The Old Problems

The 1978 agreement offered little hope of relief from the sharp upward trend in compensation costs in the industry of the early 1970s. Indeed, according to the BCOA, employment costs per man-hour, work which doubled between 1969 and 1976, doubled again between 1977 and 1980.[20] More importantly, the 1978 agreement, *per se,* offered no definite promise of offsetting gains in labor productivity or stability to mitigate the impact of increased employment costs per hour on employment costs per ton.

Surprisingly, the prospect of a continuing sharp upward trend in unit labor costs did not seem to bother many BCOA members at the time. Their sanguine attitude appeared to be based primarily on anticipation of an industry boom based on the short-

---

[20] "Bargaining Statement By Bituminous Coal Operators' Association," *Daily Labor Report,* No. 15 (January 23, 1981), p. F-4.

run, pent-up demand for coal as a result of the strike and the long-run, growing demand for coal as a result of changing energy policies, although the hope for a "miraculous" return of stability and productivity growth also was a factor in some cases. Subsequent events—specifically, the "fizzling coal boom" of 1978 and the emergence of excess capacity in the industry—should have destroyed the optimists in the industry and would have had there not been a "miraculous" improvement in productivity and stability which enabled the BCOA to enjoy at least stable per ton labor costs between 1978 and 1980.[21]

The most dramatic post-strike development in the coal industry was a precipitous decline in wildcat strike activity at BCOA mines. Such activity, which had resulted in the loss of more than 8 days per 100 days available in 1977, fell to about 1 lost day per 100 days available during 1978, 1979, and 1980, despite the absence of any new contractual controls or penalties on such action—a development not unlike that which occurred after the 1950 contract. Any number of reasons have been cited for this dramatic change, including better management, growing worker maturity, a common sense of the threat of nonunion coal and realization of the need for modernization of local bargaining structures.[22] However, the energy and resources spent in the 1977-1978 strike coupled with the layoffs of miners resulting from the "fizzling coal boom" undoubtedly also may have been a factor, as may have been the increasingly aggressive disciplinary policies and legal challenges of some companies in dealing with wildcat strikes and strikers.

The decade-long downward trend in labor productivity also was reversed during the term of the 1978 contract, despite the fact that the "fizzling coal boom" and its resultant unemployment effectively prevented the BCOA from implementing its one productivity concession—bonus systems. According to the BCOA, tons per man-day in BCOA National Agreement mines reached their post-1969 low in 1978 in underground mines (9.5 tons) and in 1979 in surface mines (19.4 tons) before experiencing "some small improvement" which, in its words, "may be only short-term." [23] The BCOA attributed the increase to the following:

---

[21] *Ibid.*, p. F-4.

[22] Everett M. Kassalow, "Labor-Management Relations and the Coal Industry," *Monthly Labor Review*, Vol. 102, No. 5 (May 1979), p. 26.

[23] "Bargaining Statement," *Daily Labor Report*, p. F-3.

The drop in wildcat strikes unquestionably has helped the productivity situation, and that help is essential. Beyond that, however, depressed business conditions have forced companies to shut down marginal mines and keep better productivity mines running. Also companies are now making greater use of newer technology such as longwall mining equipment . . .[24]

The UMWA was more "heartened" by these productivity gains than the BCOA, which continued to be concerned that increasing employment costs without offsetting productivity gains in the 1970s had made "the UMWA-National Agreement sector . . . an exceptionally high cost producer in the coal industry."[25] The root of that problem, which became evident with the emergence of excess capacity in the late 1970s, was the fact that productivity levels of non-UMWA coal miners were higher than those of UMWA National Agreement coal miners by 39 percent in underground and 55 percent in surface mine operations.[26] In the view of the BCOA in 1981, those differentials were the key factor in the shrinkage of UMWA National Agreement tonnage to under 45 percent of total U.S. coal production in 1980, making it "essential that we get our productivity back where it once was . . . ."[27]

The New Era

The phenomenon of a "new era" in labor relations following a long strike which serves to clear the air and give both parties a painful lesson in the necessity of accommodating each others' concerns and problems is not unusual. The fact that the BCOA and UMWA might anticipate such a phenomenon after their protracted 1977-1978 confrontation was not a mere product of wishful thinking, particularly in light of their 1949-1950 experience. There were, however, two ingredients in the miraculous transformation of industry labor relations in 1950 that were noticeably absent in 1978—the presence of a strong, secure union leadership able to control rank-and-file expectations and militancy and the experience of a truly shared defeat in a test of economic and political power.

The UMWA in 1978 was quite a different institution than it had been in 1950. In place of the autocracy of John L. Lewis

---

[24] *Ibid.*

[25] *Ibid.*, p. F-4.

[26] *Ibid.*, p. F-3.

[27] *Ibid.*

was the anarchy of Arnold Miller whose "inability to unify the rank and file or to resolve disputes among the leadership" has been cited as a major reason for the length of the 1977-1978 strike.[28] The democratic reforms instituted when Miller became president, which had "enabled rival factions to compete for control and weaken Miller's authority" made it unlikely that any individual could easily or quickly regain control of the UMWA, and Arnold Miller's apparent sell-out to the industry in the first agreement virtually assured that he could not maintain even that limited measure of control which he ostensibly possessed as its elected president.[29]

Arnold Miller's lack of credibility and control and the abundance of critics and competitors within the union could not realistically bode well for the future of UMWA-BCOA relations. Fortuitously, however, Arnold Miller decided to step down as president of the UMWA in 1979 for reasons of "ill health after a strife-ridden 7-year rule." [30] By constitutional succession, the presidency then passed to his vice president, Samuel Church, a man "regarded as a strong leader who is bringing stability to the union." [31] A man, however, who was still subject to all of the same constitutional constraints and political power plays as his predecessor when the time would come once again for UMWA-BCOA negotiations.

The UMWA and the BCOA had shared the economic pain of an 111-day strike. They had not shared, however, the economic fruits of that pain. The union had "won" on both principle and principal, thanks, in its own words, "to the help we got from secretary Marshall during the last negotiations"—help which enabled it to gain "things we wouldn't have had without his help." [32] The industry had lost on both and was left only with unresolved problems which were eased but hardly eliminated by developments during the term of the 1978 agreement. In combination, those two facts would seem to suggest that the parties had not solved their problem, but only deferred it and made it more difficult to solve on other than a "win-lose" basis—a possibility not foreseen

---

[28] U.S. Department of Labor, Bureau of Labor Statistics, "Collective Bargaining in the Bituminous Coal Industry," Report 625 (December 1980), p. 1.

[29] *Ibid.*

[30] *Ibid.*

[31] *Ibid.*

[32] UMWA Press Release, November 29, 1979, p. 1.

by the optimists in the BCOA and UMWA who were for the most part the "old coal" types who had finally freed themselves from their institutional constraints to conclude the final, "inevitable" agreement.

The basic premise of those who foresaw the coming of a new era was that the BCOA's defeat in the 1977-1978 negotiations had pointed out the futility of an industry initiative in contract bargaining and laid to rest productivity and stability and other "issues of principle" as subjects for bargaining. Thus, prior to and independent of the fortuitous productivity and stability developments during the term of the 1978 contract, there was a widely expressed view in the industry that the 1981 negotiations would "simply be a matter of money"—as had been the case in the 1950s. That view and the fatalistic attitude it reflected, however, were not shared by all BCOA members and, most notably, not by the dissidents such as Consolidation and U.S. Steel which subsequently threatened to withdraw from the BCOA—companies which ultimately were to gain a substantial measure of control in the BCOA as it entered negotiations in 1981.

CHAPTER XIV

The Conduct of Multiemployer Bargaining: Future Shock, 1981

The UMWA and the BCOA approached their 1980-1981 contract negotiations amidst considerable optimism regarding the prospects for a peaceful settlement by the time the 1978 contract expired on March 27, 1981. The basis for that optimism was a widespread perception, reinforced by the statements and actions of the parties and particularly the union, that both were anxious to avoid a strike in 1981. The fiirst such statement came in a press conference held by UMWA President Sam Church in July 1980, eight months before contract expiration, in which he discussed the decision of the parties to open negotiations early (six months prior to contract expiration rather than the traditional two months), indicated a possible willingness on the part of the UMWA to extend the contract beyond the deadline if negotiations were progressing satisfactorily and stated:

> We are hopeful that these agreements can be negotiated without a strike. For two years now the operators have said they don't want a strike. We will know when we get to the bargaining table. The United Mine Workers certainly don't want to strike. Hopefully, we won't have to.[1]

BCOA-UMWA negotiations did indeed officially open early in September 1980, because "both parties wanted an early start, to avoid a repetition of the costly 110 day strike that occurred in 1977-1978." [2] True to historical form, however, serious negotiations did not get underway until late January 1981, against a self-imposed deadline of March 15, 1981, set to accommodate the

---

[1] "Mine Worker President Hopes to Avoid Contract Strike in 1981," *Daily Labor Report*, No. 147 (July 29, 1980), p. A-7.

[2] U.S. Department of Labor, Bureau of Labor Statistics, "Collective Bargaining in the Bituminous Coal Industry," Report 625 (December 1980), p. 1.

UMWA's ratification procedure. Despite that return to historical form, the outlook for a peaceful settlement—"the first . . . in 15 years and 6 bargaining rounds" [3]—remained optimistic. In an article entitled "Coal's Rank and File Cools It," *Business Week* characterized the situation at the end of January 1981 as follows:

> The prospect of a peaceful settlement became apparent on January 22, when negotiations began in Washington to replace the agreement that expires on March 27. UMW president Sam Church and Bobby R. Brown, the industry's chief negotiator . . . agreed that there has been a "tremendous improvement" in coal labor relations recently. . . .
>
> Although a walkout is always possible, this new attitude is a major reason why insiders on both sides put the chances for avoiding a walkout at better than 50% this year.[4]

Those chances appeared to be further improved by the UMWA-Pittsburgh and Midway Western Agreement in early February. As a result of that settlement, "The economic pattern for a new agreement has already been set in the Western coal fields, and insiders on both sides think a peaceful settlement is likely." Thus, by early March 1981, "The chances for avoiding a strike in the Eastern coal fields this year are coming down to three major nonwage issues." [5] Those issues proved unresolvable prior to the March 15 deadline. The result was a strike which came as a disappointment to many insiders and as a surprise to many outsiders. Apparently, utilities were not among those surprised, as "entering the strike, utilities had 111 days of coal inventories on hand, enough to last through a strike exactly the length of the walkout three years ago." [6]

That strike ultimately was to last seventy-two days and to be ended, for the third consecutive time, by an agreement other than the parties' initial tentative agreement. Unlike the situations in 1974 and 1977, however, the government did not involve itself heavily in negotiations in response to union rejection of an initial agreement despite the fact that, in the words of the *New York Times*:

---

[3] *Ibid.*

[4] "Coal's Rank and File Cools It," *Business Week*, February 9, 1981, p. 62.

[5] "The Issues that Peril an Eastern Coal Pact," *Business Week*, March 16, 1981, p. 32.

[6] Douglas Martin, "U.S. seems to ride out coal strike," *New York Times*, May 30, 1981, p. 29.   ,

There is no question that the coal strike has hurt: Miners have lost more than $50 million a week in wages, the economics of the Eastern coal states have been badly hammered and the nation's second-quarter economic growth may have been held down as much as 1.5 percentage points.[7]

THE BACKGROUND OF THE BARGAIN

The optimistic outlook for the 1981 UMWA-BCOA National Bituminous Coal Wage Agreement negotiations was a product of perceived changes over the preceding two years in the basic institutional and economic framework of the UMWA-BCOA bargaining relationship. Specifically, leadership and organizational changes within both the BCOA and the UMWA, coupled with the "maturation" of their membership caused or expedited by the 1977-1978 strike, were seen as bringing to the bargaining table in 1981 two new, but older and wiser, parties. Similarly, the legacy of the 1978 agreement, coupled with economic developments during the term of that agreement, were seen as fundamentally altering the character and contentiousness of the issues facing the parties.

The Parties

The Bureau of Labor Statistics, in its prenegotiation report on "Collective Bargaining in the Bituminous Coal Industry" stated that "new leadership in the union, recent restructuring of the BCOA, and growing cooperation between the two offer hope of success in solving mutual problems."[8] *Business Week* subsequently echoed that sentiment in reporting that "one reason for greater optimism this year is that both sides have new negotiators."[9] Normally, that might not bode well for peaceful negotiations, as was noted by some members of the press, but in this case most tended to share the perception of *Business Week* that

> Church . . . is more competent . . . has strong support from the union's executive board, and . . . has tried to moderate expectations of the UMW's 39 member bargaining council . . . [while] . . . Brown has also made significant changes . . . [most notably] . . . the understanding that the industry's negotiating team would be halved to

---

[7] *Ibid.*

[8] U.S. Department of Labor, "Collective Bargaining in the Bituminous Coal Industry," p. 1.

[9] "Coal's Rank and File," p. 62.

three members [which] would prevent the industry factionalism
that occurred in 1977.[10]

The prospects that these two new teams could forge a new
peace seemed enhanced by the new era in day-to-day labor relations which emerged during the term of the 1978 contract. Insiders and outsiders alike noted and seemingly were much heartened by the "dramatic drop in unauthorized mid-contract strikes
(wildcat strikes) since the last contract." [11] The BCOA itself took
note of that fact in its formal public bargaining statement, as
did the UMWA, which stated:

> There is no doubt in our minds that, over the course of the current
> agreement, relations between the union and operators have shown
> marked improvements . . . the atmosphere that prevails between us
> now is, on balance, far better than that which existed for many
> years prior to the 1978 settlement. The sharp reduction in wildcat
> strikes is an important piece of concrete evidence.[12]

The prospects for a peaceful settlement also appeared to be
enhanced by the common economic adversity shared by the BCOA
and UMWA over the term of the 1978 agreement—adversity
which left the industry with "20,000 unemployed miners and 100
million tons a year of excess capacity," [13] most of which was in
the national agreement sector of the industry, whose market
share "has dropped to an estimated 44% from 70% in 1974." [14]
The result was a widespread perception that the parties realized
that, in the words of the *Wall Street Journal*:

> A strike could harm the industry and union for years to come. It
> would, for example, reinforce the already prevalent belief that coal
> can't be counted on. And for the weakened UMW, a strike would
> make it more difficult to organize new mines, especially in the rapidly
> expanding coal fields of the West, where nonunion miners work
> overtime when the UMW miners of the east and Midwest strike.[15]

---

[10] *Ibid.*, pp. 62-64.

[11] U.S. Department of Labor, "Collective Bargaining in the Bituminous
Coal Industry," p. 2.

[12] "Statement by United Mineworkers President Church on Union's Bargaining Demands in Soft Coal Talks," *Daily Labor Report*, No. 14 (January
22, 1981), p. E-1.

[13] U.S. Department of Labor, "Collective Bargaining in the Bituminous
Coal Industry," p. 2.

[14] "Coal's Rank and File," p. 62.

[15] Carol Hymowitz and Thomas Petzinger, Jr., "Critical contract," *Wall
Street Journal*, March 12, 1981, p. 1.

Despite the optimism which pervaded the outlook for a peaceful settlement in the 1981 coal negotiations, few expected such a settlement to be quick or easy, and few took exception to the observation of *Business Week* that "nevertheless, the negotiations are certain to turn up major disagreements. . . ." [16] Few observers, however, recognized or were much impressed by the fact that such disagreements would have to be resolved in an institutional environment.

> But for all the recent advances, harmony and cooperation between the 160,000 miners and their employers often remain unfamiliar ideas. Beneath the peaceful exterior since the last strike lies a reservoir of mistrust and suspicion by rank and file miners that makes labor-management adversity stronger in coal than in most other industries.[17]

The Issues

Much of the optimism regarding the prospects for a peaceful coal settlement in 1981 rested on the perception that those negotiations would indeed be largely a matter of money. The issues of principle which had so burdened the 1977 negotiations—stability and productivity—seemingly had been dissolved if not resolved by the drop in wildcat strikes and the rise in output per man per day experienced by BCOA mines during the term of the 1978 agreement. Thus, there seemed little reason to anticipate industry bargaining initiatives of the explosive character of those launched in 1977.

The UMWA approached negotiations seeking "wage increases, restoration of cost-of-living adjustments, improved medical and pension benefits, and revisions in the arbitration system, according to early reports." [18] Specifically, the union was expected to seek an uncapped COLA—"a sensitive issue" because "there is a strong industry opposition to a COLA, partly because most coal sales contracts do not provide for labor cost pass-throughs." [19] In the benefit area, the union "wants big increases in the $275 monthly pension for pre-1976 retirees, plus half pensions for

---

[16] "Coal's Rank and File," p. 64.

[17] Hymowitz and Petzinger, "Critical contract," p. 1.

[18] U.S. Department of Labor, "Collective Bargaining in the Bituminous Coal Industry," p. 2.

[19] "Coal's Rank and File," p. 64.

44,000 widows of retirees"—an expensive and "major" issue.[20]
Finally, the union was believed to desire abolition of the Arbitration Review Board, a demand perceived as "one of the most serious" possible causes of "major disagreements." [21]

The BCOA, which as of December had not "commented on any bargaining issues," was widely known to intend to seek work rule changes to permit continuous operation.[22] That issue had been raised by the industry in 1977 without success and seemed destined to return in 1980, particularly since "Brown, whose company has more than 20 longwalls, wants to make more efficient use of these very expensive, highly automated systems." [23] Such changes, however, "would reduce overtime earnings, result in fewer new mine openings, and probably require miners to work different shifts each week, a practice they have opposed." [24]

While much public attention was focused on the favorable productivity and stability developments in the industry since 1978, several other developments, which were profoundly to affect the BCOA's bargaining agenda and the parties' problems in reaching agreement, went largely unnoticed or unnoted by the press. The first was the court decision in AMAX Coal Company v. National Labor Relations Board, which found several provisions of Article IA, Scope and Coverage, of the National Wage Agreement to be unlawful.[25] The second was passage of the Multiemployer Pension Plan Amendments of 1980 whose provisions served to enhance the potential financial burden of existing contractual pension commitments.[26]

The problems created by the AMAX decision have already been discussed. Suffice it to note at this point that the BCOA's desire to bring the work-jurisdiction and contracting-out language of the agreement into conformity with law raised in the minds of the union some very basic issues of union and job security. Those

---

[20] *Ibid.*

[21] *Ibid.*

[22] U.S. Department of Labor, "Collective Bargaining in the Bituminous Coal Industry," p. 3.

[23] "The Issues that Peril," p. 33.

[24] "Coal's Rank and File," p. 64.

[25] AMAX Coal Company v. National Labor Relations Board, 103 L.R.R.M. 2483.

[26] Public Law No. 96-364. 94 STAT. 1295.

issues would have been sensitive at any time, but were even more so in 1981 when the UMWA and UMWA miners were keenly aware of their slipping hold on the industry and jobs. Thus, it is not surprising that resolution of these "security issues" was to prove difficult and time consuming in the 1981 negotiations.

The BCOA-UMWA multiemployer pension plan(s) embodied in the 1978 agreement entered 1980 with a fairly substantial unfunded liability, estimated at $4 billion. That unfunded liability was the product of previous benefit improvements for those already retired—more of which the UMWA seemed determined to obtain in 1981—and "the rash of mine closings in the East and the Midwest in recent years [which] has left the larger surviving companies with filling a $4 billion unfunded liability on their own." [27] The prospect that this burden would only become greater and, under law, could not be escaped and would have to be funded over thirty rather than forty years forced the BCOA to attempt to do something about "The combined costs of financing the 1950 and 1974 Pension Plans" which "throw a total pension burden on the companies that is one of the highest, if not the highest, in all of American Industry." [28] Their proposed solution was the substitution of individual employer for multiemployer plans, a step taken by Pittsburgh and Midway in the West in 1977.

Section 306(a) of the Multiemployer Pension Plan Amendments of 1980 required that "every employer who is obligated to make contributions to a multiemployer plan . . . shall, to the extent not inconsistent with law, make such contributions in accordance with the terms and conditions of such plan. . ." Kaiser Steel, which is a party to the UMWA plan, had during the term of the 1974 contract made its required contributions on coal mined in its own mines, but not on "non-UMWA" coal bought for sale or use—a practice not entirely uncommon in the industry. The trustees of the UMWA plan sued Kaiser to collect its delinquent royalty payments under section 306(a). Kaiser acknowledged its delinquency, but defended its actions on the grounds that the royalties in question constituted a violation of sections 1 and 2 of the Sherman Act and section 8(e) of the National Labor Relations Act. In a 1980 decision, the Appeals

---

[27] Hymowitz and Petzinger, "Critical contract," p. 24.

[28] "Bargaining Statement by Bituminous Coal Operators' Association," *Daily Labor Report*, No. 15 (January 23, 1981), p. F-7.

Court for the District of Columbia upheld a lower court ruling
that Kaiser's defense was inadmissable.[29] The net effect of that
decision for the BCOA appeared to be possible foreclosure of
evasion of royalty payments on nonunion coal—a prospect sufficiently onerous to lead the BCOA to press for the elimination of
that royalty obligation in 1981.

The BCOA's two pension proposals, like its work jurisdiction
proposals, touched sensitive nerves in terms of the UMWA's institutional security and its members' income security. The prospect of dismantling the union's thirty-five-year old, first-line defense against nonunion producers clearly would not be greeted
with enthusiasm by the UMWA rank and file, and indeed, it was
not. Thus, pensions were destined to become the 1981 equivalent
of labor stability issues in 1977-1978.

THE FIRST AGREEMENT

The 1981 coal negotiations did not open early as had been suggested by UMWA President Church in July 1980 because the industry lacked enthusiasm for that option. The BCOA felt that
President Church was sincere in his desire to reach a peaceful
settlement for the first time in fifteen years, but was convinced
that early talks were futile because an early settlement, if reached,
would not pass the test of bargaining council and/or rank-and-file
ratification, leaving the industry in the position in which it had
found itself in 1974 and 1978—under pressure to "sweeten" an
agreement to appease the bargaining council and possibly again
to appease the rank and file. In the hope of minimizing the
probability of such double or triple jeopardy, the BCOA rejected
the option of early negotiations in favor of the traditional approach of a two-month negotiation schedule under the clear and
imminent threat of a strike.

The BCOA leadership, like the UMWA leadership, would have
welcomed a peaceful settlement, but felt that it was more important to achieve an agreement without a repetition of the contract rejection-renegotiation pattern that seemed to have become
"traditional" in the industry. That commitment was informally
conveyed to the UMWA leadership in a private meeting between

---

[29] 206 U.S. App. D.C. 334, 642 F.2d 1302. Reversed and Remanded, S.C.
No. 80-1345 (Decided 1/13/82). See "Decision of U.S. Supreme Court in
Kaiser Steel Corp. v. Mullins," *Daily Labor Report*, No. 8 (January 13, 1982),
p. D-1.

the BCOA's bargaining team and three prominent members of its CEO committee with the UMWA leadership in October 1980. At that meeting the BCOA representatives explained the association's revised bargaining organization and informed the union that under that organization there was no latitude for end-runs around the bargaining committee to CEO's of individual companies of the type which reportedly had occurred in 1977. Finally, the BCOA representatives took pains to tell the union that there would be no economic add-ons in the event of a contract rejection in 1981. The possibility of a press blackout was also discussed at that meeting, but was rejected as politically impossible by the UMWA leadership.

With the exception of this October meeting, there was little or no formal or informal negotiation activity during the latter half of 1980. That lack of activity drew relatively little public or press attention, although the *Wall Street Journal* did note in an article entitled "Coal miners' talks off to slow start," published on November 30, 1980, that

> with memories of a four-month strike in 1978 still fresh, coal industry leaders announced in July that they planned an early start on negotiations for a 1981 agreement.
>
> So far, however, the bargaining teams have met just once, to select a site for future meetings. Spokesmen for both sides have said it is unlikely that serious negotiations will start before the end of the year.[30]

As predicted, serious negotiations did not begin until after the end of 1980. BCOA-UMWA negotiations did not begin until January 22, 1981, when the parties met jointly with the press and then privately for the first time. On that day, the UMWA made public its "Statement . . . on [its] Bargaining Demands in Soft Coal Talks."[31] On the following day, the BCOA presented to the UMWA and the public its "Bargaining Statement."[32] With those preliminaries out of the way, negotiations began in earnest against a deadline of contract expiration on March 27, with the UMWA indicating that an agreement would be needed by no later than March 18 to allow time for bargaining council and rank-and-file ratification prior to contract expiration.

---

[30] "Coal miners' talks off to slow start," *Wall Street Journal*, November 30, 1980, p. 65.

[31] "Statement by United Mineworkers President," *Daily Labor Report*, p. E-1.

[32] "Bargaining Statement," *Daily Labor Report*, p. F-1.

The Issues

The BCOA entered its 1981 negotiations with three basic substantive goals. Economically, it was resigned to a settlement commensurate with other settlements in the 1979-1980 bargaining round, but with two caveats: (1) no cost-of-living wage escalator; and (2) substitution of individual company pension plans for the existing multiemployer pension trusts, especially the 1974 pension trust. In the productivity area, it was interested in securing some concessions on scheduling issues, such as crew changes at the face, partial production shifts, and Sunday and holiday production, which could increase production time, but it was determined to resist any expansion in nonproduction time. Institutionally, the BCOA sought to "clean up" contract language which threatened to impose legal or financial liabilities on signatories—the "illegal" language in article IA, "Scope and Coverage," and the nonsignatory royalty clause provision of article XX, "Health and Retirement Benefits."

The UMWA also had three basic substantive goals as it entered 1981 negotiations. Economically, it sought a "substantial" increase in wages and a cost-of-living escalator clause "plus" increases for both 1950 and 1974 pensioners, survivor benefits for widows of 1950 pensioners, and a dental care plan. In addition, the UMWA was committed to raising the issue of reduced working time and more freedom of choice with respect to overtime. Finally, the UMWA had two contract "clean-up" issues of its own—elimination of the Arbitration Review Board and adoption of a "standard national policy" on absenteeism as part of a new agreement to replace the myriad of individual company absenteeism control policies and programs.

The basic substantive goals of the parties in 1981, unlike 1977, did not appear to place them in irreconcilable conflict on issues of principle. Gone from the bargaining agenda was the right-to-strike/pay-back/labor-stability type issue of 1977. In its place were more mundane conflicts such as COLA and working time, with the latter issue involving only conflict over desires to change the status quo versus commitments to resist changes in the status quo. Beyond these mundane and manageable economic issues, however, lay the more esoteric and emotional institutional issues inherent in changing the character of pension plans and cleaning up contract language—issues which were to thwart both the UMWA's desire for a peaceful settlement and the BCOA's desire for a single settlement.

The BCOA's disinterest and the UMWA's interest in COLA is not difficult to explain, given the performance of the CPI between 1978 and 1980. The fact that the BCOA's bargaining committee included one representative with a background in the oil industry, which has steadfastly resisted COLA, and one representative with a background in the steel industry, which has felt the burden of COLA, however, should be noted, as should the fact that COLA was dropped in 1978. The BCOA's interest and UMWA's disinterest in increased working time also is not difficult to explain. Their apparent lack of commitment on the issue, however, does require some explanation. The BCOA was of the opinion that one of the major competitive advantages of nonunion mines was in the area of working time, but was dissuaded from making the narrowing of that advantage in 1981 a possible strike issue, in the face of anticipated union resistance, by the existence of excess capacity which effectively limited the potential immediate benefits of added working time. That same excess capacity and attendant unemployment and underemployment, coupled with anticipated industry resistance to a worsening of its productivity disadvantage, apparently led the UMWA to a parallel conclusion regarding the importance of reduced working time.

The UMWA's demands in the benefit area came as no surprise to the BCOA. The level of basic pension benefits for future retirees and the lack of dental coverage placed the union behind other major unions and at least some major nonunion coal operators. The level of pension benefits for past retirees (and their widows) always has been a politically important and sensitive issue for the UMWA, given the right of retired miners to vote in union elections. The expense of such pension benefit improvements, however, has increased dramatically as a result of federal legislation and that expense was one major factor in the BCOA's desire to abandon the existing multiemployer plan in favor of individual company plans in 1981. The existing multiemployer plan encompasses not only the 130 member companies of the BCOA but almost 2,000 other UMWA-organized employers for whom BCOA members bear a liability in case of business failure. That liability, plus basic funding responsibility under law, has resulted in pension costs for comparable levels of benefits of $1.00 per hour more for the coal than for the steel operations of one firm. That cost differential constituted a major factor in the BCOA's commitment to press for individual company pension plans paralleling the individual company health plans won in

1978. The employee relations benefits of those company health plans, in terms of identifying the company rather than the union as the source of benefits, constituted a second important underpinning of the BCOA's goal to restructure the pension system.

The BCOA's clean-up proposals appear to have been in large part opportunistic in that the court decisions in the AMAX and Kaiser cases provided both incentive and leverage to rid the industry of some longstanding nettlesome constraints and requirements. That incentive and perceived leverage reportedly produced a strong BCOA commitment to eliminate the "illegal language" in article IA of the contract and to resist any new encumbering language on contracting out. The same was not the case for the nonsignatory royalty, where there was some substantial division of opinion within the BCOA as to the wisdom of pushing the elimination of nonsignatory royalties to the point of impasse at the risk of handing the union a potentially explosive, emotional issue. Despite those reservations, elimination of the nonsignatory royalties initially became a potential strike issue— a role it ultimately came to play.

The UMWA's clean-up demands were not particularly surprising or welcome to the BCOA. The elimination of the arbitration review board had been raised but not pressed by the union in 1977, as had the issue of absenteeism. The union's complaint with the review board was that "it has been responsible for inordinate delays in settling contract disputes" and the "piecemeal," company-by-company approach to absenteeism control has resulted in "unequal treatment of miners." The BCOA viewed the review board issue as a manifestation of rank-and-file dissatisfaction with a grievance procedure perceived to be stacked against them in terms of win/lose percentages—percentages biased by, in the words of one industry representative, the unwillingness and inability of the union to "filter out improper grievances." The absenteeism issue, on the other hand, was perceived as more of a leadership issue in which president Church had a strong personal interest. In both cases, the consensus within the BCOA was to retain the status quo, although few felt strongly about either issue as a potential strike or impasse issue.

The Negotiations

The first and most time consuming issues to occupy the parties in their 1981 negotiations were their clean-up issues—most notably, the BCOA's demand to clean up the language of article IA. The BCOA found it necessary to spend considerable time and effort convincing the UMWA bargaining committee of the illegality of certain provisions of article IA in light of the AMAX decision and defending its proposal simply to delete those provisions. In the view of the industry this time and effort could have been saved if the UMWA leadership had done a better job of educating its constituents about the implications of the AMAX court case. Once that task had been accomplished, the industry's next challenge was to deal with a union counterproposal involving a complex set of "union standards," restrictions on contracting out complete with an elaborate enforcement mechanism reminiscent of the 1958 protective wage clause agreement. The industry ultimately conceded the legality of such provisions but indicated it was unwilling to accept them and insisted upon simply eliminating the illegal language from the existing contract language.

The union proved equally combative about and committed to its clean-up proposals, which also consumed substantial time in negotiations. As a result, the parties entered the month of March with little discussed, and much less resolved. As late as March 16, *Business Week* reported that "the most immediate problem is solving a dispute involving the UMW's jurisdiction over nonmining jobs, such as construction work, at existing mines" and suggested that "if industry bargainers obtain an acceptable economic package, they probably will compromise on another union demand . . . to eliminate the Arbitration Review Board." [33]

The second set of issues to receive attention in the negotiations was "productivity" issues. The BCOA brought forth, discussed, and documented its proposals on work scheduling, job bidding, and work assignments, as did the union on its views on work schedules. For the most part, those issues were left lying on the table, with the possible exception of continuous operation. In late March, *Business Week* reported that the UMWA was willing to "accept an industry proposal to let miners volunteer to work on Sundays. . . . [and] to modify [its] counterproposal that Saturday work be made voluntary." [34]

The final focus of attention of the parties was the basic economic package. Negotiations over the economics of a potential

---

[33] "The Issues that Peril an Eastern Coal Pact," *Business Week*, March 16, 1981, p. 33.

[34] "A Last-Minute Snag Costs a Strike," *Business Week*, March 30, 1981, p. 46.

settlement were compressed in time and relatively free of obvious
conflict over the magnitude or shape of a settlement offer, despite
the fact that *Business Week* reported on March 30, that "the
industry is offering a 20% increase in wages and benefits, compared with the union's 41% demand." [35] The reasons for this
lack of conflict over the dimensions of an economic package were,
in the view of industry representatives, far more complex than
the following conclusion of *Business Week*: "this year's Western
coal settlements . . . have resulted in wage and benefit increases
of about 35%, including quarterly raises similar in form to cost-
of-living adjustment. Both sides are hoping for similar terms in
the East. . . ." [36]

The "pattern-setting" effect of the western 1981 UMWA agreements is strongly disputed in principle by most BOCA representatives. Practically, however, most admit that the BOCA's goal
of avoiding reinstitution of COLA was badly shaken when Peabody
Coal made a wage offer prior to its contract expiration in the
West (January 15, 1981) which included COLA. Those same
representatives privately admitted relief when the industry rene-
gade, Pittsburgh and Midway, coopted Peabody by settling in
early February on a wage package which included only "quarterly
raises similar in form to a cost-of-living adjustment." That
relief was only enhanced by the fact that "the union . . . asked
for a smaller increase in pension benefits [in the East] than it
won in the West." [37]

This analysis of where the parties were, or were coming from,
as of mid-March suggests that an agreement was within reach
by their informal deadline of March 18. Despite that, the parties
missed that deadline, thereby setting in motion the forces that
led to the strike which began on March 27, 1981. The obvious
question is why, and there are two answers. The first is the
bilateral reluctance of the parties to settle early for fear of
jeopardizing the credibility of an agreement. The second is the
existence of one major unresolved issue involving the character
of the industry's pension plan. The BCOA's basic goal as it
entered negotiations in 1981 was to do away with the existing
multiemployer plan—a goal which by mid-March *Business Week*

---

[35] *Ibid.*

[36] "The Issues that Peril," p. 33.

[37] *Ibid.*

characterized as "a strike issue with the union." [38] In the face of such resistance, and despite protestations to the contrary from some industry representatives, the BCOA's fall-back position was to seek elimination of nonsignatory coal royalties—a demand which *Business Week* characterized as the "last minute snag [which] costs coal a strike." [39]

The union's informal March 18 deadline approached and passed without an agreement, making a strike on March 27 all but inevitable. Publicly, UMWA President Church continued to be relatively optimistic about the possibility of avoiding a strike. Privately, however, he acknowledged, and the BCOA bargaining team accepted, the fact that a strike was inevitable. Despite that imposing fact, the UMWA and the BCOA were able to conclude an agreement on March 23, 1981—four days prior to contract expiration but five days after the true strike deadline.

The parties approached their March 18 deadline fairly well in agreement, at least informally, on the size and shape of a basic economic settlement. Their path to an agreement, however, was still littered by a number of "noneconomic" issues, such as the industry's productivity demands, the nonsignatory issue and a number of union demands including widows' pensions. Despite the apparent desire of both sides for a peaceful settlement, the artificial deadline of March 18 proved insufficiently compelling to force them to clean up those issues. Two reasons existed. Firstly, both sides were unsure that an early, timely agreement could be sold to the union's bargaining council, particularly if there appeared to be time to send an agreement back for renegotiation prior to the strike deadline. Secondly, that problem was compounded by the fact that there was some slack in the union's timetable by virtue of the fact that March 27 was a Friday—slack which early on had led the union to be unclear as to whether its deadline was March 18 or 22.

The negotiations recessed on March 17, and the members of the union's negotiating team were sent home. On March 20, UMWA President Church held a press conference in which he was reported to have stated, "I believe that the big coal operators want a strike because their masters in big oil want a strike. They want a strike to break the union," and he indicated that the BCOA was not willing to resume negotiations until the union

---

[38] *Ibid.*

[39] "Last-Minute Snag," pp. 45-46.

agreed to drop the nonsignatory royalty clause.[40] Private discussions the following day led to a decision to resume negotiations which reportedly began "after midnight Sunday" and culminated in a tentative settlement announced "at about 6 a.m. on March 23." [41]

Substantively, the key to the settlement was agreement by the union to the elimination of the nonsignatory royalty clause in exchange for agreement by the industry to provide $100 widows' pensions. Strategically, the key to the settlement was less a hope of forestalling a strike than of keeping it short and achieving closure by early April. That target was dictated by the fact that some key district elections, including two involving members of the union's bargaining committee, were scheduled for late April and early May—elections which, in the view of the industry, threatened to so politicize bargaining as to make an agreement impossible if negotiations dragged on into April. In short, if an agreement was to be reached, it was to be reached either then, or after those district elections were concluded. The industry, buoyed by assurances from President Church regarding his ability to sell an agreement to the bargaining council, opted to move quickly and aggressively to closure.

The First Agreement

The tentative agreement, announced on March 23, met most of the basic goals of both sides. The three-year agreement provided for wage and benefit increases generally estimated by the press at 35 percent over three years, although private industry estimates placed them at about 30 percent (an average of 9.1 percent per year). Within that package, the union had won its pension increases and widows' benefits, plus a dental plan, albeit a contributory one. The industry had won in terms of avoiding COLA, albeit at the price of a series of fixed increases in lieu of COLA.

The agreement generally met the industry's goal of avoiding further reductions in working time, but produced little progress on expanding such time. The industry did win some minor concessions on scheduling production on some holidays, but not on Sundays, nor on lateral and downward job bidding. The industry, however, failed to achieve its goal of substituting individual com-

---

[40] "Coal Negotiators Reach Tentative Contract After Abrupt About-Face," *Daily Labor Report*, No. 55 (March 23, 1981), p. A-1.

[41] *Ibid.*

pany pension plans for the multiemployer plan, having to settle instead for a "special pension plan study committee" whose mandate is "to make a complete, factual, legal, regulatory and actuarial study of the pension program . . . and to make non-binding . . . specific recommendations regarding the existing and future program . . . including the feasibility of alternative pension programs."

The industry's most visible victory came in the simple elimination of the "illegal" language in article IA and in the elimination of the nonsignatory royalty. The union, however, won parallel victories in the elimination of the arbitration review board and the institution of a standard national absenteeism plan. The union's victory on the arbitration review board, however, was slightly tarnished by contractual recognition that all its prior decisions "shall continue to have precedential effect under this agreement."

THE SECOND AGREEMENT

There were conflicting reports in the press regarding the possibility that the tentative agreement of March 23 might head off a strike. *Business Week* reported on April 6 that it was not until after a March 24 Bargaining Council meeting that "Church dropped his plan to recommend that the union's 'no contract, no work' tradition be suspended so that miners could continue working after the contract expires on March 27." [42] The *Daily Labor Report*, however, reported on March 23 that

> Church told reporters that he expects the contract to be ratified, but not without a strike of four or five days while the union completes its 10-day ratification process . . . Church has said repeatedly that he will not recommend a contract extension and that the ratification process cannot be shortened. [43]

The union's ten-day ratification process indeed was left to run its normal course. The March 23 tentative agreement was submitted to the union's bargaining council where it was approved on March 24 by a vote of "only 21-14 after an all-day debate." [44] However heated the debate or tenuous the margin of approval, that action constituted no small victory for the BCOA and President Church in that it was "the first time in its eight-year history

---

[42] "After a Short Strike, Labor Peace for Coal," *Business Week*, April 6, 1981, p. 28.

[43] "Coal Negotiators Reach Tentative Contract," *Daily Labor Report*, p. A-1.

[44] "Labor Peace for Coal," *Business Week*, p. 28.

the council has approved a contract without sending it back for renegotiation." [45] That victory, however, proved hollow when the March 23 agreement "was decisively rejected by the Union membership in voting March 31." [46] The key to the rejection was an overwhelmingly negative (75 percent or more) vote in the coal fields of western Pennsylvania and West Virginia, including Districts 4 and 17, the home districts of two bargaining committee members up for reelection in the spring.

The Issues

The fundamental defect in the March 23 agreement, from the viewpoint of the Appalachian miners whose negative votes were the key factor in a two-to-one overall contract rejection, was not economics. Instead, it was the perceived "union-busting" character of the gains won by the BCOA—gains which appeared to confirm President Church's own statement that large coal producers wanted a strike "to break the union." The combination of the BCOA's "assault," however unsuccessful, on the union's pioneering pension system and its successful assault on union's longstanding defenses against non-UMWA contractors and operators in the form of the restrictive provisions of article IA and the nonsignatory royalty requirement produced an emotional response and created a basic institutional survival issue.

The specific focal points of rank-and-file dissatisfaction were the elimination of the illegal language and of the nonsignatory royalty—both of which were to be the key issues in reaching a second agreement. On those issues, the rank and file was unpersuaded by its own leadership's rational explanations based, in the former case, on action by the Supreme Court and, in the latter case, on the financial fact of life that nonsignatory royalties had not been a major source of trust revenue, and would not be, because most operators "would do everything in their power to avoid payment." [47] Instead, they found more compelling the spectre of nonunion workers taking over their trucking and construction jobs on site and nonunion operators mining coal in their stead for their own employers.

---

[45] *Ibid.*

[46] "Membership Rejects Tentative Agreement," *United Mine Workers Journal*, April-May 1981, p. 1.

[47] *Ibid.*

The emotional character of the defects of the first agreement made those defects an ideal platform for political campaigning by those seeking office in the spring district elections. Many of those in office discerned that it was to their advantage to either not support or actively criticize the agreement, as did virtually all of their challengers. The two incumbent district officers who had been on the bargaining committee, however, were stuck with the agreement. One was soundly defeated in his bid for reelection while the other only narrowly defeated his challenger in an election whose legality was subsequently successfully challenged. Thus, the very politicization of bargaining which the industry hoped to avoid with an early settlement was not forestalled and, indeed, may have been abetted by the contents of that settlement.

From the BCOA viewpoint, the major issue created by the contract rejection was, in a sense, also one of institutional integrity. The BCOA's primary concern was avoidance of a repetition of 1974 and 1977 when renegotiation had meant a visible sweetening of the economic package. In that context, it was determined that there would be no more money except possibly in exchange for a longer contract—hopefully a forty-two-month contract. Beyond that possible rearrangement, the BCOA bargaining team stood committed to those of its basic goals realized in the initial agreement, although that commitment was not fully shared, particularly with respect to the nonsignatory royalty, by the entire BCOA membership, some of whom had argued against holding out on that issue en route to the first agreement.

The Negotiations

The BCOA, in 1981 as in 1977, was resolved not to be rushed into renegotiation of a settlement. It communicated that resolve privately to the union leadership and publicly to the union membership when, on April 1, its chief negotiator told the press that the association had "no plans to resume negotiations," citing "a disturbing lack of bargaining discipline in the U.M.W., which puts the integrity of the bargaining process in serious jeopardy." [48] Ten days later, that same message was repeated when the BCOA responded to a union request to negotiations by indicating that

---

[48] Ben A. Franklin, "No talks are set in coal walkout after pact's loss," *New York Times*, April 2, 1981, p. A-18.

it was not prepared to resume negotiations until it was assured that the union was "prepared to engage in reliable bargaining." [49]

The BCOA was also convinced that such "reliable bargaining" could not come about until after the conclusion of the union's district elections in mid-May. Despite that conviction the industry agreed to a resumption of meetings following the UMWA's April 10 request. Those meetings proved totally unproductive and were recessed indefinitely on April 17. That recess lasted until May 7 when the parties met again when "UMW president Samuel Church, Jr. began the proceedings by presenting the same list of seven union demands that the mine operators had rejected as totally unacceptable when the talks broke off April 17." [50] After five days of talks which carried the parties beyond the second district election involving a member of the UMWA bargaining team, the parties for the first time were reported to have expressed "guarded optimism." [51]

That optimism proved premature as negotiations were "recessed abruptly by union leaders [on May 18] after a meeting of less than two hours resulted in what might be a climatic deadlock." [52] That deadlock centered on the same scope and coverage (subcontracting) issues that had preoccupied the parties for so long in the early stages of their negotiations. The union resurrected its original "union standards" proposals which the industry, as before, rejected as impractical. That deadlock continued until May 27 when UMWA President Church publicly noted "that bargaining wasn't any longer stalemated by the single issue that has snagged the settlement talks for the last several weeks." [53] The deadlock was broken when the BCOA agreed to the inclusion of language barring subcontracting that would result in layoffs of bargaining unit employees.

With the subcontracting issue resolved as a job security issue to the satisfaction of both parties, negotiations moved swiftly to

---

[49] Ben A. Franklin, "Industry qualifies response to coal union bid for talks," *New York Times*, April 2, 1981, p. A-18.

[50] Thomas Petzinger, Jr., "Resumed UMW strike negotiations lag as they become union campaign issue," *Wall Street Journal*, May 8, 1981, p. 2.

[51] Ben A. Franklin, "Some optimism is reported in coal talks," *New York Times*, May 14, 1981, p. A-22.

[52] Ben A. Franklin, "Coal talks recess as new deadlock looms," *New York Times*, May 19, 1981, p. A-12.

[53] Carol Hymowitz, "Coal-labor talks surmount stalemate but many issues still impede settlement," *Wall Street Journal*, May 27, 1981, p. 6.

closure. The industry reluctantly but inevitably yielded to the union's "non-negotiable" demand to retain the nonsignatory royalty, extracting as a price for that concession a token reduction (from $100 to $95) in the widows' pension which had been the original *quid pro quo* for elimination of nonsignatory royalties. In exchange, the industry demanded a forty-two-month contract, but settled for a forty-month contract at the "cost" of an additional $0.30 per hour wage increase in June 1984 at which point the union "reluctantly" dropped its remaining demands including one to eliminate contractual recognition of the precedential status of existing arbitration review board decisions.

The basic elements of a second agreement were agreed upon on May 28 and finalized in a late-night bargaining session which carried over into Friday, May 29. On that same day the UMWA's bargaining council voted thirty-six to two to approve the new agreement which UMWA President Church reportedly indicated "would give U.M.W. members a 38 percent increase in wages and benefits" and characterized it as "probably the best agreement that will be negotiated this year in any industry." [54] Whatever its absolute size or relative stature, the April 29 agreement assuaged the anger and appetite of the rank and file who approved that agreement by a margin of more than two to one, permitting the BCOA and the UMWA to sign their 1981 contract on June 6, 1981. [55]

The Second Agreement

The most satisfying aspect of the second agreement from the industry standpoint was the fact that it did not involve a sweetening of the economic package. The additional $.30 per hour wage increase granted in exchange for the forty-month contract did increase the size of the wage package from 31 to 34 percent over the life of the contract but left the average annual cost of the package essentially unchanged at about 9 percent. Indeed, one industry representative suggested that total average annual cost was lower (8.9 percent) under the second agreement than under the first (9.1 percent). The extended contract term had one other potential benefit for the industry—it pushed the 1984

---

[54] Ben A. Franklin, "Miners' council votes to accept new coal pact," *New York Times*, May 30, 1981, p. A-1.

[55] "Contract Approved by 2-1 Margin," *United Mine Workers Journal*, June 1981, p. 1.

contract expiration date beyond the summer peak in demand for coal from utilities to meet their peak power demands. Finally, the fact that the second agreement, like the first, did not contain a cost-of-living escalator represented at least a moral victory for the BCOA.

The BCOA also was generally satisfied with the results of its prolonged battle to eliminate the illegal language in article IA, despite the last minute addition of no layoff limits on management's right to contract out. Quite the contrary was the case with respect to an equally difficult and ultimately unsuccessful battle to eliminate the nonsignatory royalty, the third of its initial basic goals for 1981 negotiations. The same was true with respect to the BCOA's fourth basic goal—substitution of individual employer for the multiemployer pension system. The second agreement, however, retained the study committee agreed to in the first settlement.

The BCOA substantially met its fifth basic goal of avoiding further reduction in working time. It did not, however, make substantial progress in changing work rules to narrow its productivity disadvantage vis-à-vis non-national agreement mines. It won only two minor concessions in this area: (1) the right to schedule production on holidays other than Christmas and Christmas eve; and (2) limitation of the number of lateral or downward job bids by any employee to two during the contract term. The BCOA fared less well in resisting the union's demands regarding the arbitration review board and absenteeism policy, but it remains to be seen whether those concessions will have a negative or positive effect on working relations and labor stability during the term of the 1981 contract.

THE LEGACY OF 1981

Economically, the 1981 BCOA-UMWA National Bituminous Coal Wage Agreement was both modest and manageable from a cost standpoint. That agreement will raise the daily wage rate of a skilled miner from $84.50 as of March 1981 to $113.32 by October 1984. Per ton royalty payments to the trust funds will increase from $1.985 to $2.236 over the same period—the equivalent of an increase from about $28.50 to $33.50 per man per day assuming average output of fifteen tons per man day. Overall, daily employment costs for a skilled miner will rise from about $113 to $147 or about 30 percent over the forty-month term of the contract—a figure which compared favorably from the BCOA standpoint with the level of major settlements of 1980 (35-40 percent), and with the level of its 1978, and particularly its 1974 settlements (39 and 45 percent, respectively).

The per ton cost-price effect of the 1981 settlement is likely to be relatively limited, particularly if the 7 percent reported increase in industry productivity in 1980 continues over the next three years. Thus, the 1981 settlement should have no serious competitive effects on the position of National Agreement mines in the long-term coal supply contract market. The same is not the case in the highly competitive spot market and may not be the case in the growing export market for steam coal. In those markets, the productivity/cost disadvantages of National Agreement mines attributable in part to such factors as working time and pension costs may have a telling effect, particularly given the existing excess capacity in the industry—excess capacity which only a miraculous boom in coal demand will eliminate.

Institutionally, the 1981 negotiations left the BCOA, the UMWA, and their bargaining relationship battered but not or at least not yet shattered. Internally, those in control of the BCOA's bargaining structure felt that structure worked well procedurally and substantively. Others, however, are not so sure, including some small and old coal companies who question the sensitivity of the BCOA's bargaining leadership to the realities of coal labor relations and its ability to relate to and deal with the "miners" who sit across the bargaining table. Internally, the UMWA bargaining structure worked more effectively in 1981 than in 1978 or in 1974, in that for the first time since democratization the union's bargaining council approved an initial tentative agreement. Beyond that, however, politics once again undermined the system, leaving the UMWA without a contract and the UMWA leadership with renewed factionalism and political opposition, most notably in the person of Rich Trumka. It was Trumka who unseated the international executive board member from District 4 in Western Pennsylvania who was on the union's bargaining team and who has now run successfully against Sam Church for the UMWA presidency.

The failures of the union's international and district leadership to sell, and of its membership in the East to buy, the first agreement of 1981 was and remains a source of grave concern to the BCOA. Many of its members now openly question whether it will ever be possible to achieve a settlement with a single agreement. Some old coal companies seem resigned to a fate of multiple agreements and are thinking about ways to build them into the bargaining process in a way that will serve to avoid or shorten strikes. Others, however, wonder whether the problem might be amenable to structural rather than procedural solution. At this point in time, members of both schools of thought are waiting to see what the union's presidential election and district politics will do to or for the union by the time the BCOA must once again contemplate and confront the brave new world of 1984.

CHAPTER XV

Brave New World:
1984 and Beyond

There is no more hazardous intellectual exercise than attempting to predict the future in labor relations, particularly in an industry like bituminous coal mining which has a long, consistent record of cycles of confrontation and cooperation. In that context, the occupational hazards of playing seer increase geometrically with the depth of the attempt to probe the darkness of the future—not unlike the hazards facing miners as they probe the limits of underground coal seams. Without laying claim to the same courage as miners, what follows is an attempt to tunnel into both the shallow (near term) and deep (long term) seams of the future of labor relations in bituminous coal.

The safety and health of the coal miner is or has become the joint responsibility of management, union, government, and the miner himself. The same sources of protection against the hazards of mining the future are available to the seer. For the past eight years, the apparent consensus of management, union, and government with respect to the future of both the industry and its labor relations was that "good times were just around the corner." Unfortunately, after eight years, the industry has yet to reach that corner. Narrowing the focus of attention to management and labor relations, one finds that after each of the last three sets of contract negotiations industry and BCOA representatives divided neatly, but not evenly, into sanguine optimists and scared pessimists—to the point of raising questions as to whether they were part of the same industry and party to the same bargain. Thus far, the record of the industry has done less to support the credibility of the optimists than of the pessimists—a fact which has, perhaps unduly, cautioned this individual miner of the potential folly of assuming all is well in the mine of the future of the industry and its labor relations.

The Future of the Industry

Throughout its history, the bituminous coal industry has been characterized by excess production capacity and strong product market competition. That was the case in 1973 when the BCOA and the UMWA entered their "democratic era" in labor relations, has continued to be the case as they have strugged through three sets of contract negotiations in that era, and will continue to be the case when they confront their next set of negotiations in 1984. In all likelihood, barring a major technological and economic breakthrough in coal gasification or liquefication, it will also continue to be the case for the rest of the decade and perhaps the century.

The foreseeable economic future of the coal industry is heavily tied to the demand for steam coal. That demand is destined to grow substantially by the year 2000, but growth will be gradual and is not likely to outstrip the growth of industry production capacity, given the industry's proven propensity to plan and prepare for the best. That propensity was most recently manifest in planned expansions of coal-loading port facilities in anticipation of an upsurge in export demand. In March 1982, the *Wall Street Journal* reported that even after a "shakeout of sorts" of planned additions to an estimated existing capacity of 160 million tons to meet an existing demand of 110 million tons, that "if all the projects still in the works are completed by 1985, capacity will jump to more than 550 million tons, more than twice what will be needed by 2000." [1]

The industry's largest market is and will continue to be its domestic market, which is dominated by the demand for steam coal for electric power generation. That demand has grown over the past eight years and will continue to grow over the next eight years, but not at the rates foreseen in the energy scenarios of the 1970s—scenarios which failed to appreciate the impact of conservation on power demand and of conversion and compliance costs on demand for coal for power generation. To make matters worse, the domestic market has been further depressed by the current recession and oil glut. The result has been the emergence of substantial manifest (short-run) and latent (long-run) excess production capacity which will not be quickly absorbed even in

---

[1] Susan Carey, "Planned expansion in coal-loading ports is scaled back as the export boom wanes," *Wall Street Journal*, March 30, 1982, p. 33.

the event of a return to prosperity and oil shortages—certainly
not by 1984 and probably not by 1990.

The domestic market for steam coal is not now a national market. Rather, three geographically distinct regional markets
exist—east, midwest, and west—each drawing primarily on its
own indigenous coal supply, particularly with respect to long-
term supply contracts as opposed to spot market purchases. Intraregional price/service competition among producers in both
contract and spot markets is active. Interregional competition
among producers to date has been limited, although recently,
western non-UMWA coal has increasingly been finding markets
in the northwestern segment of the midwestern region, as has
Appalachian-mined non-UMWA coal in the southeastern section
of that region. The general absence of interregional competition
reflects the inability of producers in one region to offer pur-
chasers in another region sufficiently advantageous terms with
respect to cost and delivery reliability to offset freight costs—a
barrier which only some nonunion firms thus far have been able
to overcome and then only after three successive UMWA-BCOA
strikes leading to very expensive settlements. What will happen
as a result of the fourth consecutive BCOA-UMWA strike and
most recent settlement remains to be seen, but whatever it may
be, it is unlikely to alter the competitive isolation/insulation of
Appalachian and Rocky Mountain producers from each other in
the domestic market.

The export market has been and continues to be an important
source of growing demand for U.S. steam coal. Unfortunately,
that market, like the domestic market, has not grown at the rate
anticipated in 1970 energy scenarios and currently is depressed
by the same short-run economic conditions that have depressed
the domestic market. As a result, the export market in 1982,
according to one exporter was a "pie" which "is large, and it's
getting larger. But it's not as large as some people thought.
The slices are getting skinnier." [2]

Despite the disappointing performance of international demand,
the industry remains optimistic about the future of export sales
as indicated by its ambitious plans to add coal-loading capacity
on every coast. World demand for coal, like domestic demand,
inevitably will rise over the rest of this century. The extent to
which that rise in demand will benefit the U.S. coal industry

------

[2] *Ibid.*

obviously will depend on its ability to supply coal on a cost/
service basis competitive with other coal-exporting nations, such
as Australia and South Africa and, looking to the future, Poland,
China, and possibly some South American nations. At the moment, it is not clear that the U.S. coal industry as a whole has
the relative competitive strength vis-à-vis its potential competitors that it would like to have to be assured of reaping the desired and much needed gains from any substantial increase in
world coal imports.

The regional character of the industry in terms of the domestic market has been reflected in its response to potential growth
in the export market. In general, eastern producers do not see
western producers as a potential competitive threat in the export
market due to the East's superior existing rail and port facilities,
despite their possible price/reliability competitive disadvantages.
That perception, however, has not precluded a mad scramble
among eastern producers to gain access to the sea nor has it
prevented unionized eastern producers from being concerned about
the possible effects of the 1981 UMWA strike on their ability to
compete with nonunion eastern producers in the export market.
The same situation appears to have prevailed in the Midwest, but
to a slightly lesser degree and with the substitution of barges for
trains and the Gulf for the Atlantic. The response of the industry in the West was similar, but far more measured, despite the
fact that it possessed the most limited rail/port capacity for serving an export market. There are three possible reasons for this
measured response: (1) the West enjoys an obvious distance/
price/reliability advantage vis-à-vis its potential U.S. competitors
in serving the Asian market; (2) the West is less dependent on
export vis-à-vis domestic sales for continued growth; and (3)
the West lacks a history of "ruinous competition" and in its place
has developed a sense of "common destiny."

The present and prospective existence of excess capacity in the
coal industry obviously suggests that the ability of any operator
or group of operators to survive, grow, or prosper requires that
they remain competitive on effective cost per ton to customers.
Effective cost is a complex and changing function of (1) price
per ton; (2) freight per ton; (3) BTU per ton; (4) pollution
per ton; and (5) delivery reliability per ton. The two of those
five variables that are directly influenced by labor relations are
price per ton and delivery reliability per ton—variables on which
the West holds a clear interregional advantage as do non-UMWA

producers on an intraregional basis. The two variables on which other producers hold an advantage are geographic and geologic— freight per ton and BTU per ton. The former two variables constitute a constraint on the BCOA, and the latter two are its cushion in dealing with the UMWA. For the most part the cushion, thus far, has proven adequate to absorb the weight of the constraint on both an inter- and intraregional basis, at least in the East and Midwest, if not nationally. Whether that will continue to be the case over the next eight or eighteen years, as it has over the past eight years, given the undistinguished labor relations record of the BCOA and the UMWA over those past eight years, remains to be seen.

The Future of the UMWA

Throughout its now almost 100 year history, the UMWA has been engaged in what has proven to be a seesaw battle to gain and maintain control of the industry. In that battle, the union scored an impressive victory in 1898 and suffered an equally impressive defeat in 1927. It regained its lost ground in the 1930s with the Appalachian agreements and solidified its gains with the 1950 National Agreement. Since then it has been steadily losing ground in a very quiet war against "nonunion" producers— losses which accelerated during the 1970s and accumulated by 1980 to more than 50 percent of the industry in terms of production. Thus, the union once again has lost control of the industry on a national basis, raising, in the light of history, two questions: (1) Can the union once again regain control of the industry as it did in the 1930s? and (2) Will the growing weight of nonunion competition result in the loss of that measure of control the union still holds, as was the case in the 1920s?

The key to regaining national control is organizing the West and bringing those mines and miners into the national agreement system. At this point, the prospects for success on either score seem dismal at best. The UMWA currently lacks the resources to mount an extensive organizing campaign in the vast space of the West and seems destined politically and economically to be unlikely to commit the resources required for such a campaign. Even if it did, it is doubtful that the campaign would yield substantial gains in the face of strong management antipathy and weak worker attraction to unions, in general, and the UMWA in particular. Finally, even if it could overcome that problem, it would still be hard pressed to bring newly organized mines and miners into the national agreement system, particularly in light of its inability to keep its western surface mine agreement mines and miners in that system either as pattern followers or participants in the pension plan.

The limited organizing gains likely to be made by the UMWA in the West in the immediate future are likely to be offset, at least in terms of national control, by mounting problems in keeping existing western national agreement mines and miners in the fold. Economically, the long run competitive viability of such mines in a regional market dominated by producers who do not share the same contractual liabilities (work rules and pension costs) and vulnerability to strikes seems doubtful. If that is the case, employers will find themselves under growing competitive pressure to break away from the national agreement, perhaps linking themselves to the western surface mine agreement system, or denied that option, to break away from the UMWA entirely as AMAX did at its Belle Aire mine. While employees are unlikely to be sympathetic to the latter course of action, they may not be so to the former, particularly after having been out on strike for seventy-two days in 1981 over a proposed contract which they overwhelmingly approved.

The "loss" of the West may be embarrassing but not debilitating to the UMWA, given the regional structure of the coal market, as long as the union can maintain control in the Midwest and East. That control, historically exercised through a combination of organization, intimidation, and contractual constraints aimed at nonunion producers, also has weakened steadily since 1950, but remains strong, as was evident in 1978. Thus far, despite its losses, the UMWA has been able to contain nonunion competition in the Midwest and East and prevent it from achieving the critical mass necessary to become an imposing constraint on the union's bargaining power and bargaining settlements. That situation, however, may change in the near future in the Midwest, but seems unlikely to change quickly in the East.

Nonunion coal from western, eastern, and indigenous sources has been a gradually increasing competitive factor in the midwestern coal market for the past five years. The fact that several "new producers" have indicated that they intended to open major new mines in the region and operate them on a union-free basis and other "new producers" quietly are planning to do the same elsewhere in the region at least raises the possibility that nonunion competition in the midwestern market will achieve the critical mass required to dominate the market. That prospect is enhanced by the depressed state of the economies of the industrial Midwest and dismal prospects for rapid dramatic recovery. The result would be powerful competitive pressure on union producers to break with the national agreement contract and pension plan and, if necessary, with the union, as at least one union producer in the largely nonunion coal field of the Arkoma basin reportedly is in the process of doing.[3]

The prospects for successful nonunion operation of major new mines or escape from national control in older union mines are uncertain at best. Such efforts pit a new "union-resisting management" against an old "entrenched" union in a region, unlike the West, where the work force is not unsympathetic to unions in general, and to the UMWA in particular. The prospect of a high paying job in a relatively safe surface mine, however, may outweigh those sympathies, particularly in the hard times which have befallen the Midwest. If so, it is not inconceivable that by the end of this decade, the Midwest, like the West, will become a separate regional labor relations system—one institutionally dominated by the UMWA districts, but economically dominated by nonunion producers. Such a development would be more than an embarrassment to the UMWA, which can be expected to resist with all its economic, political, and physical power.

The UMWA is most firmly entrenched and in control in the eastern market and there are few signs of any forces on the horizon that might alter that situation. Nonunion competition, while it exists, is not a major factor in the eastern market and there is little evidence of an impending invasion of new nonunion producers similar to that confronting the industry in the Midwest. A number of smaller union producers exist who, in 1981, voiced their resentment at being held hostage to the national agreement negotiations, but they were neither vocal nor powerful enough to gain their freedom and are unlikely to be able to do so in the foreseeable future. Larger union producers, for the most part, do not see nonunion operation as a viable alternative in their eastern operations or perceive any real hope or reason for reshaping the existing bargaining system. In short, with the exception of a relatively small number of major producers, the East seems destined for, or resigned to, business as usual for the foreseeable future.

---

[3] Ben A. Franklin, "Ex-unionist leads a coal company in bitter dispute with miners' union," *New York Times*, February 14, 1982, p. 28.

The seeming stability of the status quo in the East is the product of an expectation that the union will keep nonunion production in the region within manageable limits in the future as in the past and that geography and geology will keep sales of nonregional production in the East's markets within similar limits. At the moment, that expectation is reasonable, but it may not remain so if nonunion producers in the East or West are able to claim a disproportionate share of the growing export pie by virtue of lower cost or strike vulnerability. A UMWA "loss" of the Midwest might well enhance that possibility by adding another nonunion competitor to the export market and throwing more of the predictably increasing weight of funding the union's pension plan on eastern unionized producers—a possibility which could be forestalled by a preemptive strike by the BCOA and UMWA on pension/productivity issues as has been suggested by BCOA and rejected by the UMWA.

The Future of the BCOA

The BCOA was formed in 1950 specifically to play the role of management in collective bargaining with the UMWA. In theory, that role made the BCOA responsible for charting and steering an economically safe course for the industry through the perilous sea of labor relations. In fact, however, the BCOA did not assume that responsibility, choosing instead to cruise the sea of labor relations as a passenger on the yacht of John L. Lewis. When the crew of that yacht mutinied in 1973, the BCOA found itself adrift at sea without the services or skills of a captain or navigator. The history of the BCOA over the ensuing eight years essentially is the saga of on-the-job, at-sea training in seamanship, conducted in waters kept constantly turbulent in the 1970s by a militant and undisciplined union and a meddling and unsympathetic government.

The BCOA in 1973 was not well suited to assume its new role and responsibilities. The fact that its membership consisted of some 150 sovereign companies better suited it to be a deliberative rather than a decisive body. To make matters worse, the BCOA was "poorly structured, commercially divisive and politically impossible" in the view of at least one industry representative. Finally, the BCOA lacked an obvious, effective leader and strong professional labor relations staff among its member companies. Thus, when the BCOA took command of the ship, it was a case of captaincy by committee and navigation by naiveté. The result was the 1974 and 1978 collisions with the UMWA and the government which cost the industry settlements totalling 93 percent over six years and almost sank the industry's ship—the BCOA.

The restructuring of the BCOA in 1980 has given it a more workable and professional, but less equitable and traditional, command system. With that system came a more forward-looking approach to setting the bargaining course of the association. The result was a "moderate and reasonable" economic settlement in 1981 for which the BCOA must share credit with a non-BCOA member—Pittsburgh and Midway, whose western settlement bailed the BCOA out of the straits that its largest member, Peabody, got it into by offering COLA in the West—and a noninterventionist administration. That settlement did not include progress on several long-term industry problems, much to the chagrin of some members, and cost the industry a seventy-two-day strike, much to the chagrin of some other members. Thus, the BCOA came out of its 1981 negotiations a tighter and happier ship, although not tight enough to suit some and not happy enough to suit others.

The key to the future of the BCOA appears to be more in the hands of the UMWA than in its own hands. There was a widespread perception, on the management side, of growing understanding and maturity on the part of the union's top leaders during the course of the 1981 negotiations, which seekers of both tightness and happiness saw as a potential asset for the future. Unfortunately, that asset subsequently has disappeared.

There was considerable talk by outside observers of the growing maturity of the UMWA rank and file after the 1978 settlement and undoubtedly will be again as the BCOA and UMWA approach their 1984 negotiations. As the 1981 negotiations proved, the maturation process in coal labor relations is stubbornly slow and heavily conditioned by what one inside observer described as the anxiousness of younger miners to emulate their ancestors in "paying their dues" to join the club of miners who have taken on the operators. The possibility of buying out rank-and-file militancy on the part of the BCOA by avoiding such potentially explosive issues as pensions and productivity is one on which the BCOA is deeply divided, with "old coal" interests believing or hoping that such issues have been put to rest and "new coal" interests convinced that such issues hold the key to industry survival and growth.

The fact is that the BCOA in the 1980s, as in the 1950s, is a frail institution which may be able to survive only with the support of a responsible union—something the UMWA has not been in the 1970s and will be hard-pressed to be in the 1980s. The lack of responsible unionism over the past five years has divided the BCOA into two camps: (1) the captains—those serving to chart and steer a long-run course of competitive strength, and (2) the crew—those seeking to chart and steer a short-run course to convenient accommodation. The former are frustrated by lack of commitment by the latter; the latter are fearful of the lack of compassion of the former for the blood and sweat they are asked to give to the cause. The possibility that either group will "jump ship" is real, but is heavily dependent on where they have to go and what they have to gain. At the moment, the UMWA's still strong organizational control and rank-and-file militancy in the eastern and midwestern markets has left both groups with no place to go and nothing to gain. A weakening of that control over worsening of that militancy, however, would leave both groups with no reason to stay and nothing to lose.

It seems unlikely that the BCOA will suddenly explode, particularly by 1984. Instead, the association is likely to experience some limited but possibly accelerating defections beginning with its western members, then extending to its midwestern members, particularly if the announced nonunion invasion of that regional market is successful. When that occurs, or seems likely to occur, the growing weight of the shrinking funding base of the unions pension plan may well set off an every-man-for-himself scramble in the East unless that pension plan has already been replaced by individual company plans. If it has not, it undoubtedly would be at that point, but within the framework of a continuing eastern regional multiemployer bargaining structure.

Index

Racial Policies of American Industry Series

Order from: Kraus Reprint Co., Route 100, Millwood, New York 10546

STUDIES OF NEGRO EMPLOYMENT

Order from University Microfilms, Inc.
Attn: Books Editorial Department
300 North Zeeb Road
Ann Arbor, Michigan 48106

* Order this book from the Industrial Research Unit, the Wharton School, University of Pennsylvania, Philadelphia, Pennsylvania 19104.